Forged In Fire

The Secret Life Of A Mennonite Family

Robert Charles Graber

WestBow
PRESS®
A DIVISION OF THOMAS NELSON
& ZONDERVAN

WestBow Press books may be ordered through booksellers or by contacting:

WestBow Press
A Division of Thomas Nelson & Zondervan
1663 Liberty Drive
Bloomington, IN 47403
www.westbowpress.com
844-714-3454

Scripture taken from the King James Version of the Bible.

ISBN: 978-1-6642-5783-2 (sc)
ISBN: 978-1-6642-5784-9 (hc)
ISBN: 978-1-6642-5782-5 (e)

Library of Congress Control Number: 2022902864

Print information available on the last page.

WestBow Press rev. date: 08/04/2022

To eleven very important people in my life.

First, to the memory of my mother, whose guidance, sacrifice, and example were crucial for me during my growing-up years.

To my sister, who supported me in this effort and always believed that I could do anything I put my mind to. Her support and contributions were momentous.

To my loving wife, who has been my marriage partner for over fifty years and supported me in publishing this account of my life.

To my loving children and grandchildren, who have made me proud to be called their father and grandfather, and who I am confident will make this world a better place to live in.

I wrote this book for all of you.

CONTENTS

Introduction ix

Chapter 1   Swiss-Volhynian History. 1
Chapter 2   The Beginning of It All 7
Chapter 3   The Early Years. 26
Chapter 4   The Primary Times 34
Chapter 5   Living with Abuse. 56
Chapter 6   Country Living 65
Chapter 7   Double-Dealing. 109
Chapter 8   The Extended Family 120
Chapter 9   The Secondary Years. 131
Chapter 10   Alternative Service 142
Chapter 11   The College Years. 150
Chapter 12   Left Alone. 160
Chapter 13   The Deception Exposed 166
Chapter 14   Life after Graduation .181
Chapter 15   Other Fires to Face 187
Chapter 16   The Choices We Make 191
Chapter 17   Professional Tips, Hints, and Pointers. 202
Chapter 18   What's Important 210

INTRODUCTION

This book is the true story of a young boy growing up in a small, cliquish religious community, who experienced rejection and hardships. This is a true account of the events and adversity this boy's family faced. This unusual narrative explains the loss of trust in those who should have been able to be trusted. It tells of physical and mental abuse this family endured and overcame, and the successes achieved because of determination and good choices made. It describes the events that led to fear of losing their lives because of poor decisions their husband and father made, and actual situations where the young boy had to physically stop his father from physically abusing his mother and sister. What is surprising about all of these events is that they happened to a Mennonite family living in a Mennonite community.

All scripture passages referred to in this book are taken from the King James Version of the Bible.

CHAPTER 1

SWISS-VOLHYNIAN HISTORY

The twenty-third day of March 1947 was cool and dreary, and it was the day I was born, the second child to my parents. I was the boy my mother had dreamed of having. She had feared she may not be able have another child after my sister came into the world four and a half years before me. My father, on the other hand, never showed the excitement that most fathers exhibit when a son is born. The father-son relationship that generally develops as the years go by never materialized in my case.

This story is a true recollection of a boy growing up in a small, cliquish religious community, who throughout the years experienced rejection and hardships. My mother, sister, and I faced more than four decades of ill treatment, which I will describe in this narrative. Now at the age of seventy-two years, I am telling this very unusual story of what seemed to be a typical Mennonite farm family living a normal life in a small, central Kansas community. With both of my parents gone now, I feel free to tell this improbable story of what my family endured.

When one thinks about what it would be like growing up in a predominantly Mennonite community in a small Midwestern town, one develops a mental picture of what they assume it would look like. Growing up in a small Mennonite community, or in any small community for that matter, is often not what it is perceived to be. Most people think that Mennonite communities are low-conflict, loving, caring, peaceful communities, but that is not exactly how my community acted toward my family. Unfortunately, my community had a faulty perception of itself. Hypocrisy was alive and well. Some of the community people professed one thing but lived a much different way of life.

As I share my story, it is my hope that this account of my life will help bring an end to judgments based on faulty expectations and show that all children are in need of acceptance, encouragement, recognition, support, and love. It doesn't matter if one is rich, poor, smart, or living with disabilities. Every child's needs are the same.

I grew up with a feeling of being inadequate and inferior to other people in my community. These feelings resulted from such things as doubt, fear, guilt, rejection, and shame. For me, inadequate and inferior feelings resulted from the rejection I felt because of a father who demonstrated a lack of concern for his family, his lack of a true moral standard, and the ill treatment I experienced from some in my home community because of who my father was. My mother, sister, and I were deceived by a man who was a husband, father, and someone we trusted and loved. This was a man who some in the community were unable to respect, and rightly so, yet it appears that my father was singled out when some in the community lived similar lives. This all led to my family's life of continual pain, rejection, isolation, and fear.

Before I begin to tell you my story, a little historical background on the lives of my ancestors will be helpful in understanding why our lives took the direction they did. The genealogical and historical events recorded in this book are written as they were told to me or were written in my family's ancestry books.

The Mennonite community I grew up in was of the Swiss-Volhynian Mennonite tradition. These Swiss-Volhynian people migrated to central Kansas in 1874, during a time often referred to as the Great Migration. They migrated from the Emmental Valley in Canton Bern, Switzerland, with stops in France, Austria, Poland, Russia, New York, and South Dakota. The ship on which my ancestors sailed to America was called the *City of Richmond*.

Throughout the Mennonite historical experience, totalitarian governments were a major problem for them. They were persecuted because of their religious beliefs. The governments would require Mennonites to serve in their countries' military. This Mennonites could not bring themselves to do so because of their pacifistic beliefs.

These people were what is called Anabaptist, which means they believed that baptism was only valid when the candidate for this religious act confessed his or her faith in Christ and wanted to be baptized. Thus, they were opposed to baptizing infants, who were not able to make a conscious decision to be baptized. This belief caused doctrinal conflicts with other religious groups and the state religion in most places they lived. Mennonites were nonviolent people who believed in the separation of church and state, meaning the state should not determine what is to be believed or practiced religiously. This desire to believe as they wanted and to live their lives as they wished was the driving force behind their migration to America.

Historically, Mennonites were often considered martyrs because they would not sacrifice their religious beliefs for what the world considered the "good life." They held to the belief that God would bless them greatly if they lived the life they thought Jesus would want them to live. They, however, suffered many hardships, severe persecution, and adversity. At times, they became angry at the situations they had to face.

Mennonites were a very proud people and felt that being Mennonite made them a special people in the eyes of God. This feeling of supremacy is exemplified by the fact that they believed there would be a special place in heaven for only Mennonites. These believers considered themselves as more godly people than their non-Mennonite neighbors, even though that definitely was not always the case.

Mennonites became very wealthy because of their unparalleled farming skills. They were such superior farmers that Catherine the Great asked these Mennonite farmers to come to the Ukraine and teach the Russian people how to farm more effectively. Being wealthy and superior farmers probably had a lot to do with their feeling of superiority. However, wealth can be fleeting, and the Mennonites' wealth lasted until the governments took everything away from them.

With this historical background, I can now share pertinent

information about my extended family, as was told to me by my mother during our evening conversations. When my paternal great-grandparents settled in the area where I grew up, I was told that the community expected everyone to be a superior farmer. Even today, many people consider the Mennonites to be excellent farmers, and when my great-grandparents came to America, they were expected to follow the farming tradition. However, farming was not every Mennonite's strong point. My paternal great-grandfather was considered a very poor farmer by the farming standard of the Mennonite community. He made decisions that the community considered foolish. He bought what they considered unproductive sand hill pastureland. This pastureland was only productive or beneficial for grazing cattle. That simple fact caused the farming community to consider it extremely inferior land. However, that so-called unproductive, inferior sand hill pastureland had other redeeming qualities.

I am told that in the 1920s, oil was discovered under this so-called worthless land, and my paternal great-grandparents became very wealthy. I am told that they received more than $5,000 a month in oil income, which at that time was unheard of. Needless to say, my father's family did not have to become superior farmers to be influential in the community.

Being wealthy allowed my great-grandfather to become a very generous person. People would come to see him to request money for purchases of farmland, homes, and so forth. He would give whatever was requested of him and never require repayment. He would go to orchards and purchase large amounts of fruit to hand out to the people of the community. I wonder why a man would give away his assets to people who never thought of him as a successful person. I suppose he did this to gain a feeling of self-worth.

After my paternal grandmother, whom I will refer to as Grandma from now on, grew up, married, and lost her husband at the age of forty-four to complications of diabetes, money became a very important resource to her because it meant financial stability, power, control, and influence, and it gave her the ability to sway people to her way of thinking, wants, and wishes.

Grandma was dearly loved by her family but resented by some of her fellow church members and criticized by many in the community. She controlled her family with what could be called a heavy hand.

Because of her extreme protection of her children, the community blamed her for her rebellious son's actions. She also made every effort to ensure that her daughters married individuals with the same religious background and who would provide them financial security. I have always felt that because Grandma used the almighty dollar to control her son, he never learned how to be responsible for himself or his actions, how to give and receive love, how to work hard for a living, or how to take pride in a job well done. My father grew up never experiencing the feeling of what it is like to be in need of material things. Money was always available for anything and everything. My father learned to become what one might call self-centered and used money to manipulate and impress other people, to the detriment of his own family.

While he was alive, my grandfather was extremely strict with his sons and rather lenient with his daughters. Because of my grandfather being this way, Grandma was just the opposite of him. She was strict with her daughters and lenient with her sons. Because of the tough treatment from his father, my father developed a major dislike for him. As an example of my grandfather's strictness, one day, when my father asked a young lady out on a date, his father refused to give him the car to drive and did not allow him to contact her to explain why he was unable to keep that date. Of course, this situation embarrassed my father greatly. Because of situations like this, my father expressed a deep feeling of hatred for his father and carried that feeling with him to the grave.

When her husband passed away, my grandma did what was traditional for a Mennonite family to do in that situation. She decided to put her eldest son in charge of the 160-acre farm, her family, and the checkbook, even though he was only nineteen years old at the time. At that young of an age and not having been given any prior responsibilities, my father was not prepared to take over the family's farming operation and manage their finances. But my unprepared father became the man of the house with the passing of his father.

After the passing of his father and an unlimited supply of money coming into the family's bank account from oil production, my father was able to do whatever he wanted to do, whenever he wanted to do it. Controlling the family's cash flow made life for my father a piece of cake, so to speak.

My parents' generation was expected to carry on the Mennonite traditions that had been brought over from the old country, along with the new traditions that were established in the new land. In the old country, Mennonites made and consumed wine, and my paternal grandparents did the same until one major event happened. They had made wine, bottled it, and stored it in the basement of their home. One night, all of those homemade bottles of wine they had filled fermented and popped their corks, causing an immense mess in the basement for them to clean up. My grandparents, with their knowledge of what the Bible has to say about consuming "mixed wine" or enhanced fermented grape juice (Proverbs 20:1, Proverbs 23:30, 33; Isaiah 5:22), took this incident as a sign from God that they should no longer consume beverages with an alcohol content. So, from that time on, drinking alcohol was considered against God's Will and a sinful activity. Their wine production and consumption ended abruptly with that particular incident, but their eldest child had already been exposed to family and friends consuming wine at home and at social gatherings.

Other social traditions also changed. Before my maternal grandfather was married, he played the harmonica in a folk dance band. When young, my parents even folk danced at their church's youth activities. I am not sure how it came about, but dancing of any kind became a lewd, lascivious, sinful activity. So, my parents grew up in a time of transition. Things like drinking alcoholic beverages and folk dancing were no longer acceptable. This transitioning, for some Mennonite young people, was very difficult to accept. What had been an acceptable activity for them to participate in at one time was no longer considered acceptable. My father was one of those young people who did not make the transition well. I expect not accepting these social changes and having wealth had a lot to do with the way my father lived his life.

CHAPTER 2

THE BEGINNING OF IT ALL

My father and mother grew up in the same community where my sister and I grew up. They attended the same church assemblies and went to high school together for one year. I use the words *church assemblies* because it is not a service to God; it is a gathering of people for the purpose of worshiping God, to remember Christ and what He did for us and to edify or build up one another in the faith.

Before my parents dated, my mother's older brother and my father were close friends and socialized together. Even though she was three years younger than her brother and my father, my mother would often ride along with them when they went somewhere together. This made it easy for my parents to get to know each other. With money not being an issue for my father, they would go places and do things that other young people were not able to afford to do. My father was very personable, which made it easy for him to pull the wool over people's eyes. He was also very generous with money he didn't have. He used his personality and generosity to his advantage his entire life, and he became very skillful at deception.

My father grew up with a fondness for being thought of as rich. This prideful feeling became a major problem for him. Where arrogance and pride exist, people will suffer. The Bible teaches us that when pride exists in one's life, knowledge of God's will is set aside. Personal feelings become more important than what God requires. First John 2:15–17 tells us to "Love not the world, neither the things that are in the world. If any man love the world, the love of the Father is not in him. For all that is in the world, the lust of the flesh, and the lust of the eyes, and the pride of life, is not of the Father, but is of the world. And the world passeth away, and the lust thereof: but he that doeth the will of God abideth for ever." James 1:14–15 tells us, "But every man is tempted, when he is drawn away of his own lust, and enticed. Then when lust hath conceived, it bringeth forth sin: and sin, when it is finished, bringeth forth death." My father was tempted with pride and social status, which he was unable to set aside. The desire for being thought of as well-to-do controlled his life and supplied him with what he was missing, the feeling of self-worth.

Since Mennonites considered wealth as an extremely important asset, marrying into an affluent family was especially appealing. So, my mother and her parents viewed marrying into my father's family as very desirable. But having money isn't something on which to base a marriage. When marriage or friendship is based on money and money becomes in short supply, things start to fall apart, and that is exactly what happened to my family.

Both sets of grandparents had regrets. My maternal grandfather felt responsible for what my mother had to endure throughout her lifetime because he encouraged the marriage based on the financial security my father represented. My grandma felt responsible for the way my father lived his life. She realized that she should have provided more financial supervision, teaching her son how to manage his financial affairs. Unfortunately, she was also unable to teach her son just how to have a normal functioning family.

In 1940, my parents were married and started their life together. They lived with my grandma and my father's siblings, cultivating Grandma's 160-acre farm and rearing livestock for her. Needless to say, this was not the most ideal situation for a newlywed couple, but with her husband gone, my grandma needed her son to operate the family farm. My parents spent the first two years of their married life in this situation. Both my grandma and my father basically ran things their way, causing my mother to become submissive to their wishes. After two years, my father's mother felt that her son was being careless with the handling of her finances. Too much money was disappearing from the family bank account with no regard for where it went. Upset with how her son was handling the family finances, my grandma thought it was time for her careless son to be on his own. So she purchased a two-hundred-acre farm for him. Purchasing a farm for my father was not an unusual thing for my grandma to do. She purchased a farm for each of her children when they married. My grandma told her son that it was time for him to make his own way in life. Thus, my father lost control of the family's checkbook and its unlimited supply of money.

My father had never experienced having debts, so paying off debts was foreign to him. Saving for unexpected situations that may come along was an unfamiliar concept as well. His financial learning curve was immense, and reality became apparent when he was forced to provide for himself and his family. After spending two years under the control of her mother-in-law, my mother had become very passive and remained stifled under her husband's repressive control when they moved to their own farm.

The old white clapboard (redwood lap siding), two-story farmhouse into which my parents moved, and where they spent the next eleven years of their marriage, and I the first five of my life, was not fancy but was very livable, according to the standards of that time. Today, people would consider it extremely primitive because it was equipped with only cold running water to the kitchen and washroom sinks, and there were no bathroom facilities located in the house.

This farmhouse had a large kitchen area with a Formica-topped table and metal chairs located in the middle of the room. There was a front door leading from the kitchen to a screened-in front porch, and a second door opened into a washroom.

The washroom had a concrete floor with a drain in the center of the room. This washroom was a multipurpose room, used for many things like bathing during the summer months and laundering our clothes and drying them on an inside wash line during rainy days and winter months. After the clothes sloshed around inside the wash machine's tub for a while, my mother would hand rinse them and then wring the water out of the clothes, using the wringer attachment located above the washing machine's tub. You had to be very careful when using that wringer attachment. It was never a good thing to get your fingers between the rollers. When that happened, the wringer attachment pulled your fingers and arm between the two rollers and squeezed them severely.

Mom would hang the washed clothes on a wire line to dry outside during the summer months, and to this day, I can still see the washed clothes hanging on the line, flapping in the Kansas summer breeze. I am not sure why, but clothes that are dried outdoors seem to smell so much better than clothes dried inside a dryer. The only exception was when a bird flew over the drying clothes and left a streaky deposit on them. When this happened, the bird-soiled clothes had to be rewashed and dried.

The washroom also housed my sister's potty chair and a commode for adult use during the night since there wasn't an indoor toilet. No one wanted to run outside to the two-hole outhouse in the middle of the night. This washroom had been added to the southeast corner of the original farmhouse.

There was a dining room used for entertaining guests and a parlor converted into a master bedroom. A stairway was located between the north wall of the kitchen and the south wall of the dining room; it led upstairs to one bedroom and a storage room. Lastly, there was a second stairway located under the stairs that led to the second-floor bedroom. This stairway led down to a dirt-floor basement with limestone rock walls.

The farmstead also had a very large, wood, vertical-sided red barn that could accommodate sixty milk cows, a hayloft that my sister and I loved to play in, a thirty-foot-tall concrete silo, a long white chicken house, a small white structure used as a shop and utility building, a round, metal storage Butler grain bin, three garage-sized buildings, a two-sided wooden grain storage building with four individual grain storage areas, and an open drive-through between the two sides.

When I was two years old, our parents decided to put a real porcelain toilet stool inside our farmhouse. They located this porcelain toilet stool on a small landing at the top of the basement stairway. This toilet area had two doors, one leading into the kitchen area and the other leading into that scary dirt-floor cellar. This underground room was spooky because snakes, mice, and bugs were often found down there, and it was dark. As a child, I thought a big snake, a nasty, repulsive mouse, a gigantic spider, a huge bug of some sort, or some other type of scary creature was just on the other side of the door leading into that basement. Because of these images in my mind, I didn't spend too much time there.

Now we had a modern toilet but no bathing facilities inside the house. So the concrete-floor washroom was still the place baths were taken during summer months. Because there was no heat in the washroom, during the cold months, baths were taken in the kitchen. A round, 28-gallon, 13-inch-high galvanized metal tub served as our bathtub, and everyone had to use the same metal tub for baths. This metal tub was of a size that when an adult took a bath, only the adult's bottom would fit in the tub. The children used this galvanized tub first, and the water could easily become polluted. So my sister always wanted to be the first to bathe. Being older, my sister usually won the bath order privilege, and she would bathe first. I guess since I was the baby of the family, I wasn't trusted to not pollute the water.

Since we didn't have hot running water inside the house, our mother would heat the bathing water in a large metal container on the kitchen stove. She would pour the heated water into the tub. I am not sure, but I suspect the water got changed after the children bathed. Bathing happened at least once a week, on Saturday night, for church attendance the next day. Of course, there were times we got dirty playing outside, and baths had to take place more often.

It was my mother who made sure that we attended church assemblies every Sunday. Mom was a big fan of cleanliness, and to her, cleanliness was next to godliness. The church building we attended was located fifteen miles from our farm, and on our way to those church assemblies, Mother would make sure her little boy was clean. I hated when she would spit on a Kleenex and wipe behind and inside my ears, making sure they were clean. She would ask if I had washed behind my ears, and I always replied that I had washed carefully.

My mother knew just how carefully I washed behind my ears, so my answers were never good enough for her. It never failed. I had to put up with the spit-wet Kleenex, even though no one saw behind my ears.

During the summer, after my parents had moved to their two-hundred-acre farm, disaster struck. Their farm was hit by a massive hailstorm that stripped the trees of their leaves, destroyed all of their crops, and killed the birds and small farm animals. The hail was so severe that it caused the cattle to bleed from their back injuries where the hailstones tore into their hides.

Their injuries were so severe that the cattle had to be sold for slaughter. Needless to say, my parents lost almost everything they had. They had no income from the farm that year. This was a major financial tragedy for them, but a few weeks later, an even bigger tragedy struck my mother's family. This tragedy happened to my father's best friend, my mother's two brothers, and forever affected all those who saw the incident happen.

My father was standing next to his best friend when the tragedy took place. This tragedy left scars on my parents and my mother's family that only we cousins, now as adults, can begin to fully understand. The gruesome details of that incident and how it affected my uncle and the family have stayed with me my entire life. The men of my mother's family were out hunting rabbits one afternoon from the back of a farm truck. The older uncle stood up in front of his younger brother just as he shot at a rabbit. My grandfather was driving the truck when his younger son was accidentally killed. This tragedy was clearly hard on my uncle and grandfather and changed the family in ways that I am unable to explain. This tragedy was no doubt hardest on my surviving uncle. Understandably, my uncle's life was so affected by what happened that he never truly recovered from it. The close relationship of my uncle and father somehow faded after that day. Their relationship was never quite the same again.

My mother told me that the incident was so gruesome that my father did not want to talk about the details of what he saw happen. She did say that my father told her that her brother tried to put his brother's brain back into his skull after it happened. The brother who shot the gun was so distraught that he jumped out of the bed of the truck and ran screaming at the top of his lungs. My father said that he had to run after him and tackle him to stop him from running. It was a devastating experience for everyone. The brother who died and his wife had their first child on the way when the accident happened. I can't imagine how hard it was for my uncle to live the rest of his life with that tragic experience always on his mind.

With these two tragedies happening within weeks of each other and my parents with no money to live off of until the next harvest season, surviving was a priority. Unfortunately, my grandma was still upset with how her son had handled her finances and refused to help them financially. She expected my father to handle his financial situation, but being without unlimited funds was something my father found difficult to deal with. He came to realize that borrowing money from the local bank by mortgaging the farm was an easy way to put money in his pocket.

In 1942, my sister was born a bit too early. My mother was very concerned for her firstborn child's well-being. She told my sister her fingernails were not fully developed when she was born. An undeveloped fingernail was a sign of being a premature baby. Our mother had painted the nursery for my sister the day before she was born. The doctors assumed it was the paint fumes our mother inhaled that caused her early birth. Even though a premature baby, my sister was a cute, feminine baby girl.

As a toddler, her talent for singing became apparent. Our grandma would have her stand on a wooden stool and sing the song "Jesus Loves Me." At two years of age, she could sing the song, word for word, pronounce every word correctly, and sing in tune. God blessed my sister with a beautiful singing voice. Our grandma was extremely proud of her granddaughter's singing ability because Mennonite people consider having musical talents as a very valuable asset for a family, the church, and the community.

Before I was born, my parents and maternal grandparents spoke the Switzer-Deutsch language to one another to prevent my sister from knowing what they were talking about. That would have worked well, except my grandma had sat my sister down on that same kitchen stool when she was cooking and taught her to understand the Switzer-Deutsch language. Not realizing my sister understood every word they were speaking, my parents and maternal grandparents spoke sensitive things to one another in Switzer-Deutsch while she was present. One day, as my mother and maternal grandmother were talking to each other, my sister laughed at what was said. Once they realized she understood what they were talking about, the use of the Switzer-Deutsch language became less important and stopped being spoken in front of her. By the time I came along, my father and mother had already stopped speaking Switzer-Deutsch to each other, and I missed out on learning the language like my sister had.

When I was in the oven, so to speak, my mother had a very difficult time carrying me to full term. She was bedridden for the last three months of the pregnancy. My mother told me that she had prayed if God would allow my live birth, she would give me to Him and help instill in me the importance of being faithful to Him! She kept that promise! I have a very strong Christian faith. My sister told me that our mother was extremely proud of her baby boy and considered me to be a special child.

I was a chubby baby with an olive complexion and a full head of dark hair. My sister says that I was a very calm, cheerful, good-natured child with a pleasant personality. I was an obedient type of kid and very easy to raise. All through my growing-up years, I had no problem entertaining myself. I played for hours, using my imagination to create my own entertainment.

I was a true farm kid and loved to play like I was farming. I played with toy tractors, farming equipment, trucks, and farm animals. I built farms out of anything I could get my hands on. The farms I built inside our house would take up one-fourth of our large dining room floor. When I played outside in the dirt, I made fences out of sixteen-penny nails and string. I would hammer the nails into the ground to serve as fence posts. I would wrap string to and around each nail, stretching the string tight between the nails. This string served as barbed wire fencing. I played with my toy farm animals so much that I wore the legs off of my toy cows. Legless toy cows didn't stop me from playing with them. I knew that there wasn't enough money to buy replacements, so I made do with the legless cows.

My sister was very protective of her baby brother and enjoyed mothering me. She had a real live doll to play with. When my mother was working outside of the house, she would take over the mothering duties. One time, when I was a month or two old, our mother's parents came to our farm. While they were busy helping Mom with some outside chores, I became hungry and cried. I am told that I didn't cry unless I was hungry. No one outside the house could hear my cries, so my four-and-a-half-year-old sister decided to take care of her baby brother's problem and feed me a bottle of milk. She looked everywhere for milk and found a bottle lying around the house. What she did not realize was that the milk she had found was cold and had gone bad. Doing what she thought Mom would do, she proceeded to feed me this cold, spoiled milk, which satisfied me for a while. Cold milk, let alone spoiled, isn't good for a baby to consume, and this less than desirable milk gave me a major tummy ache. I had been hungry, but now my tummy hurt for a much different reason. I was told that I cried extremely loud because of my upset tummy. My maternal grandmother had feared there was something seriously wrong with me since I never cried when she was around. This time, however, I used my lungs, putting her fears to rest.

My sister's early-childhood memories are somewhat different from mine. Until I was born, our father was around the family more often. During my sister's early years, until the age of about five, she was very close to our father. My sister was truly what one would call Daddy's little girl! She would sit on his lap during the church assemblies. When she was feeling sick, he would hold her, which helped her feel better. When he was reading the newspaper, my sister would crawl up under the newspaper and onto his lap. When this happened, he would read the comic section to her. Our father would also tell her Peter Rabbit and the Uncle Remus stories. Up until I was two years of age, I am told that I got in on some of those Peter Rabbit and Uncle Remus stories. My sister claims that the Peter Rabbit stories our father told us were so sad that I would cry when hearing them. I was too young to remember being told those sad stories. Our father made Mr. McGregor so mean to Peter Rabbit and his family that my sister developed a major dislike for Mr. McGregor. Her dislike for that character had a real impact on my life.

When I was born, my parents named me Gregory Gene, but that name and my first birth certificate lasted only one day. When my parents told my sister that I was named Gregory Gene, she cried and threw a terrible fit. There was no way she was going to have a brother named Gregory because it was too much like the name Mr. McGregor, who was so awful to Peter Rabbit's family in our father's stories.

Because of my sister's insistence that her brother could not be named Gregory, my parents were compelled to change my name. The next day, they ripped up my first birth certificate and made a new one with my new name on it. My new name, Robert Charles, was just fine with my sister. So, thanks to my father's sad stories about an awful Mr. McGregor and my sister's extreme disapproval of the name Gregory, I have the unique distinction of having had two birth certificates and two different names in the first two days of my life.

As an infant, I slept in a crib at the foot end of my parents' bed, but when I was older, my sleeping arrangement changed, and I was made to sleep in an upstairs bedroom, shared with my sister. She slept in a regular-size bed in the middle of the room. I slept in a crib-type bed located at the top of the stairway.

When the weather was cold, it was necessary for us to sleep with a lot of blankets over us. There was no heat in this upstairs bedroom. The only heat we had was what would rise up the stairway during the night if the bottom stairway door was left open. In the mornings, when we got out from under all of our blankets, it did not take us long to get ourselves dressed and hustle our little bodies downstairs, where it was warmer. When thunderstorms occurred, my protective sister would come to my crib, wake me up, and take me downstairs to our parents' bedroom. During these times, we would sleep on an area rug at the foot of our parents' bed.

The floor wasn't the most comfortable place to sleep, but it was better than sleeping upstairs by yourself during strong gusts of wing, lightning flashes, and loud thunder. I only remember my mother, sister, and me together during those times. Thunder and lightning were very scary for my sister and me. But our mother would comfort us by saying there was no reason to be afraid because lightning was God's way of getting our attention, and thunder was just His way of talking to us. At that young age, I thought that God talked extremely loud, but I knew God was only telling me not to worry because everything was going to be all right!

When I was two years old and my sister was six, our father became much more restless and would go to the nearest town to play dominoes in the local pool hall during the day and most nights instead of doing the farm work to keep it operational and support his family. At times, he would win money playing dominoes, which encouraged him to continue gambling. However, there were more times that he lost money. More and more, my father became eager to be away from the farm and our home, especially at night. The first time that my sister says she remembers our father not being home at night was an evening when she had a severe earache and needed her daddy to hold her so she would feel better, but her daddy was not there for her! So, our mother held her instead and told her that her daddy would be home soon. But he didn't get home in time to hold her before she went to sleep. To my sister, that was the beginning of her realizing that our father was not home in the evenings, especially when she needed him. I was far too young to remember my father being at home much, especially at night. During the early years of my life, my mother demanded that my father be home with the family at least on Sunday evenings. For a few years, he complied with her demand, and we would spend those Sunday evenings visiting our extended family and friends. I do not recall, during my entire life, a single evening that my father was home with just his family.

In an attempt to regain the money lost on playing dominoes, the farm income he spent, and the mortgaged money he thoughtlessly used on his own pleasure outings, my father searched for quick, easy ways to obtain money. Wouldn't you know ... a man came to their small community with just such a get-rich-quick opportunity! My father saw this get-rich-quick scheme as very inviting. So inviting that he took the risk and borrowed more money to invest in it. Securing money from the local bank was not a problem for him because of his family's financial status. My father soon saw mortgaging things as an easy way to obtain the money he needed to continue his deceitful lifestyle. This get-rich-quick financial opportunity was investing the borrowed money in a gold mine located in Mexico.

Now, one would think, being asked to invest money in a sight-unseen gold mine in Mexico would send up red flags. But a number of very wealthy men in the community had invested in this mine and encouraged my father to do the same. Since these wealthy men had invested, my father thought it would be a good, safe way to regain his financial losses and supplement his spending habits. He assumed that if these wealthy men thought it was a good investment, who was he to question their thinking? My mother, on the other hand, felt much differently about investing borrowed money. She feared losing the money they had borrowed on such a questionable investment, but my controlling father borrowed $2,000 and invested the money anyway.

My parents received stock certificates for the shares of stock they had purchased in this gold mine. After a period of time and no money coming in from the mine, those wealthy men who invested along with my father decided to travel to Mexico to see, firsthand, why there was no return on their investment. Surprisingly, a gold mine actually existed, but there was a problem. The existing gold mine was not producing enough gold to pay for the expenses of mining it. So, my parents were $2,000 more in debt and part-owners of an unprofitable Mexican gold mine!

When my father traveled to Mexico with the other investors to see the mine, he took an eight-millimeter movie camera with him to film the entire mining operation. The film of the mining procedures showed them to be very primitive and inept. That film is very old, but I still possess that mining film and those stock certificates to this day.

My mother's family felt that my father was not the same person after he returned from that Mexico trip. They felt that something had happened that changed him. My mother's family realized, for the first time, that my mother, sister, and I and the farming operation were not priorities of his. Left with little money to live on and not being accustomed to having limited funds, my father again tried to make money in another get-rich-quick endeavor. Unfortunately, he listened to one of the same men who had lost money along with him in that gold mine calamity. This, of course, turned out to be another bad idea. This new idea for making money was speculating in oil with this man and some other investors. It is easy to understand why the oil business was very appealing to my father. His family's wealth had been obtained from oil production. The man who my father associated with was not a moral man. In fact, it could be said that he was immoral, unethical, unprincipled, and dishonest.

It is true what the Bible says in 1 Corinthians 15:33: "Be not deceived: evil communications (companionship) corrupt good manners (moral habits)." This man my father associated with was, as the scriptures describe, an "evil companion" with corrupt "moral habits." Evil companionship will not tolerate us unless we embrace their lifestyle. The only way we can maintain our character is to live according to the highest standards at all times. In Ephesians 5:11, the apostle Paul wrote this, "And have no fellowship with the unfruitful works of darkness, but rather reprove them." The word translated "fellowship" in this passage carries the meaning of sharing in and participation. The word translated "reprove" carries the meaning of to expose, convict, and show to be guilty. So, we can see that choosing the wrong people to associate with is detrimental to us, making our choices of companionship of great importance. Unfortunately for my family, my father was easily influenced, and he developed a liking for immoral activities.

The oil speculation story was hardly an adequate reason for my father to be away from home each evening. Consequently, he needed another believable excuse to go along with the oil business fairy-tale fiasco to alleviate my mother's suspicions. To continue the immoral lifestyle he had learned to enjoy, my father concocted a story that my mother was able to believe.

The fabricated story my father came up with was that he was secretly working as an undercover agent for the Kansas Bureau of Investigation. According to him, this secretive and very hazardous work had to conveniently be done at night, giving him the perfect excuse he needed to be away from his family and the farm each evening until four or five in the morning. Getting home at that time each morning left my father tired and incapable of helping with the daily farm operation.

Of course, my mother became skeptical of his stories and often questioned him about them, especially since she did not see any money come into the home from any of his evening activities. All she could see was being abandoned by her husband, and money from the farm and his so-called evening work went elsewhere. My father defended his secretive ventures by claiming that the money made from the undercover work, oil speculation business, and farming were needed to cover the expenses incurred during his evening work. My mother felt that his so-called work activities were not worth the sacrifices the family had to make, and she wanted him to get a regular job instead. My father did not want to give up his evening activities and pacified my mother somewhat with the claim that in twenty years, he would be able to retire from the KBI with a pension they could live off of for the rest of their lives. My mother was disappointed with my father's choices, but what could she do to change things, having become a passive person and under the control of her abusive husband?

My father needed my mother, sister, and me to keep quiet about his evening absences. If his mother, uncles, and siblings found out about his unethical activities, he would be ostracized from the family and would lose out on his inheritance, and his inheritance was very important to him. My father kept us silent about the miserable, depressing life we were forced to live and his absences from home by telling us that if we told anyone about the situation, his life and our lives would be in extreme danger because of the nature of the undercover work.

The real tragedy in all of this was that my family continually lived in fear of losing our lives because of what my father told us. He claimed to have been responsible for some very bad people being sent to prison, and if these very dangerous people found out that we were his family, they would probably have someone come to the farm and kill us to get back at him. The thought of losing her children to some disgruntled criminal kept my mother from saying anything about her husband's evening activities. The possibility of my sister and me losing our lives and possibly losing our mother was an effective way of keeping us from saying anything about why our father was away from home so much.

Things always seemed to happen to make my father's stories believable. One would think that his concocted stories would become exposed due to a lack of support for them. However, my father's claims became very real due to three situations that happened to us. The first had to do with a strange man coming to our farm one afternoon and knocking on the front door. I was closest to the front door, so I answered the knock at the door, and this strange man asked for my father. When my father came to the door to see who it was, he recognized the man and pushed me back into the house, closing the door behind him. Inside the house, I was unable to hear their conversation.

As I looked through our large living room picture window, I saw this man and my father get into a very heated argument that became physical. Being only five years old, I was scared by what I was witnessing. I had always been taught to be nonviolent, and here my father and this strange man were physically fighting, wrestling, and punching each other. When the altercation was over and the strange man left our farm, my father told us his account of what had happened. He said that through his undercover work, he was responsible for this man's wife being arrested and going to jail for illegal drug sales and use. In the early 1950s, drugs were not something we were familiar with. I had never heard of illegal drugs. My father went on to say that this man was upset with him because of my father's part in what had happened to this man's wife. My father told us he could not guarantee that this same man would not return when he was gone and take his anger and frustration out on my mother, sister, and me. That was a scary thought for us! Being beat up or even killed was not something we took lightly. As a result of this incident and the possibility of people doing us physical harm, we became very suspicious of people we did not know who drove by our farm or came to our house and those we came in contact with during our daily routines and activities. We kept our doors locked, and if we didn't know the person who came to our farm, we would not answer a knock at the door and hide until they were gone.

Only my father and this strange man knew what the real story was behind this situation. Not knowing the truth about this situation has caused my sister and I to speculate about what the real story was. Since there always seemed to be a teeny bit of truth my father based his stories on, my sister and I now believe the real story behind the conflict was probably due to our father having an affair with the man's wife. This brawl happened because the man was upset about the affair taking place. This man may have even had suspicions about his wife being involved in immoral activities, and he may have asked my father to keep an eye on his wife's activities for him. A situation like that would have provided my father with the prime opportunity to have an affair with her himself. We do not know the truth behind this situation. We can only speculate as to why that confrontation took place.

The second scary situation happened to my sister shortly after the first confrontation with the strange man coming to our farm. My sister was approximately ten years old at the time and was often allowed to walk home from the country school with some neighboring children her age when the weather permitted. I was too young to go to school and walk home with her, so she would walk with the neighbor children for the first three-quarters of a mile. After that point, she was on her own for approximately one more mile.

One day while she was approximately one quarter of a mile from our home, an unfamiliar car approached her from behind. My sister had been warned about what could happen to her by strangers, so she became fearful of the situation she was about to face. As the car approached her from behind, she was near a small, wooden, country road bridge. Feeling uneasy about the situation with the unfamiliar car approaching, my sister left the sandy dirt roadway and crawled down through the tall grass and weeds covering the deep ditch into a dry creek bed. This unfamiliar car actually stopped on top of the bridge above her. The car window was rolled down, and an unfamiliar man stared at her out of the open car window. This sinister-looking man smiled at her. Being scared of what this man might do to her, my sister quickly made the decision to crawl through the barbed wire fence at the bottom of the creek bed and run through our pasture to our farm buildings, where she could hide from this man. While she was running through the pasture, the unfamiliar car drove away. To this day, my sister can still see, in her mind, the vivid image of the scary man's villainous-appearing face staring and smiling at her, and she still feels the intense fear for her well-being that came over her that day.

Upon reaching the house, she told Mom about what had just happened to her. Mom listened to her account with great concern, yet tried to comfort her. This incident helped solidify the deep-seated fear of physical harm that could happen to us. My sister had never seen this unfamiliar man before, nor did she after that day. Needless to say, from that day on, our mother would not allow my sister to walk to and from school alone.

The third frightening incident that happened definitely convinced my mother and me that our lives were in danger. I was approximately fourteen years old, and my sister was out of the house, living on her own in a city fifteen miles away from our farm. Fortunately, she missed out on experiencing this frightening situation. Early one morning, around two o'clock, my mother and I were jolted awake in our beds. A vehicle drove by our farm, slammed on its brakes, and skidded to a stop on the sanded roadway at the end of our short driveway. Then gunshots were fired through our yard. Feeling shot at by some unknown vengeful person that early morning convinced us that our lives were truly in danger and we could be killed at any time. That horrific experience put a justifiable, real, honest-to-goodness fear into my mother and me. This incident definitely confirmed our fear of losing our lives and served as a warning to us to never speak to anyone about why my father was always gone at night. When my father came home a few hours later, Mom recounted what had taken place. He didn't act surprised or even concerned for our well-being. He simply replied that he had warned us about what could happen if certain people he helped put into prison found out that we were his family. So, for sixteen years of my life, I lived with real fear of losing my life or a family member because of some vindictive person's actions. To this very day, I do not know who fired those shots into our yard that morning, but I suspect that my father was somehow involved in this terrifying event. Could it have actually been my father who fired those shots to scare us into silence? Maybe! Could he have had someone else do it for him? Maybe! I do not know! In any case, this shooting was an extremely effective way of scaring us into silence. It convinced my mother and me that my father had to be involved in very dangerous activities, that life was uncertain for us, and that it was in our best interest not to speak to anyone about what my father claimed he was doing or why he was away from home so much. So our fears were reinforced, and we never spoke to anyone about my father's evening activities or about the things we had experienced. Through the years, I learned to keep things that happened to me to myself. I spent a good part of my life fearful of saying who my father was when asked by anyone.

Because of the fear I lived with, even to this day, when asked about who my father is, I get a hesitant feeling inside of me to say who he was, despite the fact that I know all of his stories were fabrications. I guess a deep-seated fear never really leaves you. My mother, sister, and I had no knowledge that my father was actually running around womanizing along with the man who got him into the so-called oil speculation business! We thought my father was working in a very dangerous occupation and that it was imperative we remained silent about it. Of course, there were times when we questioned his truthfulness, but incidents always seemed to happen that verified his claims. It is my understanding that my father's mother and siblings had no knowledge of his immoral pursuits.

Now, you would think that someone within the Mennonite community would have known about my father's escapades and would have approached us with what they knew. Unfortunately, no one ever did. Instead of helping us that way, they treated my sister, mother, and me as if we were inferior to the rest of the community and lepers in their midst! I never understood why we were treated like that in a supposedly loving, caring, and peace-centered Mennonite community, from the late 1940s through the early 1970s. It is hard for me to comprehend. This poor treatment was at the hands of "good" Mennonite people with whom we went to school and attended weekly church assemblies. Being ostracized, especially by our peers, made it impossible for my sister and me to develop close friends. If we had what could be thought of as friends, they might turn on us in a second! They were nice to us one minute but hateful to us in the next. So, I never was able to trust any of my peers to treat me well. In the back of my mind, there was always this feeling of mistreatment eventually coming my way. Growing up in these stressful conditions was not helpful for developing a trust in those I was supposed to be able to trust. Actually, to this day, if someone I consider to be a friend treats me poorly, I am taken back to my growing-up years and how it felt to live that way. Not being able to say anything about the fear we lived with, not even to our relatives, was extremely difficult for me, and as a result, I grew up very frustrated and a bit defensive.

Why wasn't my mother more forceful with my father? Matthew 19:9 tells us, "And I say unto you, Whosoever shall put away his wife, except it be for fornication, and shall marry another, committeth adultery: and whoso marrieth her which is put away doth commit adultery." If she had known about my father's adulterous ways, she would have been scripturally justified to divorce my father on the grounds of adultery and marry someone else. But Mennonite people, at that time, believed there wasn't any reason for a divorce to happen. So, a divorce was a big no-no, even though Jesus said there was one and only one reason for a divorce and remarriage to take place.

Those in the community who divorced were excommunicated from the church and ostracized from the Mennonite community. Basically, divorced individuals were forced to move out of the community, even if they were not the guilty party in the divorce situation. If a person wished to remain in the church, divorced Mennonites could go before the entire church, plead to remain in the church, and apologize— even for something they had not done. That pleading and apology seldom kept them from being excommunicated. So, the possibility of being cast out of the church and community, even though my mother wasn't guilty of anything, was another reason she did not divorce my father.

My mother's parents believed that one should not retaliate against mistreatment, be it verbal or physical. The belief of not responding to abuse by a corresponding act of ill treatment was instilled in Mother as a child. This credence controlled my mother's way of life, and she taught her children the same.

My father's violent temper and the physical and mental abuse my mother endured kept her from pushing my father too hard. She feared what he was capable of doing to her. She was a battered woman and suffered the battered woman syndrome.

Another reason our mother did not push our father out of the house was that she did not want her children growing up without a father. The stigma of that would be too great. But growing up without a father is essentially what happened anyway. My sister and I grew up ill-treated for who our father was and what people expected of us to become because of him. The shoddy treatment from members of the community, along with my father's lack of interest in me and my activities, caused me to feel unwanted, inferior, inadequate, and, to some degree, worthless.

CHAPTER 3

THE EARLY YEARS

I am told that during my parents' first seven years of marriage, my mother was a very happy person, and our family functioned as what appeared to be a fairly normal family. Mother was a pretty young woman who laughed and played practical jokes on those she loved. Unfortunately, due to all she endured throughout her life at the hands of my father, she became a woman who felt no self-worth, fearful of what life might bring and unsure of how to react to what was happening in her life. As years came and went, my mother became unable to make a decision without fear of what the consequences might be.

Once I was old enough to remember things, I realized that my father was never around and did not seem to care much about us. Growing up without a father to nurture me and show me that he loved me left me not knowing how fathers really treat their children—how they show the love and guidance every child needs. When my sister shares with me stories of how our father was in her first five years of life, I realize what I missed out on. I never heard the bedtime stories, got tucked into bed, or shared evening prayers with my father. I grew up not realizing that these things should have been the norm for me. Feeling that my father rejected me and was never really there for me left me with no fond memories of him. I am told that he was a very giving person but never to us, his family, only to other people. People thought of him as a kind, generous, and good-natured person. When I became a father, I strove to give my children what I had missed out on. I can somewhat empathize with orphaned and adopted children who grow up wondering why their birth parents didn't want them. I grew up wondering why my father, who I knew, didn't seem to want to be around me.

My earliest memories have to do with our mother cleaning the dirt and wax out of our ears. This ear cleaning was done in the kitchen, after the evening chores and supper were over. Our mother would sit on one of our old kitchen chairs and have us lay our heads across her lap. She would clean the dirt and wax out of our ears with hydrogen peroxide and bobby pins. Sixty-eight years later, I can still feel how good that felt. Even though I was very young, I fondly remember those times.

Another early memory I have has to do with my great-uncles. Because of my interest in animals and the farm at a very young age, my two great-uncles on my father's side of the family took an interest in me, and I gravitated to them because they did what my father wouldn't do. They gave me attention. When my father's family would gather together at my grandmother's farm for Sunday noon meals, I would squeeze in between my two great-uncles while they were sitting on the living room couch. I would proceed to tell them all about "da boo," meaning the big, mean Holstein bull at our farm. I assume I did a lot of talking about da boo, and my great-uncles never seemed to tire of hearing me tell them about that bull. They must have enjoyed our conversations very much because they would take me out to my grandma's barn to see the Hereford bull she had. Of course, that encouraged me to continue to talk to them about da boo. I always wanted to see my grandmother's bull, so every time we were together, I would tell my two great-uncles about the bull at our farm, knowing they would then take me out to see my grandma's Hereford bull.

Our grandma loved to have my sister and me come and stay with her overnight. She always had us sleep in her bed with her. I had to sleep in the middle of the bed, with my sister on one side of me and Grandma on the other side. I suppose Grandma thought I was too little and would fall out of bed if I didn't sleep between her and my sister. Before we could go to sleep, we would say our bedtime prayers and sing the German song "Gott ist du Lieber" ("God Thou Beloved") in the Switzer-Deutsch language. I learned the Switzer-Deutsch words to that song, but at that very young age, I didn't know what the words meant.

My sister says that during the evenings when our father was away from home, we would sit on the living room rug and talk with our mother. She would tell us about God and the importance of remaining faithful to him as we grew up. Our mother would take the time to rub our backs, which we really enjoyed. After she gave us our back rubs, she would have us walk on her back. As I got older and heavier, she would have me drive my toy trucks all over her back as a replacement for a back rub. My sister remembers laughing a lot during those times. I wish I had been old enough to remember those happy times. My sister and I were extremely fortunate to have had a devoted mother who put the well-being of her children above her own needs, unlike our father. Our mother sacrificed much for us, and we always had our mother's undivided attention. She was a good example for us, and to this day, I remember what she would say when things didn't go right. She would say, "Ach du lieber himmel staunch," meaning, "Oh my goodness, gracious friend." She would use this Switzer-Deutsch phrase instead of saying any bad words.

There were times, however, when my sister would find our mother in tears, which, of course, saddened my sister greatly. To make things seem better, our mother would always reassure her that everything would be OK someday. She never spoke poorly of our father, which revealed the type of person she was.

I am told that my sister and I sometimes played in an upstairs closet where our mother stored her crystal and china dishware. My sister would sneak into the closet to play, and I, of course, would follow her in there. With us both in that small closet, at times things would get broken. Being the youngest, I would get the blame for the broken dishware. I was too young to remember if the broken dishware was always my fault. In any case, I got the blame for us being banned from the closet.

My sister was a very active child. When I was young, she would run circles around me. I was the kind of kid who was content with just standing in one place, watching my sister run and jump around. We even have eight-millimeter movies of that happening. My sister was very entertaining to me!

Older siblings seem to take advantage of their younger brothers and sisters. Being the older sibling, my sister often took advantage of me. At times, our mother and paternal grandmother would give us gum to chew. Our grandmother always had Black Jack gum in her purse and offered it to us every time we were together. Black Jack gum tasted like black licorice to me. When my sister and I were given a stick of gum to chew, my sister would quickly put her stick of gum into her mouth and then tell me that my stick of gum had rotten ends. Of course, I didn't want to chew anything that was rotten. My cagey sister would lead me to believe that she was such a kind person in offering to bite off those rotten ends for me. That would leave her with a stick and a half of gum in her mouth and only a half stick for me. Even though I was very young, it didn't take me long to catch on to what was happening. Her trickery abruptly ended.

When my family traveled by car, my sister would pester me, as older siblings often do. To keep the peace between us, we each had our half of the back seat, divided by an imaginary line. Our halves were not to be infringed upon by the other sibling. I was one who generally adhered to that rule, but my sister often did not. She knew that she could get away with pestering me on my half of the car seat. I was the one to fuss about her infringement on my side, and, thus, I was the one to get into trouble. One Sunday evening while my family was driving home from my paternal grandmother's house, my sister was harassing me. It was a time when my father was actually home for the evening. His patience left a lot to be desired, and in this case, he, in no uncertain terms, warned us that he would put us out of the car if he heard another noise from either of us. I was about four years old at the time, and my sister did what she wasn't supposed to do. She touched me on my side of the back seat. Of course, I was the one to make a noise. It was nighttime and very dark outside, around nine o'clock. We were about a quarter of a mile away from our farm when I made that noise. My father stopped the car, took me out of the back seat, stood me up on that country dirt road, and drove off. There I was, this little four-year-old kid, standing alone on that dark country road, feeling abandoned by my father. My sister was very scared for me and extremely sorry that she had a part in what happened. Of course, at four years of age, I was extremely scared of the dark, mainly because of the numerous coyotes that roamed our area. The coyotes would howl at night, come around our farmhouse after dark, and chase our dogs around the house. They would try to make an easy meal of one of them. Standing alone on that dark country road with coyotes nearby made my imagination work overtime! I knew I couldn't run as fast as our dogs. So I feared that I would become the next easy meal for one of those coyotes. I hustled home as fast as my little legs would take me. I made it to our house unscathed, but, needless to say, that event caused me to fear my father and what he was capable of doing to me.

Since my father was gone so frequently, my mother often went to visit her parents, and we kids would go along with her. On one of those days, my grandfather was out in his old wooden garage working on two wooden rocking horses for my two older cousins. My grandfather told me that he was making these two rocking horses for my cousins' birthdays. I loved horses and wanted a rocking horse for myself. Since I was two years younger than the younger of the two cousins, I figured that my turn was still coming and my grandfather would be making me one too. I had a special request of him. I told my grandfather when he made my rocking horse, to make mine alive! He did eventually make me a rocking horse, but it wasn't alive as I had hoped it would be. When I got older, I did get my live horse to ride. Her name was Daisy.

When I was five years old, my father went to help a neighbor build a rock dam across a small creek that ran through his pasture. This dam was constructed in a wooded area of the pasture, with animal trails along the banks of the creek. I am not sure why, but I was able to go along with my father that day when he helped our neighbor construct the rock dam. I suspect that my mother probably talked him into taking me with him. While Dad and the neighbor were building the rock dam, I played along the banks of the creek. I ran along the animal trails, and as I was running along one trail, I thought I stepped on a small tree branch that flipped up and poked my ankle. I had stepped on small branches before that poked my ankles, but this time it hurt for a much longer period. In spite of the pain in my ankle, I continued to play along the creek bank that day. Later that evening, I complained to my mother about not feeling well and wasn't really hungry. I was always a good eater, so not being hungry was very unusual. It was a sign that I wasn't feeling well. I always liked to eat, especially meat and potatoes, probably due to the fact that I didn't get meat and potatoes that often.

The next day, we had a family meal at our maternal grandparents' home. I still wasn't feeling well and didn't eat much. I complained to my mother that my ankle hurt. Upon examining my ankle, my mother found two small fang holes at the base of my Achilles tendon. The snake that bit me had to have been a small prairie rattler, but it was far too late to worry about the injected poison hurting me. I was an extremely fortunate young boy. The snake that bit me didn't inject enough venom into me to kill me. It just injected enough venom to make me sick. That snake must have been very small or had just eaten something, having injected its poison into its meal before I came along. I didn't feel well for a few days, but I survived that ordeal. It had to have been the providence of God that I survived that situation. Some people would say that it was a miracle that I survived that snake bite, but a miracle is a supernatural event, and surviving this snake bite was not a supernatural event.

Siblings have their little disagreements, and even though my sister and I got along well, there were times we got upset with each other. From my sister's mastery of the Switzer-Deutsch language at a very young age, when disagreements happened, we would call each other names in Switzer-Deutsch, like "du bist ein küh schwanz," which means "You are a cow's tail," or "du bist ein henne foos," which means "you are an old chicken foot." When we got really upset with each other, we resorted to what we considered the really big gun of insults in the Switzer-Deutsch language. That was "ein eber schweine furz," which meant "a big boar pig's expelled gas."

Calling one a boar's expelled gas was as bad of a name as we could think of. So we would try to be the first to call the other a boar pig's expelled gas in Switzer-Deutsch. For some reason, it always sounded so much worse in the Switzer-Deutsch language than it sounded in English.

My father placed a wooden outhouse a short distance from the southwest side of our old farmhouse. If a person was outside of the house and needed to relieve themselves, they were expected to use that two-hole outhouse. I can tell you firsthand, being inside the outhouse was never a pleasant experience. It smelled so bad in that privy you'd want to hold your breath the entire time you were in there.

The problem was I never could hold my breath long enough to get in and out of it fast enough. Children and young adults today have no idea how fortunate they are with inside toilets.

Mom was a very frugal woman. She would put *Sears and Roebuck* catalogs in the outhouse to be used as toilet paper. Sometimes, if we were lucky, we had corncobs to wipe with. The white, fleecy-soft corncobs were so much nicer to use than those old, stiff, scratchy red ones. If you have ever had to use corncobs, you know what I am talking about. If you have never used corncobs, you have missed out on a unique experience. But I am sure you can imagine what that was like.

Sometimes we would feed our pigs corn that was still on the cobs. The pigs would eat the kernels of corn off of the corncobs, leaving the cobs lying on the ground in their pen. Gathering clean corncobs from the pigpen was my sister's and my job. We would have to get into the pigpen and look for the clean cobs for the outhouse. Good, clean cobs were not always easy to find in a pigpen, so the *Sears and Roebuck* catalogs were most often used. During my sister's first year of school, she was in awe because the school's one-hole outhouse had real store-bought toilet paper in it!

Both my sister and I loved springtime with warmer weather and green grass. We got to go outside and play. My sister and I would play in the mud puddles after spring and summer rains. We would play in the hog houses, making mud pies that, of course, we did not eat, and in the winter months, we played in the snow, making snow angels and tunnels in the deep snowdrifts. As I think back to the winters, when I was a kid, the volume of snow we received back then seemed much more than the amount of snow we receive today. There were snowdrifts across our country roads higher than the top of our farm trucks. Those drifts were higher than eight feet tall. Maybe the snow depths I remember receiving seem to be so much more than what we receive today because I was much smaller then, and eight feet of snowdrifts looked much deeper.

When my sister was six years old, our grandmother took her along to visit our aunt's family in South Dakota. On this particular trip, a young service man was hitchhiking along the highway. Our grandmother surprised my sister by stopping and giving the young man a ride. That seemed very unusual to my sister since Grandma was a pacifist and the young man was in the military. The soldier and our grandmother had a very cordial and meaningful discussion about serving in the military and being a pacifist. The young man was very polite and understanding of our grandmother's position. My sister wondered if that young man would be going to heaven when his life on earth was over since he was in the military. Killing of any kind was considered wrong by the Mennonites, and that belief was drilled into my sister and me at a very young age. When my sister got home from the trip, she told Mom about it and asked if that young man would be going to heaven one day. Our mother's answer to her question was "Heaven has a lot of different rooms in it, and there is a very special room where all of the Mennonites will go after they pass from this life." By answering my sister's question that way, our mother did not say the young man would not be going heaven, but she did reveal that Mennonites felt they were a superior people. Things have greatly changed in many Mennonite churches since then. Things that were condemned then are now considered acceptable to say and do. Homosexuality, abortion, using tobacco products, drinking alcoholic beverages, cussing, and other such things happen among Mennonite people today. It seems many Mennonites have become worldly, and these practices are no longer condemned or looked down upon.

CHAPTER 4

THE PRIMARY TIMES

My sister and I attended a rural, redbrick, two-room grade school. Our story-and-a-half schoolhouse had one metal fire escape and two white, side by side, wooden exterior doors with a number of small windowpanes in them. These two wooden doors opened onto a small concrete interior landing. From the small interior landing, a wide, traffic-worn stairway led up to another large wooden landing. To the left of the landing were two coatrooms. One room was for the boys to hang their coats, put their snow boots in, and place their lunch boxes or lunch sacks on the shelving above the coat hooks. The second coatroom was for the girls. I am not sure why there had to be different coatrooms for the boys and girls, unless the changing of clothes was sometime necessary. At the end of this landing were two wood-floor classrooms. One of the classrooms held grades one through four, while the second room held grades five through eight.

A second concrete stairway led down to a large concrete-floor basement. At one side of the basement was a room that held a potbellied, wood burning stove and a large stack of firewood. On cold days, it was always a treat to be selected to go to the basement and add wood to the fire in the potbellied stove so that the upstairs rooms would stay warm. When the weather got extremely cold, our classrooms also became cold. This was because the entire school building was heated by this one potbellied stove. I remember the times that we would go downstairs and sit around that potbellied stove to stay warm during the school day. We would hold our classes around that stove. These few days were special and very enjoyable for us because it broke up the monotony of the regular school day. The basement doubled as a lunchroom and recess area. When the weather was rainy or too cold to go outside, recess was held in the basement. I remember playing dodge ball in that basement and hiding in the stove room when playing hide-and-seek.

After my second grade year of school, a third classroom was constructed along with a hallway, bathrooms, showers, and a metal, round-top gymnasium, with a stage and dressing rooms at one end of the tile basketball court. Until this new addition was built, we had to use a one-hole outhouse even during the winter months. These inside bathrooms and showers were a great addition to our school building. The gymnasium ended the need to play on an outside basketball court, which had consisted of a dirt court, a pole, a plywood backboard, and a rim. When the weather permitted, we could shoot the ball through the metal rim, but dribbling the ball on the uneven dirt court was very tricky. And with no net on the rim, it was often difficult to see if a shot was made or missed.

Above the two bathrooms was a room used for crafts. We made a large, wooden duck cutting board and a wicker basket. I made both of these items for my mother. I loved working with my hands and was very diligent in making my projects. My mother told me that the duck cutting board I made was the best constructed and finished cutting board made by any student. My mother treasured that cutting board so much that she never used it. It was only for display. A kitchen was also added to one end of the basement to serve hot lunches. A modern furnace replaced the potbellied, wood burning stove. These additions changed our school building greatly. Until this kitchen was built to serve hot lunches, we had to take our cold lunches to school in lunch boxes or paper sacks.

Hot lunches were a big improvement over having to take cold lunches to school. Since ladies of the community would prepare our hot lunches, the food was very tasty. We could have second and third helpings as long as we ate everything that was served on our plate the first time we went through the lunch line. I always had third helpings, even when cooked spinach or pineapple was served. I hated cooked spinach. That stuff was nasty! I would drink my milk, and when no one was looking, I would stuff the cooked spinach into the empty milk cartoon. That worked well for me, and I ate very well at school. I would always compliment the ladies who cooked our meals on how good the meals tasted. These ladies would smile at me and give me extra-large helpings. I learned that compliments and kindness helped me get what I wanted.

Our education was not a high priority for my father. He was never around to express any interest in how our education was progressing. That task was left up to our mother. But without our dad's help, she was too busy handling the farming operation and the household chores to closely monitor how my sister and I were advancing. She was satisfied as long as our grades were Cs or above. Without much parental supervision concerning our academic progress, my education was not a high priority for me either.

When my father started his formal education, he spoke only the Switzer-Deutch language, and on his first day of school, he was sent home and told he could not return until he learned the English language. His mother taught him and his siblings the English language so he could return to school the next year. Dad was originally left-handed, and his teacher changed him to a right-handed writer. He did not adjust well to this change, and his handwriting was never very legible.

My school experience was somewhat similar to my father's experience. When I started school and the teacher said it was time to practice our handwriting, I would take my pencil, put it into my left hand, and start writing the numerals, alphabet letters, or words on my red-covered Big Chief writing paper. When the teacher would notice me writing with my left hand, he would come over to my desk and instruct me to put my pencil in my right hand. My writing lessons thus consisted of one half of the lesson being completed with my left hand and the other half of the lesson being completed with my right hand. Without realizing what he was doing, my teacher made me ambidextrous.

My sister was left-handed as well, and she must have complained to our mother about having to write with her right hand, because our mother would not let my sister's teachers change her dominant writing hand. With me, however, my mother did not realize what the teacher was doing to me. I was never one to complain about things. I thought the teacher knew which hand was to be used in writing. So, ambidextrous I became.

During the first year of my formal education, I was introduced to sports in a rather unusual way. In October 1953, the Brooklyn Dodgers and the New York Yankees were playing against each other in the Major League Baseball World Series. The boys in the second through eighth grades got together at lunch and voted to see which team would win the World Series that year. Wouldn't you know, there was an even number of boys, and they were split evenly on who would win the World Series. The older boys came to me and told me that I had to cast the deciding vote on who would win the World Series. I was the only boy in my class with four girl classmates. It was up to me to cast the deciding vote with no knowledge of baseball. Well, my choice was between the Dodgers or the Yankees. The name Yankees didn't sound appealing to me, because it gave me the idea of jerking or yanking on something, which seemed physically abusive to me. The name Dodgers was much more appealing to me. It carried the idea of being elusive and evading. Based solely on the sound of the names and what I perceived them to mean, I chose the Dodgers. From that day on, I became a Dodger baseball fan.

In 1955, when Sandy Koufax became a rookie for the Brooklyn Dodgers, I bought a pack of baseball cards with the five cents I had saved. Sandy Koufax's rookie card was in that pack. I started paying attention to how he was doing, and he became a sports figure I looked up to. I had always wanted to see a Dodger game at Dodger stadium. On my sixtieth birthday, my two grown children took me to Los Angeles to see the Dodgers play. I enjoyed that experience immensely, and to top it off, the Dodgers beat the St. Louis Cardinals that day.

As a result of the absence of a father's attention, I never liked being left out of anything. So, because of my new interest in baseball, I decided that I wanted to play fast-pitch softball with the older boys before the school day started. Sometimes it was also played during recess in the fall and spring of the school year. Being the youngest and littlest guy out there, the older boys would put me in the outfield where they thought I would do the least amount of damage and see the least amount of action. I never got the opportunity to swing a bat. I just stood out in the outfield waiting for the ball to be hit my way. I was just fine standing out there, watching the grass grow and the butterflies flying around. One day, however, while I was standing in the outfield, a fly ball was hit to me, and I almost caught that fly ball. Since I didn't have a ball glove on my hand, I dropped the ball. The older boys, seeing that I would have caught the fly ball if I had a glove, moved me to a position where there would be more opportunities to catch fly balls. They made sure that I had a glove to use so I would catch the fly balls when they were hit my way. To teach myself how to catch fly balls, I used the visualization technique. At night, after saying my evening prayers and looking at the picture on the wall at the foot of my bed, I would go to sleep picturing, in my mind, catching the fly balls hit my way. In my mind, I would see the ball going into my glove. I sensed how it would feel to actually catch the ball. Sure enough, the visualization technique worked, and I was catching fly balls at a very young age. My successes on the softball field didn't help endear me with the boys a year or two older than I. I was already an outcast to them, and being successful at sports didn't cause me to be any more accepted by them.

When I was six years old in 1953, my parents mortgaged land to build a new L-shaped house. It was a modern, experimental-type home and had both hot and cold running water piped into the kitchen sink, a shower, a toilet, a utility room sink, a bathroom sink, and an actual tub. This house was a one-story structure with a concrete slab floor. The concrete floor had copper pipes running back and forth throughout the entire floor. Those copper pipes were for heating purposes. Heated water circulated through the copper pipes contained in the concrete floor and wall heating registers. Because of the heated water circulating through the pipes, the floors were warm as long as we had propane to heat the circulating water.

The walls were constructed out of concrete blocks with steel rods though each layer of blocks. These steel rods held the concrete block walls together to prevent wall cracks from appearing. The living room floor was covered with a beige shag carpet; the family room and the three bedroom floors were covered with dark brown cork tiles, which helped cushion the concrete floor; and the kitchen, utility room, and bathroom floors were covered with linoleum floor tiles.

The house's exterior walls were covered with white asbestos corrugated tiles. The roof trusses and sheeting were wood construction and covered with tar paper and green interlocking asphalt shingles. The concrete block walls kept our house cooler in the summertime, and a ceiling-mounted attic fan located in the hallway above the kitchen doorway made the summertime evenings very comfortable.

My sister and I had our own bedrooms, and at the foot of my bed, a picture hung on the wall. This picture was very meaningful to me. I looked at that picture every night after I said my bedtime prayer and before I went to sleep. The picture showed a lost lamb lying in the snow during a severe snowstorm. A large collie dog stood over the freezing lamb, barking for help. Birds, appearing to be like birds of prey, were located in the background and seemed to be waiting for the little lamb to die. But the collie dog was standing over the lamb as the lamb's protector and rescuer. I think I know why it was so impactful to me. The lamb appeared to be alone, like I often was. This lamb appeared to be in great need, just like I felt at the time. The lamb had a protector and rescuer in the barking dog, who came to comfort it, save it from birds of prey and the dangerous snowstorm, and stay with the lamb during its time of need. Like the lamb, I had a loving, caring mother who was my comforter and protector, but what I was missing was a rescuer from the distressing situations I was facing. My mother was unable to be that rescuer for me. Just like me, she was trying to survive the situations she had to face. She needed a rescuer just like I did. When I look at that picture today, it still affects me like it did as a child. I realize that the haunting feeling of having to face rejection and abandonment on my own still exists inside of me.

Thinking he could make easy money by operating a dairy business like all of the other farmers in our area were doing, my father followed the crowd into the dairy business. Soon after the new house was built, my family started a dairy business and built a modern, two-stall dairy barn. The milking parlor consisted of a milking pit to stand in, so you could place the milking machine teat cups on the cow's teats at shoulder-level height. This dairy barn was equipped with a modern milking pipeline system that ran from the two milking machines to a milk vat (tank) located in a separate room. This milk vat held the milk until the company's milk truck came to get the milk for the company. This milk truck would come to our farm twice a week, so the milk vat had to be refrigerated and large enough to hold up to five hundred gallons of milk.

Our dairy farm was called the Cedar Fur Farm. At the time we began our dairy business, we had a few rows of cedar trees that functioned as a windbreak north of our house, and we raised mink and rabbits. Thus, our dairy farm was named the Cedar Fur Farm. When my mother inherited some farmland, my father sold the land to purchase Holstein milk cows to expand our dairy herd to sixty individuals, and we produced grade A milk for human consumption. We sold the milk our cows produced to a major milk company in a larger city, thirty-three miles from our farm.

Before we had the modern dairy barn and the automated milking pipeline system, we produced grade C milk not for human consumption. The two milking machines' cups would be placed on the cows teats, and gravity would have the milk run into ten-gallon milk cans. The milk cans had to be picked up every day, morning and evening, after the milking of the cows was finished.

One morning, while I was watching my father unload the empty milk cans from the milk truck and load the full ones, he accidentally set one of those empty milk cans down on top of my head. The bottom rim of the can put a large bump across the top of my skull, which I still have sixty-five years later.

The dairy business was very profitable for my family, but my father would not use the profits to pay off the mortgages he had made. Instead, he used all of the money that was made from the dairy, crop sales, and the one oil well on his evening activities. With my father gone so often and not getting home until four or five each morning, milking the cows, feeding the animals, and attending to all the needs of the animals were left up to my mother and me. Since Mom was always busy milking the cows, attending to the needs of the animals and repairs around the farm became my work. At five years of age, I had to climb a thirty-foot silo to feed silage (chopped-up corn or grain sorghum plants) to the dairy cattle and feed hay from the hay barn's hayloft each evening and many mornings. Having to climb that thirty-foot tall silo at that young age helped me overcome my fear of heights. At first, it was a very difficult task for me and quite a scary experience. Before I was school age, to overcome my fear of heights, I would periodically practice climbing up and down the exterior of that silo during the daytime until my fears were gone. I knew my mother was not able to do all of the work around the farm by herself. So I took it upon myself to help her. I knew if I was going to be of any real help to my mother, I had to overcome my fear of heights.

I fed a milk-replacer product to all of the baby calves we had most mornings and every evening and cared for all of the other farm animals. I taught myself how to repair fences and do other farm repairs. Being self-taught probably helped me develop my problem-solving skills and become a very independent person. After I finished feeding all of the animals and other chores, I would help my mother finish milking the cows. During those times I helped Mom finish milking, she would quiz me on the four basic operations of arithmetic. Mom thought it was extremely important that I be able to do addition, subtraction, multiplication, and division, so she would quiz me every day. Because of her efforts and insistence, I became very efficient in those four areas. Repetition is definitely the best teacher.

While my sister was still living at home, she was responsible for the housework. After she left home, the housework became my mother's and my responsibility. My father was either sleeping in the morning because of his early-morning arrivals at home, or he was gone by late afternoon and evening, doing what he claimed was undercover work or oil business. After my mother and I finished all of the chores, I would take a bath, and Mom would prepare our evening meal. We would pray before each meal, thanking God for what He had blessed us with. While we were eating, my mother and I talked about what had happened that day. If it was during the school year, what happened at school. We would talk about why my father was always gone, why we couldn't say anything about it, stories about what our relatives were like when they were younger, and events that happened in their lives.

We had genealogy books, but most of this information was orally handed down from generation to generation. Mom would tell me stories about my grandparents, great-grandparents, uncles, and aunts. She would tell me what our ancestors were like in the old country and how different their lives would be if they were living in our time. Many of those stories had a great impact on my life. The story about an uncle who accidentally shot and killed his brother while rabbit hunting from the back of a farm truck was one of those impactful stories.

When my mother would talk about my maternal grandfather, she would always say that he was a great man who she never knew to tell a lie. One evening, my grandparents came to visit us. It was during chore time, and since my father was gone and my mother was milking the cows, I went to do my job of feeding the animals. My grandpa thought I needed help feeding the cows since I was so young. He didn't know that I was already an old hand at feeding those hungry cows. I had been doing those difficult chores by myself every day—and most of the time twice a day.

I had a coal-black horse named Daisy, who I fed along with the dairy cattle. While my grandfather and I were feeding the cows, my grandfather told me that I'd better be careful and not feed my horse any spoiled silage. He explained that feeding her spoiled silage would cause her to "kick the bucket." I looked out into the feedlot, and there was one old, bent-up, rusty bucket half-buried in the ground. I thought he was talking about that bucket in the feedlot, and it would be real interesting to see my horse kicking a bucket. I thought that one old bucket was too limiting for Daisy to kick, so the next day, I gave her a better chance of connecting a kick to a bucket. I went around the farm gathering up all of the buckets that I could find, even the old, bent-up, rusty ones, and placed those buckets around the cattle feedlot so my horse could easily kick one. To my disappointment, Daisy never kicked a single bucket.

A few evenings later, Mom came out to see how I was doing with feeding the cattle. She was a bit puzzled to see all of those buckets lying in the feedlot and asked me if I knew why those buckets were there. Of course, I knew why they were there. I had put them there. I told her that my grandfather, who never lied, lied to me one time. He had told me that if I fed Daisy spoiled silage, she would "kick the bucket." I said that I had placed all of those buckets in the feedlot so Daisy could easily kick one when I fed her spoiled silage. But Daisy never kicked a single bucket. Mom started laughing at my reply since I did not understand that Grandpa meant my horse would die from eating spoiled silage. After she got herself under control, Mom explained what Grandpa meant by using the slang term "kicking the bucket." I never fed Daisy any spoiled silage again.

My grandchildren have ask me what kinds of birthday and Christmas gifts I received back in the old days. They were shocked when I explained that I never received Christmas or birthday gifts. During my growing-up years, celebrating a holiday was not something my family had the opportunity to do. Living eight and a half miles from the nearest town and with my father always gone, holidays like Halloween, Valentines' Day, and St. Patrick's Day were observed only at the grade school we attended. Since the Fourth of July holiday was a summer holiday, I never really got to experience shooting off fireworks. Mom and I never had the money to purchase fireworks, except for one time. Mom thought I needed to have the experience of shooting off fireworks and saved enough money to purchase two Roman Candles. We lit those Roman Candle fireworks with matches and watched the flaming stars shoot into the sky. The exploding stars were awesome to see. But that was the one and only time we were able to purchase fireworks.

There was one time when I was about twelve years old, after the Fourth of July celebrations were over, my father brought home a partial pack of leftover Black Cat firecrackers. Even though it was long past the time that one was to be shooting off fireworks, I popped a few of those leftover firecrackers to see what they were like. I sent a few small cans up into the air about treetop level. The explosions inside those cans were powerful enough to expand the metal can. Because of not having fireworks to ignite on the Fourth of July, I did not ignite all of those leftover firecrackers. I saved most of them so that I would have some left to shoot off on the Fourth of July each of the next few years. I would pop no more than five firecrackers a year. Not having things like firecrackers or toys made me a saver. I was not a hoarder. I never had things to accumulate. You may find this hard to believe, but I never actually popped all of those leftover Black Cat firecrackers.

As children, my sister and I never knew that families gathered together and read Christmas stories or that children anticipated what was in the wrapping paper under the tree Christmas morning. My sister and I cannot remember receiving gifts for birthdays and Christmas unless our mother had sewn them for us. There just wasn't enough money for us to receive gifts. Mom did sew clothes for my sister, but they were never wrapped and put under the tree. There wasn't enough money to buy wrapping paper. The clothes were just given to my sister, unwrapped and a day or two early. For my sister and me to receive gifts, our mother would have had to hide some of her hard-earned money. Whatever my father didn't take of her earnings had to go for bills or groceries. If the bills were not paid, there were no lights to see at night, no heat for the house in the wintertime, no stove to cook meals on, no water to drink for us or the animals. Since Dad was always celebrating the Christmas holidays elsewhere, Christmas celebrations didn't exist for us. I did get one real Christmas gift that I can remember. It was when I was a fifth grader (1957). I loved playing basketball and was asked to play with the seventh- and eighth-grade team. My mother saved enough money to buy me a real, honest-to-goodness basketball for Christmas. She put it on a layaway plan at the store and paid a little out of each paycheck until she had it paid off. This basketball was expensive. It cost about seven dollars back then, which meant it was very expensive, and it took her quite a while to pay for it. I asked my mother about the gift being so expensive, and she explained that she was able to save the money for it. I felt bad that she spent that amount of money on me because money was always in short supply. But she said that I hadn't gotten gifts in the past and I deserved to have this one. It was the only true gift I remember receiving, and I loved that basketball. I dribbled it everywhere I went and even slept with it in my bed at night. I still have that basketball today. It is now over fifty-eight years old and still holds air, even though it is quite worn. When I think about or look at that basketball, a special feeling comes over me. I know just how much Mom had to sacrifice so that I could have that basketball.

There were times that Dad would bring home broken toys for us as so-called gifts to play with. I do not know why he did that. Maybe he considered them substitutes for the birthday and Christmas gifts we missed out on. He brought home those malfunctioning toys only a couple of times, long after our birthdays or Christmas were over. These broken and defective toys were never fun for us to play with because they didn't work and pieces were missing. Old plastic musical instruments that wouldn't play anymore and an erector set that was only half there were examples of what my father would occasionally bring home. It was frustrating for me to receive toys that didn't work, and I knew they were merely someones rejects.

Not receiving gifts on Christmas or for birthdays made me feel inferior, unimportant, and unworthy to receive nice things. Yet I always felt that I needed to act appreciative for what I received because my mother had taught me to be thankful for whatever I was given. I do not know where Dad got those worthless things. But I acted thankful for them.

As young children, my sister and I did have children programs on Christmas Eve at the church we attended. We were given treat bags of candy, nuts, and one orange. I always looked forward to receiving that brown bag of goodies, especially the orange. I seldom had an orange to eat, and it was something I was given that was worth something to me. After the program was over and we received those treat bags, we would go to our grandma's house and enjoy eating the contents of the treat bags with our uncles, aunts, and cousins. We would trade the bag items we didn't care for with each other for items we preferred. As we got older and our grandmother aged, that tradition ended, and Christmas became just a day like all the other days for us.

Each year, the country grade school my sister and I attended would perform Christmas programs and end-of-the-school-year plays. My sister and I always enjoyed performing before crowds. Even though I enjoyed performing in front of crowds, I did not feel important enough to be selected for a part in the productions and tried to make myself unnoticed until someone told me I had been selected to perform.

My sister and I were given parts in the school plays and sang during the school performances. We sometimes were even given leading roles in these performances, yet our father would only attend our performances when he didn't have something else he considered more important to do. Most of the time, he was elsewhere. Unlike our father, Mother always attended our performances. At the end of my eighth-grade year, I was surprised that I was given the leading role in the school play and a leading singing role in the Christmas program. My father's younger brother attended that end-of-school-year play and was impressed with my performance. He made a special effort to come and tell me about how impressed he was. I did not get other compliments for my performance. My peers and the people of the community certainly weren't going to compliment me. My uncle's compliment meant a lot to me. From him, I received the acceptance, approval, and encouragement that I so desperately needed. Like usual, Dad had other plans that he considered more important than my performance.

New Year's Eve was another holiday I was unable to celebrate before I graduated from high school. So, New Year's Eve celebrations never became special to me. After graduating from high school, I did attend a few college New Year's Eve parties at students' homes or buildings where college students gathered to bring in the new year. Generally, there was the consumption of alcohol at these New Year's Eve parties, and the punch bowls were often spiked. Since I never drank alcoholic beverages or used illegal drugs or tobacco products, I felt out of place. I stood on the sidelines, so to speak, and didn't enjoy attending those celebrations. Celebrating anything with alcoholic beverages, tobacco products, or drugs was not a part of my life. As usual, my father was elsewhere, celebrating the incoming new year with people other than his family.

In the early 1950s, my father unexpectedly brought home a Sylvania console television set. It was in a large, dark wooden cabinet. The large greenish-appearing picture tube was located at the top of the cabinet, and a large fabric-covered speaker was below the picture tube. It had what we called "rabbit ears" (television antennae) to receive the television signal. I have no way of knowing for sure where my father got the television set. I know that particular television set was not a new set when we received it. By what I've been told by people in the know, I am confident that this TV was left over after my father purchased a new television set for one of his mistresses, and he needed a place to dispose of this old, used one. Like usual, we were just an easy place to dispose of that old television set. But unlike all of the other things he would bring home, this television had redeeming qualities. It was still in working condition.

In our community at that time, most people didn't have a television set in their home. Until my father brought this television set home, I didn't know what television was. My mother, sister, and I truly enjoyed watching the television programs. Mom would make us rest our eyes by closing them during the commercials. My sister and I think that she wasn't so much interested in our eyes being rested. We think she did not want us to see all of the alcohol and tobacco commercials.

Our grandma thought that television was an evil, worldly thing and that we would be going to the unpleasant place for eternity because we were watching what she considered an evil device. But with the passing of time, I got to see the day when my grandma purchased one for herself. She claimed that she did it so that she could keep up with the daily news, and her male family members needed a television to watch the NFL football games after the Sunday noon meals were over.

The television programs that I enjoyed watching were the *Mickey Mouse Club*, the *Jackie Gleason Show*, the *Martha Ray Show*, *Rawhide*, and *Gunsmoke*. My sister liked the *Lawrence Welk Show* and *Toast of the Town,* and we both enjoyed watching the *Lone Ranger, Roy Rogers, Howdy Dowdy, I Love Lucy*, and the *Ed Sullivan Show.*

During those days and probably because the television set was used, the picture tube would get dimmer and dimmer and dimmer. It would get so dim that we would have trouble seeing the picture during daylight hours. To see the picture during daylight hours, we had to put a blanket over the television set and crawl under the blanket, where it was dark enough to be able to see a faint picture. My mother permitted us to watch television on Saturday mornings, after school until chore time, and after the milking and chores were done. When the dimming of the picture tube occurred, it would take my father a very long time to have the television set repaired. He was never home to watch the television programs with us, so it wasn't important to him to have it repaired. To have it repaired, he would have to spend some of the money he would have otherwise been able to use on his evening activities. Obviously, spending that money on the TV repairs was not something he wanted to do. One time, my mother took it upon herself to have the television repaired. My father was not happy with her because he didn't want to have to pay for its repair.

After Dad passed away at the age of ninety-seven, a person who had firsthand knowledge of his extra activities told me that over the years, my father had purchased brand-new cars, new furniture, jewelry, television sets, and more for the women he was involved with. Being told these things about my father verified that my mother, sister, and I were never really important to him. This revelation helped explain where all of the money had actually gone over the years. We suffered physically, emotionally, and mentally because of my father's selfish and uncaring actions.

When my sister was in high school, she would either drive me to my country grade school, where I had my first eight years of schooling, or I would walk, ride my bike, or drive an old 1941 Chevy Deluxe Coupe to and from school. At the age of ten, I had learned to drive that old standard transmission Chevy by driving it into our pasture to get the cows for milking each morning and evening. By the age of twelve and only on good driving days, my mother would allow me to drive that old 1941 Chevy to and from school, as long as she was sitting in the front seat beside me.

Due to our father's spending habits, there was not enough money to buy a school car for my sister when she started high school. The old 1941 Chevy Coupe was not trustworthy enough for her to drive the seventeen-mile round trip to high school each day. Our grandma, seeing our predicament, bought a new car for herself and gave my sister her old black 1951 two-door, automatic transmission Chevy to drive to high school. My sister was not the best driver in the world at that time in her life. She often made my life interesting with her driving skills. When the weather would not allow me to walk, ride my bike, or drive that old Chevy, she was expected to drive me to my country grade school on her way to her high school. Far too often, we would not make it to where we wanted go, especially if it had rained or snowed. We are talking about only one and three-fourths of a mile. For some unknown reason, when my sister drove, ditches were a car's magnet, and we would end up in a ditch along the way. She had a natural lead foot, and traveling too fast on muddy roads meant a journey into the ditch. We, of course, didn't have such things as cell phones, so it would take some time for someone to drive by, see us in the ditch, and notify someone to come and pull our car out.

I eventually got tired of ending up in ditches and refused to ride to school with my sister. Since I refused to ride with my sister, during bad weather, my mother had to drive me to school. Dad was either too busy or not concerned about me getting to and from school.

As a prank, someone put a little cow manure on the engine manifold of my sister's 1951 Chevy, and when the engine heated up, the manure also got hot. Hot manure doesn't smell good. That car smelled pretty bad, especially when the car heater was turned on. I do not know if it was a silly, fun prank played on her or if it was a mean trick done to her because of who her father was. I suspect it was because of our father, and she was an easy target. Even though that burnt manure smell faded some over the years, the smell stayed with that car as long as we used it.

For what appears to be strictly for their entertainment, older siblings find ways to harass their younger brothers and sisters. My sister was no different. When she was bored, she found pestering me to be an enjoyable activity. Her being four and a half years older was a big disadvantage for me, but I found an equalizer. When my sister would start to pester me, I would run to the utility room, grab the cane broom, and chase her around the house. I think that she not only enjoyed pestering me, but she seemed to enjoy me chasing her around the house with that broom in hand. As I chased her, I would take a few swings at her before she would run into her room and lock her door. I never told her, but I never wanted to hit her with that broom. I just wanted to chase her into her room, making her lock herself in, which gave me some peace and quiet for a while.

By the time I was a fifth grader, Dad had reduced the milk cow herd from sixty cows to twenty. He did this reduction so that he would have money to spend. The reduction in milk production left us in need of more finances. Due to the lack of money for bills, groceries, and to purchase fabric to sew clothes for my sister, Mom took on a job outside of the home. The job she took on was at a local egg hatchery and poultry butcher shop, where she butchered turkeys and chickens. Her salary was meager, but we were able to survive off of what she earned.

After my sister graduated from high school, she moved to a city about fifteen miles away from our farm. A year later, she got married, and my sister's absence left my mother and me alone to keep the house up and the farm operational. With my mother and I at home alone and my father no longer able to secure any money by mortgaging something, surviving got extremely tough for us.

The local banker loved to see my father come into the bank to borrow money. This banker saw it as an opportunity to take whatever my father owned. My father's need for finances caused him to take the leftover money my mother had earned at the butcher shop after utility bills were paid, leaving us basically penniless.

By the time I was an eighth grader, my father had for the most part mortgaged everything we had. He had mortgaged the two-hundred-acre farm and everything he could find to fund his evening activities.

The only thing he hadn't mortgaged was the one oil well located on our farm. But he soon mortgaged it without my family's knowledge. Now, there was nothing left to mortgage. Thus, money got extremely tight. The hard times that we faced included times that our propane tank was empty during the winter months. We had no money to fill the propane tank or to even buy groceries. The milk we had from the few cows left of the dairy business saved our lives. We had milk to drink, and with a little flour, Mom could make milk gravy to eat. Sometimes we had homemade bread that we could pour the milk gravy over. When we still had chickens, we would have eggs, and my mother would fry or scramble the eggs, or she would make what we called "ribble soup." Ribble soup was a soup with very small clumps of egg (ribbles) in it, and when the chickens were gone, clumps of flour similar to dumplings were dropped into boiling milk.

Since Mom and I often didn't have money to have the propane tank filled, some nights the house would become extremely cold, especially when the outside temperatures would drop below twenty degrees Fahrenheit. The temperatures could get as low as twenty degrees below zero. I can't tell you just how cold it got inside our home, but I can tell you that it got extremely cold.

My mother and I were fortunate that we had an electric stove in the kitchen. Since there were no doors to the kitchen, to keep from freezing, numerous times we hung blankets over the kitchen door openings. We would use the electric oven to heat this kitchen area, which kept us semi-warm. You may think that hanging those blankets over the three kitchen doorways was not a major task, but there were no wooden door casings around the door openings. That meant we had to hammer nails into the smooth stucco covering over the concrete blocks. Hammering nails through the stucco covering and into concrete blocks without destroying the stucco wall covering was a bit tricky. Once we had three nails in the smooth stucco walls above each door, we were able to hook blankets over the nails. This preserved what little heat we were able to get from the electric oven. We used every blanket that we had left to wrap up into and slept on the tiled floor in front of the open oven door. Our problem was that since heat rises, the heat never got down to where we were sleeping. So it was not that warm on the concrete tiled floor, making it a very unpleasant experience. When a person is extremely cold, the type of sleeping surface isn't the main concern. Warmth becomes the main concern, and the comfort of the sleeping surface is merely secondary. Of course, my father was not home to experience these cold sleeping conditions with us, and our physical comfort was not a high priority of his anyway.

Because of my father's absences and his spending all of the family's money, my mother, along with doing the farming, dairy business, and butchering poultry at the local hatchery, had to take on another job. This job consisted of cleaning the building where I attended grade school. She would arrive at the school after her work at the butcher shop was over. Due to my mother being overwhelmed by the amount of work she had to do to keep us alive, I took it upon myself to help her out. While my mother was cleaning the classrooms, I would sweep the gym floor, clean the boys' and girls' restrooms, and sweep the hallway between the gym and restrooms. My mother would tell me that when I finished cleaning the gym floor, restrooms, and hallway, I could shoot hoops in the gym until she was finished cleaning the rest of the school building. So, I quickly swept the gym floor and the hallway and cleaned the restrooms. Then I was free to practice shooting the basketball every day on my own for the two hours it took my mother to clean the rest of the school building. During that school year, I spent many hours shooting the basketball and never tiring of it. I would have loved to have had a basketball goal at home, but having a basketball goal to play ball with was not a high priority for my father, so it never happened.

After my mother was through cleaning the school building, we would go home and do the chores, milk the cows, feed the animals, and all the other chores around the farm. With the depleted herd of dairy cows, it took us only about an hour to do the chores each evening before we could go into the house to eat supper. It was generally after seven o'clock before we were able to go into the house, and then it took my mother some time to prepare us something to eat. Of course, we didn't have the luxury of having a microwave oven. They were not invented yet, so meal preparation took some time, even when it was only milk gravy.

When my mother and I would finish eating and talking, I would take two empty pork n' bean cans, with both ends of the cans removed, and tape one can to the wall at each end of our long hallway. I would use a very small rubber ball to dribble from one end of the hallway to the other end of the hallway and shoot that small rubber ball into the pork n' bean cans. I spent a good deal of time dribbling that little rubber ball and shooting it through those cans. I do not know why I took such a liking to the game of basketball. Maybe it was because I didn't need others to accept me. I could spend time by myself shooting in the gym or through pork n' bean cans and not have the feeling of being mistreated or ostracized because of my father. For whatever reason, I learned to love the game by the time I was in the third grade. During the winter months, while other students were playing other things, I would at times spend recess shooting the basketball in the gym by myself. Not being a favorite person of my peers because of my father, spending so much time by myself, shooting the basketball during recess, turned out to have a positive effect to go along with all of the negative ones I encountered. When I was a fifth grader, the man who coached our school's seventh- and eighth-grade boys' basketball team asked me if I would be willing to play with the team. Of course, I was excited and jumped at the chance to play with the older boys. Even though I was only a substitute, I was excited to be a part of the team. From that point on, the game became my passion, and I made every effort to learn every aspect of the game. I was not a gifted athlete, so I had to work hard and learn the fundamentals of the game to be successful and to see the court in high school and college.

One day, my teacher / basketball coach did something that had a lasting effect on me. When I was in the seventh grade, my basketball coach came to me and informed me that the rural grade school we were scheduled to play would not come to play that scheduled game with us if I played in that game. My coach told me that the opponent coach had talked with him about what kind of players we had. My coach told him what we were like, and the opposing coach said that since their basketball team was not very good, they didn't want to drive an hour and a half to play a game where they would get blown out, so to speak. The opponent coach said that my playing skills were too advanced for me to play in that game. So, to keep from having to cancel the game, it was agreed that I would not play in the game. Because of my father's lifestyle, I had already faced many disappointing things by that time in my life. Of course, I was disappointed that I couldn't play in that game, but I handled the disappointment just like I had handled all of the other disappointments I had faced.

Without knowing what he was doing for me, my coach came to me and asked me to coach the team during that game since I wasn't allowed to play. Of course, I jumped at the chance to coach my peers. It was my first experience at coaching basketball, and I loved every minute of it. No doubt it helped that we won that basketball game. So, my first basketball coaching experience was successful, and my coaching career, from that point on, spanned fifty-eight years. I actively coached basketball for forty-three years, forty years in the same school district, which I am told is very unusual. I understand that the average length of a basketball coaching job in one school district is about seven years. So, I have been very fortunate coaching basketball over all these years.

Today, and rightly so, our society rejects bullying as an acceptable behavior, and there is support for those who face this form of abuse. When I was young, the term *bullying* did not exist, and that activity was not something people were concerned about. I faced being bullied by my peers, and there was no support for me. Without any kind of support, being bullied by someone can be devastating, especially when it is at the hands of one's peers. I faced this peer bullying far too often, yet I never complained or physically retaliated because I was taught not to retaliate against physical or verbal mistreatment. The Mennonite community held to the belief that one should be nonviolent and peaceful in every instant, no matter what, even if the situation left it impossible to be peaceful. A person was expected to walk away from every mistreatment. Because I was taught that being a Christian is to live the peaceful life, I endured the persecution from my peers, except for one time. During recess, when I was in the sixth grade, an eighth-grade boy would often kick me in my shins with his cowboy boots. No one seemed to want to do anything about the situation, and I got extremely tired of being kicked with those sharp-toed cowboy boots. Not having a father around to ask what I should do to prevent the cowboy boot assaults from taking place, I asked a neighbor high school–aged boy what he thought I should do about it. He told me that the next time this boy kicked me, I should punch him in his nose with my fist so hard that his nose would bleed. While he was crying and holding his bleeding nose, I should tell him that if he ever kicked me again, I would hit him harder. So, with this advice, the very next day during recess, when this older boy kicked me with those cowboy boots, I punched his nose so hard that his nose bled, and while he was crying and holding his bleeding nose, I told him that if he ever kicked me again or anyone else, I would hit him harder the next time. That older boy must have believed me, because he never kicked me or anyone else again. My retaliation caused me to feel a little guilty. I did not act as peaceable as I had been taught I must be. I didn't walk away from that abusive situation. I learned a valuable lesson that day. I discovered how one must handle bullies. You have to stand up to them and not allow them to mistreat you. Of course, it is always right to be a peace-loving person, but I have come to realize that there are times a person is not allowed to live peaceably. Romans 12:18 says, "If it be possible, as much as lieth in you, live peaceably with all men." Even though a person makes every effort to live peaceably, there may be times when other people do not allow one to live peaceably with them. Bullies are those kinds of people.

After I nailed this boy's nose with my fist, that eighth-grade boy tried to become my friend. I was taught to be a forgiving person, so when that older boy wanted to ride his bike home with me, I rode with him. When I walked home, he often walked with me. I learned that once you've made your point, you treat everyone like you want to be treated. I can't say that we became good friends, but after I made my point, he treated me better than any of my other peers did. I do not know why this older boy chose me to pick on. It is likely that this peer abuse of kicking my shins stemmed from me being my father's son.

Because of how we were treated and how we were looked down on, my mother told my sister that she would have to date boys outside of our Mennonite community when she was of dating age. Mom was right. None of the Mennonite boys in our community would date my sister, even though she was a very pretty girl. Our mother knew that the families of the Mennonite boys in our community would not consider my sister as marriage material because of her father. As for me, when I became dating age, I needed to date girls outside our community as well. This was not all bad, however. Most of the girls that I dated in the community were second or third cousins and thus were not suitable for marriage. Not being considered marriage material by many in the community encouraged me to look elsewhere to socialize and find a lifelong mate.

I am not sure why, but both my sister and I had the ability to speak in public. I am told that my sister was quite the talker, from a very early age, and her talkativeness carried her through her formal education years. In high school, her talkativeness was beneficial in her high school debating performances. My sister was very talented and loved to dance and sing on our front porch. She would see her reflection in our big picture window and dream about having a wonderful and successful life. My sister has a very beautiful singing voice, and as the years went by, she would sing solos at many different engagements. When she was in high school, she was selected to sing on the nationally televised *Jerry Lewis Muscular Dystrophy Telethon*. That was quite an honor for her, and after she had sung her song on national television, Jerry Lewis tried to get her to sing a second number, but she had already left the stage, and they couldn't find her backstage. I am not sure why, but my sister never pursued a singing career after high school.

I got to attend my sister's televised performance and meet both Jerry Lewis and "Rusty," the young boy from the *Danny Thomas Show*. Rusty was my age, in fact one month older, so I thought meeting Rusty was a pretty neat experience.

CHAPTER 5

LIVING WITH ABUSE

My mother had a difficult time enduring her husband's absences from home and his chosen lifestyle. She would find empty alcohol bottles in the truck of the car. Drinking alcoholic beverages was something she totally opposed. She was seeing her husband's way of living change before her eyes, and life was getting difficult for her to handle.

When I was eight years old, my father decided that my mother and sister needed to go to North Carolina to see Mom's sister and brother-in-law. He wanted Mom out of his way for a while. She was having a difficult time with him being away from home and his family so much. So he talked my mother into going to see her sister by train. With my mother and sister away from home for ten days, it meant that Dad had no one to answer to and only me at home to take care of. Of course, I was not of any concern to him, and instead of him having to take care of me, my father talked his mother into coming to our farm each day and caring for my needs. Grandma would come during the morning and early-afternoon hours of the day. Dad told her that he was sending my mother to see her sister in North Carolina because she really missed her sister and needed to go see her.

The truth of the matter was my father liked the idea of his wife and his thirteen-year-old daughter being gone, out of his hair, for ten days. With my mother and sister away from home and his mother looking after his eight-year-old son during the day, my father could easily do as he wished. Grandma agreed to help her son out and came over to our house in the mornings. She would fix my breakfast and noon meals and then go back to her home around four o'clock each afternoon. To prevent my grandma from knowing that her son left his son home alone at night, Dad would wait until grandma left the farm. Then he would leave for the evening, leaving me at home alone each night from four in the afternoon until four or five in the morning.

The first evening that my mother and sister were gone, Grandma did not have to come and look after me. For some reason, my father took me along with him that first evening when he went to the small town eight and one-quarter miles from our farm. He parked the pickup truck in a parking space on Main Street and told me that he needed to go into the local pool hall to see someone. My father told me to stay in the pickup and he would be back shortly. He said that I couldn't go into the establishment with him because they served alcoholic beverages, and minors were not allowed in there. That made sense to me; at eight years old, I was far too young to be able to go in with him. So, I willingly stayed in the pickup truck by myself while my father went into the pool hall to see someone. I am not sure why Dad didn't leave the truck keys in the ignition since I stayed inside of the truck. It wasn't like I was going to drive it away, stranding him there. At that time, it was a normal practice to leave your keys in the ignition of unlocked vehicles. No one would steal unlocked vehicles. Times sure have changed. For whatever reason, he took the keys with him when he left.

After a few hours of sitting in that cold pickup truck, waiting for my father to return, I thought he should have returned already and probably got involved in a game of dominoes, losing track of time. It was late October, and at that time of the year, it got extremely cold outside, especially at night.

I was getting really cold and decided to go into that forbidden pool establishment, in spite of my age. I assumed that the people in that establishment couldn't do more than tell me I had to leave. I felt that going into the pool hall would be a good way for me to warm up a bit and see if my father was ready to go home. So I crawled out of the pickup, making sure I didn't lock the doors so I could get back into it if I needed to. I walked on the Main Street sidewalk the short distance to the front door of the establishment, opened the door, and stepped inside.

Upon entering the dreary, smoke-filled pool hall, I looked around for my father, but he was nowhere in sight. I was shocked that he was not there. I wondered where he could be since I saw him go into the pool hall, but now I didn't see him anywhere inside this forbidden place, and I hadn't seen him walk out the front door. The only other possibility was that he had walked out of the back door. But if he did that, why did he do it and where did he go? Why did he leave me sitting in that very cold pickup truck when he said he'd be back shortly?

There was a group of men playing dominoes at a wooden table near where I was standing, so I asked the men playing dominoes when my father had left the pool hall. To my surprise, not one of those men could remember even seeing him come in. I knew that he went into that establishment. I had seen him go in. At that point, a feeling of abandonment came over me, and I wondered what I could do about the situation I was facing. I realized that I had to take care of myself. No one was there to do it for me. As I thought about my options, four possibilities came to mind. I could go back to the pickup and wait for my father to return. I could walk to my maternal grandparents' home about a half mile away. I could walk the six miles to my grandma's farm, or I could walk the eight and one-fourth mile home. None of those choices seemed to be good options, but they were all I had.

I eliminated walking to my maternal grandparents' home because my father would have no idea where I was when he returned, and upsetting my father would be very detrimental to my physical well-being. I eliminated walking the six miles to my grandma's farm and the eight and one-fourth miles home because it was dark, there were coyotes out there at night, it was very cold outside, and it would take me a long time to walk to Grandma's farm or home. So I concluded that my best option was to go back to the pickup truck and wait for my father's return, hoping he would be back soon.

I walked back to the pickup, opened the passenger door, crawled inside the cab, locked the doors, and waited for my father to return.

I feared telling anyone about the situation because I had been told that I could not trust anyone. As I waited for my father to return, my mind went back to the time he put me out of the car and left me on that dark country road, when I was only four years old. That same feeling of abandonment I felt at that time came over me, and since my mother and sister were gone, I felt that I was alone in the world with no one to help me or care about what was happening to me. I felt that if I was to survive situations like this one, I had to learn to take care of myself. My mother and sister might not always be there for me when I needed their help. They were not there with me now, and I sure could have used their help. So, I became self-reliant and never expressed my true feelings to anyone.

I have no idea where my father went that evening. He never told me. He was gone for a very long time. In fact, he was gone for about eight hours while I sat in the cab of our pickup truck, with the temperature getting extremely cold. If my father had not taken the keys to the pickup with him, I could have periodically started the pickup and used the pickup heater to stay warm. I did have a coat on, but it got so cold inside the cab that the coat didn't help much. I sat there shivering for three hours before I lay down on the truck's seat and tried to go to sleep. That did not work well. I was so cold and shivering so much that I couldn't go to sleep. I shivered for the entire time that my father was gone and was happy for the coat I had. It kept me warm enough so I didn't freeze to death. Without that coat, I am not sure what would have happened to me.

When my father returned and opened the pickup truck door, he saw me lying on the seat, shivering in the cold. At that point, he realized that he had forgotten about me being out in the cold for the entire eight hours he was gone. He never apologized for what I had to endure, and that experience with my father's lack of concern for me reinforced what I already felt. It reinforced my feeling that I was unimportant to my father. He could leave me out in the cold for eight hours and never think about me once during that entire time. I never told anyone about that experience. If I had said anything about what had happened to me, I would have reaped my father's wrath, and it wasn't worth the abuse I would have had to face. I thought it wouldn't have solved anything anyway. That feeling of abandonment was powerful. It put me in a survival mode, which stayed with me throughout life.

After that first evening, my father never took me along with him any of the next nine nights he was gone. He just left me at home alone to fend for myself. I had to find and prepare things to eat each evening on my own. Being just eight years old, living over eight miles from the nearest town and one mile from the nearest neighbor, staying home alone at night was a bit scary for me. As I spent the evening hours, I thought about all the terrible things that could happen to me. The possibility of strangers coming to the farm and doing me harm, and the coyotes just outside the house doors waiting for a chance to get me caused me to be on edge. Of course, I locked all of the exterior doors, closed all of the window blinds, and locked myself in my room. But I knew that if someone really wanted to get into the house and hurt me, all they had to do was break a window, and I would be at their mercy. I knew the coyotes, who chased our dogs around the house at night, and other scary animals couldn't get into the house as long as the doors were locked or someone didn't let them in. For sure, I was not going to let them inside or go outside where they were.

What I could not understand was how my father could forget about his eight-year-old son being out in the cold or leave his young son home alone for nine straight nights. Needless to say, my father and I were never close. I feared my father for what he could do to me and was never able to trust him to be concerned about my welfare.

My sister and mother took the train to North Carolina and were not sure just how to make the train connection in Cincinnati to get to their final destination. While they were traveling on the train, they started a conversation with a very nice man sitting in the seat across from them. He was traveling to Cincinnati just like they were. This nice man told them not to worry about making the train connection in Cincinnati because he would make sure they got on the right train. He helped them change trains, and they got to their destination with no problem. My sister said that never before had she met a man as nice as this man was. Her comment included the men of our community, the men who attended the same church assemblies as we did, and our father. When she got back home, Mom seemed very relaxed. She had a great time visiting her sister and truly enjoyed the trip. My sister said that she had not seen her mother as relaxed as she was for a very a long time.

After returning from her trip to North Carolina, Mom decided to go see a psychiatrist by herself. When she explained the life she was living, this psychiatrist told her that it would be in her best interest health wise to leave our father, but Mom could not bring herself to do that because of her children. That was my mother; she always put her children's well-being before her own. Somehow, maybe through threatening him, she was able to convince my father to go with her to the next session with the psychiatrist. At that session, the psychiatrist told my father that he was a very selfish and unloving person who was treating his family awfully and that he needed to stay home with his family or he could lose them. Upon hearing what the psychiatrist said to him, my father became extremely angry and stormed out of the session. He refused to go back to see the psychiatrist, and from that time on, he became extremely mean, and the physical and verbal abuse happened more often and became more intense.

My father possessed a quick and violent temper. There were times when I witnessed him being physically abusive to both my mother and sister. My father attempted to strangle my mother on three different occasions that I know about. During one of those strangulation incidents, if I had not come to my mother's rescue, I am confident that he would not have stopped soon enough, and he would have strangled her to death. I was about eight to nine years old when I heard my mother scream for help. Not knowing what was happening, I hurried into the living room, where my father had my mother pinned down on the living room rug. He had his hands around her throat, choking her to the point of her passing out from the lack of oxygen getting to her brain. At first, I didn't realize what he was doing. But when I saw his hands around her neck and her not able to breathe, I realized that the situation was critical and began hitting my father with my fists, trying to get him to stop, but he wouldn't stop. I had to grab his body and pull him away as hard as I could to get him to release his grip. That was a scary situation for me and I am sure for my mother as well. This physical abuse reinforced our fear of what he was capable of doing to us. We not only had to fear strangers coming to our farm and killing us, we had to fear our father and husband doing the same.

One evening, soon after this choking incident, after we had finished doing the milking and the other chores, I asked my mother about that choking situation when we talked during supper. She was confident that my father would have strangled her to death that time if I hadn't been there to prevent it from happening. She had lost consciousness and was close to death. She then told me there were other times that my father tried to strangle her. She said that one incident happened when she approached him about his lipstick-smeared underwear that she had found when washing his clothes. She told me that when she showed him the lipstick-smeared underwear and accused him of cheating on her, my father became violent. He grabbed the underwear out of her hand, wrapped it around her neck, and twisted it to stop her ability to breathe. My mother said that she was at the point of passing out when he released his grip on the underwear, and she could breathe again. She didn't know why he released his grip. Mother was definitely afraid of what my father would do to her if she ever tried to divorce him or push him out of the home. She told me that if anything ever happened to her, my father would probably be responsible. Mom was definitely an emotionally and physically battered woman.

One morning when my sister was eighteen years old, I witnessed my father physically attack her. He pinned her up against the kitchen wall and was choking her. It took both my mother and me to pull him away from choking her, or he may not have stopped in time. My sister had confronted him about seeing him cross a street in a larger town with a group of people. The unusual part of this incident was that my father was dressed to impress. He was wearing an expensive suit and white saddle-back shoes. As far as we knew, Dad never owned a fancy suit or saddle-back shoes. The clothes he had at home were always rather shabby, and he hardly ever wore anything that resembled a suit. To justify him being dressed to the hilt and being with that specific group of people, my father said he had to dress like that for that particular undercover assignment. The problem with his explanation was where he kept these clothes. He never kept them at home. My father made the claim that the clothes were not his. They were only borrowed, and he just had to wear them for this one undercover situation.

In some ways, I see myself as fortunate that my father wasn't around enough to be physically abusive to me. I knew what he was capable of doing to me, so I kept my distance to prevent him from being physically abusive to me. However, he was very verbally abusive to all of us. When I was about thirteen years old, I started a penny collection. I checked the dates and mints of every penny I could find.

Checking the dates and mint of each penny I came across was a bit time-consuming, but I filled a complete Lincoln Cent Penny collection book from the dates of 1909 to 1958. Pennies are made of copper, but an unusual thing happened in 1943.

In that year, the US Mint changed the makeup of pennies from a copper penny to a zinc-coated steel penny. This change from copper to zinc-coated steel was for only one year. My completing this book was not an easy task. Unfortunately for me, one day my father needed money to continue his evening activities, so he took my hard-earned penny collection and sold it for one hundred dollars. One hundred dollars in 1959 was a considerable amount of money. My father told me that he would replace my penny collection sometime. But I knew that sometime would never happen. *Sometime* had never happened in the past, so why would I expect it to happen this time? It was difficult for me to lose my penny collection and even more upsetting to know that he never intended to replace it as he promised.

While other families of the community had family vacations, my family did not. Due to a lack of funds and Dad's activities, we never went on family vacations. The family trips and the summer experiences I would hear my peers describe at the first day of school were difficult for me to listen to. If my family traveled anywhere, we would travel to South Dakota to visit our cousins. The only states I ever visited as a kid were Oklahoma, Nebraska, and South Dakota. During one of those trips to South Dakota, a situation happened that was especially memorable, and we are brought to laughter every time we talk about it. The reason we traveled to South Dakota was for a cousin's wedding. We stayed with my father's sister's family while we were there. After the wedding ceremony was over, for some unknown reason, my father was in a big hurry to get back home. So, as soon as the wedding ceremony was over, we went back to our uncle and aunt's house to change clothes for our long drive back home to Kansas. It so happened that a cousin left her dog in my uncle's house during the wedding ceremony. While everyone was gone, that dog deposited a small pile of poop on the bathroom floor.

Being in a big hurry, Dad didn't pay any attention to the floor when he went into the bathroom to change his clothes. Not noticing the dog's deposit on the floor, he slipped his socks on his feet and stepped down onto the floor and the dog poop. Without realizing what he had just done, he slid his dog-poop-covered sock into the pant leg of his jeans. When he slid that messy sock into his jeans, it left a long, dark streak of dog poop inside the pant leg. Dad finished putting his jeans on, but things didn't feel quite right in one pant leg.

There was this wet, slimy feeling on his leg. When Dad realized that there was dog poop on his sock and inside his pant leg, he was not a happy camper, to say the least. It was a very good thing that the little dog went into hiding and was nowhere to be found when my father realized what had happened. Those jeans were the only extra clothes my father brought along, and he was not going to drive all the way back to Kansas in a Sunday-go-to-meeting type of pants. My father took off his dirty sock, deposited both socks in a wastepaper basket, washed the poop off of his leg, and tried to wipe the poop out of the inside of his pant leg. Unfortunately, for the rest of us traveling in the same car as he was, the inside of his pant leg still carried the smell of that poop for the entire trip home.

CHAPTER 6

COUNTRY LIVING

Farm life is unpredictable. Hazardous situations may arise at any moment. These dangerous situations are more common when a young mother is left to perform farming tasks while her husband is away from home.

One of those hazardous situations happened when I was just a few weeks old. After milking the cows that evening, my mother went to feed the cows silage from a concrete silo. She needed to cross a twenty-yard area between the hay barn and the thirty-foot-tall silo. A cow had just given birth to her calf, and cows can become very protective of their newborn calves. When my mother ran from the hay barn to the silo, that cow attacked her, knocking her down and butting my mother's face with her head. Mom wisely turned on her side to prevent the cow from stepping on her midsection and causing her internal injuries. The cow dropped to her front knees while straddling my mother's body and proceeded to headbutt Mom's face. Mom wisely played dead, and after a period of time, the cow stopped headbutting her.

Since my mother appeared dead, the protective cow walked away to join her calf. Once the cow had left to join her newborn calf, my mother tried to get up and get back to the barn for protection. But upon seeing Mom move, the cow returned, knocked her down, and started headbutting my mother all over again. This attack lasted a very long time, and this cow nearly killed my mother. Fortunately, the newborn calf walked away from where my mother was lying, and the cow got up and followed her calf. This time, my mom played dead until the calf and cow were completely out of sight. After they were out of sight, Mom made her way to the safety of the barn. She was bruised and beaten up extensively. My sister and I were very close to being motherless children. Of course, my father wasn't home at the time to help my mother.

Before I was old enough to go out into the pasture by myself to get the cows for milking, my sister would walk with me. Together we would complete our task of retrieving our herd of dairy cows. One afternoon while we were walking in the pasture, we faced a very serious and unexpected situation. There were a few horses in the same pasture where our milk cows were grazing on the native buffalo grass. We had never had any problems with any of the horses before that. Our horses had always been tame and well mannered around us.

However, this time was different. While my sister and I were walking in the pasture, one of those horses came galloping up to us. For some reason, this horse reared up and pawed the air with his front hooves. His hooves made contact with the ground just inches from hitting us. This horse's actions surprised us because that type of thing had never happened before. To keep from getting hit by this horse's flailing hooves, my quick-thinking sister grabbed my hand and told me to pet the horse's nose because he would like being petted and then stop rearing up on us. Her instructions worked perfectly, and the horse stopped rearing up and pawing at us, as long as we were petting his nose. But the second we stopped petting that horse's nose, he would proceed to rear up again and paw at us. My sister, being a smart girl, had us work our way over to the pasture's barbed wire fence, between the petting of the horse's nose and his rearing up on us. When we reached the wire fence, my protective sister told me to crawl under the wires of the fence while she petted the horse's nose. It worked great, and once I was on the safe side of the wire fence, my sister quickly crawled under the fence to safety while I petted the horse's nose through the wires of the fence.

Our parents, realizing that it was not safe for us to be around that particular horse, got rid of the animal as soon as possible, before something catastrophic happened. The next day, our father took that horse to the nearest sale barn and sold it for what he could get for it. The horse was not very cooperative when loading it into a farm truck, and it took my father and his brother a couple hours of struggling with it, pulling and pushing that horse into the truck.

When I was old enough, five to six years old, I was able to retrieve the milk cows by myself and do other chores around the farm. My sister, being a girly girl, didn't have to go outside the house to help with the chores anymore. I was capable of handling those things on my own, and as long as she was still living at home, she had the responsibility of doing the housework. That arrangement was perfectly fine with me. I hated doing housework and especially washing dishes. Yet, somehow, my sister used her subtle skills to railroad me into helping her with washing the dishes. With Dad gone and Mom doing outside chores, my sister was able to convince my mother that she needed help, and I was enslaved into assisting her. Neither my mother nor my sister was fond of washing the dishes, so, being the youngest, I was relegated to that activity. My sister would dry the dishes and put them away while I was the one to get my hands wet. I think the reason my sister didn't enjoy the washing and rinsing part of doing the dishes was that she did not want dishpan hands from being in the water so long.

For most of my life, I have not been a fan of mustard and for a good reason, at least in my own mind. My lack of appreciating mustard goes back to our family having a dairy farm. My mother was never one to joke with us children, even though I understand in her younger days she was quite a practical joker. As my sister and I grew up, she became more serious about things, and we never saw her joking. On the other hand, my father was never one we could trust or believe. One day, one of our dairy cows gave birth to her calf. This calf was located way out in a secluded part of the pasture. When this happened, we would drive a converted old Model-A Ford with the back seat removed out into the pasture to pick up the newborn calf and bring it back to the barn, where we could feed it and care for it. It was always my job to stand in the back of that old Model-A and hold the baby calf as we drove it back to the barn. I loved holding the baby calf because newborn calves are so cute. Well, one day, as I was holding a calf in the back of the Model-A, it defecated all over the place. Of course, it was yellow in color, much like mustard appears, and its texture was similar as well. When we got to the barn, my mom, who was always serious about things, turned to me and told me to run to the house and get a glass jar so we could save as much mustard as possible.

That calf poop was extremely gross. If my father had told me to get a jar, I would have known that he was not serious about it. But my mother saying to get a jar for mustard was a different story, since I never knew her to joke. Reluctantly, I crawled out of the vehicle and started to walk toward the house. Mom, seeing me headed toward the house, stopped me and asked me where I was going. I replied that I was going to get her a glass jar for the mustard. My mom promptly explained that she was merely joking about the mustard. Even though it was only a joke, to this day, I am not a great fan of mustard. It is not the taste, the texture, or the color that I dislike or bothers me. What causes me to have adverse feelings for it is the thought of the closeness in appearance of that calf's poop and mustard. I will never put mustard on anything I eat, but if mustard is already on something or in something, I will go ahead and eat it anyway. To the day my mother passed away, she felt bad about her mustard-joking incident and how it affected me.

Even as a very young child, I had the responsibility of mowing the lawn and farmyard, which included mowing the areas around the house, farm buildings, and ditches. I have always enjoyed mowing grass, so it was not a dreaded activity for me. Of course, we didn't own a riding lawn mower. I had to mow the entire area with a manual push lawn mower. Mom worried about me pushing that dangerous, gasoline-powered lawn mower around, especially when I mowed the ditches. I was always very careful not to do anything that would cause me to be injured, and I never had a mowing accident.

One day when my father was home during the day, I tried riding my horse, Daisy, around the farmyard and was having some difficulty making her cooperate with me. He walked by and noticed the obstinate horse, so to get her to respond to my commands, he picked up a long metal pipe to poke her with. Dad rammed that pipe into Daisy's rear end, giving her a very sore sphincter muscle and me the ride of my life. That horse took off on a very fast gallop, with me bouncing up and down as she ran, jumped, and bucked. Daisy and I even cleared an electric fence before I could get her to stop. That pipe incident was not a nice thing to do to a horse, but it was a very effective way of getting her to cooperate. After that experience, Daisy was always cooperative with me.

That was not the only time Daisy gave me a wild ride. One day while riding her bareback in the pasture, she walked up to a large, wooden cattle self-feeder. I thought she just wanted to see if there was any hay in that self-feeder for her to eat, but Daisy had a different reason for going there. She attempted to scrape me off of her back by rubbing up against that wooden structure. When she rubbed against the feeder, it stirred up a nest of yellow jackets. Those wasps stung Daisy's rear end, and I got another wild ride with her bucking, kicking, jumping, and running. I was fortunate because Daisy outran those upset yellow jackets, and I didn't get stung by a single one.

My mom was not the most athletic woman in the world, but she accomplished something that I still marvel at today. Her fear of mean cows was well founded, and in our herd of dairy cattle, we had one cow that didn't like women in dresses. This cow had a mean disposition, and one day while Mom was helping my father round up the milk cows and driving them into a corral, my mother forgot about this mean cow being in the herd and her dislike for women in dresses. While she was driving a pickup truck to help round up the milk cows, a few cows tried to break away from the herd. Without thinking, Mom reacted by stopping the truck, jumping out of it, and running to stop the cows from breaking away from the rest of the herd. She accomplished the task, stopping the cows from breaking away from the herd, but she was wearing a dress and opened herself up to an attack from this mean cow. When that mean cow saw her standing there between the pickup truck and the barbed wire fence, wearing a dress, she attacked my mother. When Mom realized that this mean cow had seen her and was coming after her, she thought about running back to the pickup for protection. But the pickup was too far away for her to make it back before the cow got to her. So she chose to run to the fence. When she reached the barbed wire fence, she jumped over it, clearing it without a scratch. The only mishap was that my mother left the lower half of her dress hanging on the fence. That cow spent a good part of that day standing at the fence and headbutting the part of the dress that was still hanging on the barbed wire and flapping in the summer breeze. The top wire of the four-wire fence is at least four feet off of the ground and has sharp barbs on each wire. It is amazing what Adrenalin can do for a person when fear is involved.

My sister and I loved to care for baby animals. A neighbor had two orphaned baby lambs that he needed help with. Since the lambs took so much effort and time in caring for them, he gave my sister and me the orphaned lambs to care for and raise. We loved caring for those lambs and bottle-fed them until they were old enough to wean. Caring for and raising any kind of animal can be very rewarding and beneficial for the animal as well as for the caregiver. It is my opinion that every child needs some kind of animal to care for and be accountable for as they grow up. Caring for animals instills a feeling of being responsible for something and provides a sense of satisfaction when the task is completed.

One morning, our dad brought home a cute little puppy. I assume that someone he knew did not want that puppy anymore and gave it to him to dispose of. My father, for whatever reason, was not able to say no and brought the cute puppy home. Over time, my sister became very attached to that cute little puppy. Sadly, one day, an uncle, who likes to drives very fast, and our grandma drove into our yard and accidentally drove over that beloved little puppy. The death of that puppy was hard on me, but it was especially hard on my sister. Our uncle felt so bad about what had happened, but there wasn't anything he could do to soothe my sister's pain. About the same time as the death of the beloved puppy, one of the many cats we had around the farm gave birth to a number of kittens. When I found the kittens in our hay barn, they still had their eyes closed. Knowing she was still hurting from the loss of the puppy, I told my sister about the kittens and that she needed to come to the barn to see them. She was reluctant to do so because she was still hurting from the loss of her beloved puppy She was afraid of getting close to those kittens, for fear something might happen to them. My description of those cute little kittens was appealing, and I convinced her to come see them. Of course, she became very attached to them and loved to run out to the hay barn and play with those kittens.

Unfortunately, when our maternal grandparents found out that we were playing with little kittens, they feared that we would get ringworm (a common fungal infection of the skin) from them. So one day while my sister and I were at school, our grandparents came to our farm and took those cute little kittens away with them. Our grandparents thought they were protecting us from getting a fungal skin infection, but they were just making the pain from losing the beloved little puppy worse. After losing a puppy that she dearly loved and those kittens that she enjoyed playing with, my sister never let herself get close to animals again.

Baby animals are the cutest things, and in the spring, our mother would sometimes bring home around one hundred baby chicks from the local hatchery where she worked. We would put those baby chicks in a brooder house, feed them, and raise those little chicks until they got to what we called "fryer" size. My sister and I loved to go out to the brooder house and watch those baby chicks interact with one another. Since baby chicks scare easily, we had to be very quiet and move very slowly around them. If the baby chicks became startled, they would pile up on one another and suffocate the ones underneath the pile.

When those chicks got to be fryer size, it became butchering day, and, not surprising, butchering those chickens was not a favorite activity for my sister. Being a very clever girl, she knew how to disappear into the house undetected. Her disappearing act allowed her to escape seeing the chicken's heads being chopped off, the flopping around of the headless bodies, with blood splattering everywhere, the scalding of the carcasses, and the plucking of their feathers. With my sister conveniently in the house, I was the one relegated to those nasty jobs. My sister, however, never seemed to have a problem with eating those chickens when they were fried.

Another job my sister finagled her way out of was gathering the chicken eggs. Gathering the eggs was not a fun job to do. The reason it was not enjoyable had to do with an old black hen. This old black hen loved to sit on her eggs and would not get out of the nest box. So, to gather her eggs, we had to reach into the nest box and underneath her. When we tried to reach in under this hen to retrieve the eggs, that old bird would peck our hands and arms. Her pecking was a bit painful. My sister would again finagle her way to get out of doing the task and convinced me that it was best for me to get my hands pecked doing the unpleasant task because I was the tough one; I was the boy, and she was the girly girl. Since I always wanted to be the tough one, my smart sister was able to convince me to do the unpleasant jobs.

This chicken was what we called an old "cluck," which meant that she was an old hen trying to sit on and hatch the eggs she had laid. Along with that old black hen that didn't like anyone retrieving her eggs, we always had to look very carefully into the dark areas inside the nest boxes before we reached into them to retrieve eggs. Big bull snakes and opossums also liked to crawl into those nest boxes and collect the eggs for an easy meal. Reaching into a dark nest box and feeling a snake or opossum instead of eggs was not an enjoyable experience. My sister was not fond of grown-up chickens, and she was scared of snakes and opossums. So, the egg-gathering task became strictly my job, since I was the tough guy. I would take a long stick to poke in the dark corners of the nest boxes to detect unwanted critters inside. Our chickens were free-range chickens. That meant they were not in cages or a pen. They were able to freely roam the farmyard. Because of the freedom, they would sometimes lay their eggs in other places, like on the hay in our barn's hayloft. Not being found for many days, those eggs could become rotten inside. One evening, I found a number of those rotten eggs in the hayloft of our barn and thought I needed a good target to throw those rotten eggs at. The milk cows were handy, so I peppered some of our milk cows with the rotten eggs I had found. When broken, rotten eggs have a very strong, stinky sulfur smell. So, the cows I plastered with the rotten eggs looked pretty nasty with the broken shells and the stinky insides dripping off of them. They also carried a very foul sulfur odor with them. Wouldn't you know it … one of the few times my father milked the cows was the next morning. Needless to say, Dad wasn't pleased to have to milk those foul-smelling cows. It was the first and last time I threw rotten eggs at the milk cows.

We had one very healthy, old, bad-tempered white rooster with a large red clump of skin the shape of a comb on the top of its head, a large red clump of skin under its neck, and long, sharp leg spurs. This clump of skin hanging underneath the rooster's neck is called the wattle. Wattles are the same color as the fleshy skin on a rooster's head. The shape and size of the wattle varies depending on the breed of the bird and the health of the individual. The red clump of skin on top of its head is called the coxcomb, also known as just the comb.

This rooster also carried very dangerous weapons on the back of its legs known as spurs, which are very long, pointed, rigid growths that are hard like a person's fingernail. This aggressive bird liked to bully my sister and me. That old rooster would attack us when we would go outside to play. It seemed to us that the old, vile-tempered rooster spent his time just waiting for us to come outside. When he would see us, he would attack us with his long, sharp leg spurs. Those leg spurs would hurt and even draw blood if they connected with our skin. Whenever that old rooster was around, we were never safe, and after a lot of complaining about the ill-tempered rooster bullying us, Mom ended that bad boy's life with a hatchet blade to his neck. Neither my sister nor I was upset the day Mom chopped off that old boy's head. His fried carcass was tasty, and we had a very enjoyable time eating that rooster.

Even though that ill-tempered rooster was out of our lives, we still had a few problems with bullying fowl. There were a number of large geese that freely roamed our farmyard, and they were not always friendly to us. When we came too close to them, these tame geese would chase after us, trying to peck us and beat us with their wings. Until we were older, my sister and I would have to sprint away from those large, ill-tempered geese to keep from being attacked. They were especially aggressive when the females were sitting on their nests, hatching their eggs. These geese were far too useful to get rid of them like we did that old ill-tempered rooster. They ate what we called sand bur stickers. A sand bur is a problem weed that produces a seed pod that sticks to clothing and fur and, unfortunately, pokes the skin. The painful stick of a bur is very painful and annoying, so the geese eating those sand burs was worth us facing their annoyances, and our grand parents would come to our farm, pluck some of their down feathers, and use their feathers for feather-filled pillows.

When my father needed some money for his evening activities, he would take an animal or two or some bales of alfalfa hay to the local sale barn a few miles away from our farm and sell them. When this happened, sometimes I was allowed to go along and attend those livestock sales. I learned to enjoy going to livestock sale barns and watching the animals come through the sale ring. One day, I attended a livestock sale at the local sale barn, and while I was watching the livestock coming through the sale ring, a large group of red Duroc weaning pigs came into the ring. This group of over thirty weaning pigs looked awesome except for one little, red, skinny runt piglet. This runt piglet was about half the size of all of the other pigs. Since the runt piglet was so much smaller than the rest of the pigs, the man who purchased this group of pigs did not want that little piglet. So, he sent that piglet back through the sale ring again, to be auctioned off by itself. I had twenty-five cents in my pocket, which I had earned by swatting flies that came into our house. My mother would find loose change in my father's pockets when she would wash his clothes. She paid me one penny for each fly I swatted. When I had killed twenty-five flies, she gave me a quarter.

When the auctioneer started the bidding for the little piglet, Dad was not there to prevent me from bidding on it. If the price was within my twenty-five-cent budget, I decided that I would bid on the scrawny little pig. To my surprise, the auctioneer started the bidding at twenty-five cents, so I raised my hand to bid. Wouldn't you know ... no one else bid on that piglet, and its owner told the auctioneer to let me have it for twenty-five cents. So, I bought the skinny, little runt piglet, took her home with me, fed her, cared for her, played with her, and raised that little runt into a massive 450-pound sow. This sow acted more like a pet dog than a pig. That sow became an interesting pet because she would follow me everywhere I went, just like a pet dog does. I always enjoyed riding animals, and this pet 450-pound sow was definitely large enough for me to ride. So, I would take my horse saddle, saddle her up, and ride that sow around the farmyard like you ride a horse. To make that sow go where I wanted her to go, I would get a stick, long enough to be able to sit in the saddle and tap the side of her head. When I wanted her to go forward, I would tap her rear end, and she would walk forward. When I wanted her to turn a certain direction, I would tap the opposite side of her head where I wanted her to go.

Around harvest time, we would have the gasoline deliveryman bring gasoline to our farm. One day, while I was riding that sow around the farmyard, the gasoline deliveryman drove into our yard to fill our large gas barrel. The gas barrel was located on the top of a tall metal stand. The gas was used to fuel up farm machinery, the pickup, the farm truck, and the car. While the gasman was sitting on top of the gas barrel, waiting for the barrel to fill with gasoline,

I rode that sow into his view. It must have been a very unusual sight for him, because he laughed so hard that he almost fell off of the gas barrel. After that, every time he came to deliver gasoline to our farm, he would request that I go saddle up my sow and ride her around the farmyard for him to see. Obviously, the gas deliveryman enjoyed watching me ride that saddled sow. I am confident that he had a great time telling other people about this kid on his delivery route who saddled up a sow and rode her around like you ride a horse. I doubt there were any other kids on his route or anywhere else in this world who rode a saddled sow. I am not sure why I was not allowed to continue keeping this sow for a pet.

I suspect that Dad was in need of some money for his evening activities, as one day when I got home from school, my pet sow was gone. I asked my mother if she knew where my pet sow was, and she informed me of some very bad news. My father had taken my pet sow to the local livestock sale barn and sold her for the hot dogs, bacon, pork chops, and hams she would provide. Selling my pet sow without my knowledge was hurtful, and I was upset that my father had taken my pet and sold her for money he needed. I not only lost my riding sow, I lost the money she was sold for.

After losing that pig, I moved on to riding half-grown calves, along with riding my horse, Daisy. These half-grown calves were perfect riding size, and I was back in the animal-riding business. I would ride these calves until they would buck me off of their backs. After they got used to me riding them, they would not buck anymore. So, like they do with rodeo bucking bulls, I enticed them to buck by tying baling twine over their backs and around their rear flanks. That baling twine, cinched up tight, would make them uncomfortable, and they would buck for me. My calf-riding days came to an end when my mother noticed that the calves were looking a bit swayback. I knew then it was time to move on to riding something else.

One might think that I was a sucker for cheap animals at livestock sales. One day, as I attended the weekly livestock sale with Dad, while watching the animals go through the sale ring, a small, mostly black nanny goat came into the sale ring. I thought she was cute, with those two curved horns sticking out of the top of her head, and thought she would make a good pet for me. But I didn't think I had enough money with me to buy her, and my father probably would not allow me to bid on her anyway. Just as I thought, the auctioneer started the bidding too high for me to bid. He asked for ten dollars for this little goat. At ten dollars, no one bid on the animal. So the auctioneer dropped the bid to one dollar. Still no one bid, and I was thinking it would be nice if I had a dollar to bid on the goat. But all I had was twenty-five cents in my pocket. Now, wouldn't you know … the auctioneer dropped the starting bid to twenty-five cents. I told my father I had twenty-five cents in my pocket and pleaded with him to allow me to bid on the little goat. As usual, my father wasn't real interested in what I did and said that he didn't care if I bid on the goat or not. I do not think he expected me to outbid other bidders for the little goat with a measly bid of twenty-five cents. I bid what I had in my pocket. Now, either no one wanted that goat or no one wanted to bid up a little kid, because no one bid on that little nanny goat but me. Like the little runt piglet, I paid my twenty-five cents, and the little nanny goat was mine.

To get that little goat home, like I did the piglet, I had to kneel in the bed of the pickup and hold the goat as my father drove us home. I worked with her each day so that she would become a good pet. I thought that she was eating a lot of grass and weeds, because her stomach area was getting pretty big for a little goat. To my surprise, a few weeks after I bought her, she gave birth to triplets. Now I was in the goat business without even trying to be. One of the baby goats, however, fell into a pond and drowned soon after it was born, so I had three goats instead of just one.

About a year after I bought that little nanny goat, my grandfather, who lived in town, got tired of feeding and milking the three nanny goats he had. He milked the three goats twice a day and sold the excess milk to other people who were lactose intolerant or could not drink cows' milk. To me, goat milk tastes terrible. I could never understand why anyone would want to drink that nasty-tasting stuff. One day my grandfather surprised me by hauling his three nanny goats and his one male billy goat out to our farm. He wasn't interested in taking the time to haul them to a sale barn to be sold. So, it seemed logical to him to just bring his goats out to our farm to be with the three goats I already had. The goats he brought me were three big red nanny goats and one very large white billy goat. Now I was blessed with seven goats instead of just one little nanny goat that I paid twenty-five cents to get.

Goats can get into all kinds of mischief and eat anything and everything. The good thing about those goats was that they ate grass and weeds, which helped cut down on my lawn mowing responsibility. These goats all became like pets except for the billy goat. One day, when I was outside the house and home alone, the telephone rang our number. We were on what was called a party line. A short ring and two long rings meant someone was calling us. So, when I heard the telephone ring a short and two longs, I ran into the house to answer the phone. Wouldn't you know … the back screen door didn't close completely behind me. A partly closed screen door is an extremely inviting situation for inquisitive pet goats. While I was talking on the telephone, six goats came into the house and walked past me. I quickly finished talking on the phone because there were six goats running around the inside of our house. A goat inside of the house is not a good thing. I could just see those goats breaking something, chewing on something, or leaving little, round potty droppings on the floor of our house. So, it was of utmost importance to get them out of the house before something broke and I had to clean up a big mess. My mother would not have been pleased if she had learned about the goats being inside the house. I chased six goats around the house and herded them back outside. Fortunately, the billy goat did not get into the house, and the goats did not leave any droppings, but after I removed the goats from the interior of the house, I took the vacuum cleaner and ran it throughout the house, just in case they had left any evidence of their presence. It was important to me that my mother not find out about what had happened. As long as everything went well when she and my sister went shopping, I did not have to go along with them. I could stay home alone. Shopping was definitely not a favorite pastime of mine. I would do almost anything to not have to go shopping. I would even wash dishes.

The old billy goat that my grandfather gave me was white and big, smelled bad, and had a nasty disposition. He would knock me down given half the chance. I think that old goat enjoyed headbutting things, especially me. Because of his bad disposition, I always kept my distance from him. One morning when I was in the hay barn feeding alfalfa hay to the milk cows, my father thought I was taking far too long to get the job done. He was not a man blessed with a lot of patience and had a quick temper. I had thrown the bales of hay down from the hayloft into the barn's alleyway. I would then distribute the hay for the cows to eat into the feed bunks located on both sides of the alleyway.

The reason it was taking me longer than usual was because of that old, mean-tempered billy goat. He was standing at the bottom of the ladder, below where I had to climb down. I tried to climb down the ladder, but the billy goat wouldn't let me come down. When my dad came to the barn to see why it was taking me so long to feed the cows, he did not know about the billy goat's bad temper. I warned him about what the billy goat would do to him if he upset the goat. But my impatient, quick-tempered father didn't believe me. He picked up a bale of alfalfa hay and proceeded to use the bale to knock the billy goat out of his way. That was a very big mistake. Being hit with that bale of hay only upset that goat, and he took it as an invitation to fight. The billy goat shook his head, reared up on his hind legs, and rammed his head into my father's midsection. The force of the hit to his midsection was hard enough to knock Dad down onto his backside. This, being knocked down by the billy goat, happened at one end of the barn's alleyway. While he was on his backside, my father's anger elevated even more than it already was. All kinds of bad words and unusual names for the billy goat came out of my father's mouth. He was determined not to let that billy goat get the best of him. But each time he stood up, the billy goat would rear up and headbutt him again, knocking him down each time. This getting knocked down happened so frequently that the billy goat knocked my father from one end of the barn, down the alleyway, to the opposite end of the barn.

Billy goats have extremely hard heads, and about three-fourths of the way across the barn, my father was able to grab a piece of hedge post (Osage orange wood) to defend himself. This piece of hedge wood was about a foot and a half long and three inches in diameter. A hedge post is an extremely hard piece of wood. Each time, as my father stood up, he would hit that billy goat on the top of his head, as hard as he could. The old billy goat would just shake his head, rear up on his hind legs, and headbutt my father again, knocking him down, time after time. My father destroyed that piece of hedge wood over that billy goat's head. The hedge post broke into splinters, but it had no real effect on the billy goat. To escape the goat's wrath, Dad climbed into the cattle feed bunk, and the goat, unable to fight my dad any longer, lost interest and went to rejoin the rest of the goats. At that point, I was able to climb down the ladder to finish feeding the hay to our patiently waiting dairy cows. Each time we describe this event to family and friends, smiles come over our faces as we picture that encounter of Dad and the billy goat in our minds.

That billy goat was not the only animal my father hit with a piece of hedge post. He cold-cocked a cow with a piece of hedge post when she wouldn't go where he wanted her to go. A cow's head is not as hard as a billy goat's head, and that cow lay on the ground, not moving. We thought he had killed that cow. But while we were preparing to butcher her, she regained consciousness and rejoined the herd. I had never seen a cow knocked out before, nor have I seen one since that time.

Another exciting event that happened involved the same mean billy goat and my protective dog. That billy goat had a unique taste for things. One day, he chewed a hole into the plastic window screen of my sister's bedroom. My sister was a beautiful, long-blonde-haired teenager and attracted the attention of the non-Mennonite boys in the area. These boys would sneak into our yard at night and scratch on her window screen to talk with her. The first time it happened, she thought it was just the old billy goat chewing on her window screen again, so she opened the window to chase the billy goat away, but it wasn't the billy goat at her window. She talked to the boys for a few minutes, and they left. My sister wasn't happy with these boys sneaking to her window at night to talk to her. However, their sneaking to her window created big problems for them. My great-uncle found a litter of puppies under his house and gave me one of those puppies. That puppy was a boxer, German shepherd mix who became extremely protective of me. If anyone got near me or grabbed me and I yelled help, my dog would attack them viciously. He would continue his attacks until I went over to him and reassured him that I was OK. It did not matter who it was, family member or not. But when it was other people bothering my family, my dog would protect them as well. So when these boys came back the second time, this dog found the boys at my sister's window. The dog's protective instincts kicked in, and he taught those boys how to sprint quickly to their car.

My sister had complained to my mother about the boys bothering her at night. To prevent the boys from wanting to come back, we put up an electric fence, so when the boys took the shortest distance sprinting back to their car, they would have a very unforgettable experience running into our "Weed Chopper" electric fence. That electric fence would give them quite a jolt of electricity when touched.

The last time these boys snuck back to my sister's window, my dog found them before they reached the window, and they sprinted the shortest distance back to their car. All of a sudden there was screaming and yelling, with the dog on their heels. These boys ran into our Weed Chopper and were electrified. With all the yelling and screaming going on, my sister, mom, and I woke up and had a good laugh about what had just happened.

I've always loved animals and caring for them. I would attend to sick and injured animals, setting broken bones, helping cows to birth their calves by pulling the calves when the cows were not able to birth them on their own, and nursing the sick and injured animals back to health. One day, one of my dogs got its leg stepped on by one of our cows, breaking the dog's leg. Of course, my father would not spend the money to take her to the veterinarian, so I took the dog to the hay barn, made a nest for the dog in the hay, set the leg, splinted the leg, and fed the dog as much milk as it could drink every morning and evening until her leg healed.

One day after a cow birthed her calf, we brought the calf to the barn to be cared for. This calf became seriously ill with pneumonia. Animals that get pneumonia seldom survive, especially the very young and very old animals. So, my father did not expect this calf to live. My mother talked him into giving me the opportunity to try to save its life since I had a knack for healing sick and injured animals. So, Dad came to me and told me if I could nurse the calf back to health, it could be my calf. That was an exciting proposition for me. No matter what kind of animal it was, I enjoyed playing veterinarian and nursing it back to health. I fed that little calf three times a day and gave it some antibiotics by injection, and it responded to the antibiotics and my care. That calf supposedly became mine. However, that lasted until my father needed money. A healthy calf was worth some money, so he sold my calf and kept the money he received. I was brokenhearted again because I was unable to keep that calf I worked so hard to save.

I did not understand how my father could lie to me about that calf being mine. I was hurt, but more than that, I was scared of what he might do to me if I tried to stand up to him.

Just like the pet sow, when my father needed money, he sold all of the goats, calves, chickens, sheep, dairy cows, and even my horse, Daisy. Even though my father was responsible for me losing many of my pets, he wasn't always responsible for my losing a pet. One of my pet calves got its hoof caught in a cattle guard, which is a row of horizontal metal pipes welded together a few inches apart. It allows vehicles to be driven over it, but it prevents livestock from crossing over it. The calf's hoof was small enough to slip between the pipes, and when the calf tried to pull its hoof out from between the pipes, its leg broke. Again, I felt miserable, because I knew that the calf would have to be butchered and made into hamburger, steaks, and the like. I knew the calf would not survive, and meat was in short supply for us. After it was butchered, I tried hard not to think about where that meat came from when we had beef for meals. Tough life-and-death situations like this happened many times and conditioned me to handle the many sad experiences that I had to face throughout my life.

Another animal health problem that I dealt with had to do with a critical situation. While working for a local farmer/banker by doing field work for him, I spotted a bloated cow in the pasture. I informed the owner's son, who was working with me, that the cow was very sick and needed immediate attention. The owner's son did not know what to do and wanted to go to town to notify his father that the cow was sick. But I was persistent and talked him into allowing me to handle the situation. The cow would have died by the time a veterinarian could arrive. So it was crucial that I helped this cow immediately. The gas buildup in this cow's stomach was immense and needed to be removed as soon as possible.

There were two ways to solve this cow's problem. You could take a pocket knife and stab the knife into the cow's stomach just in front of its hip bone or have the gas escape through her throat and mouth. I didn't have a pocket knife, so I looked for and found a piece of galvanized pipe about two foot long and a garden hose. I placed the pipe into the cow's mouth to prevent her from biting down on the garden hose as I pushed the hose down the cows throat and into her stomach, to allow the gas causing the bloating, to escape through the garden hose. You have to be careful to make sure the garden hose goes into the cow's stomach and not into her lungs.

This situation with the bloated cow gave me the opportunity to play a joke on the farmer's son, who was my age. I guess I have a lot of my mother in me. I have always been what people would call a practical joker. I would play tricks on people, and this situation was a perfect opportunity for that.

The escaping fermented gas had a very unpleasant odor, and I convinced the owner's son to put his nose close to the end of the garden hose that was sticking out of the pipe so he could smell the escaping gas. At first he wasn't excited about doing that, but I told him that the escaping gas had a unique sweat odor to it. So, he complied and smelled the escaping gas. Upon smelling the fermented gas, he almost fell backward off of the wooden fence he was sitting on. Needless to say, he wasn't happy with me, but he couldn't get too upset since I saved that cow's life that day. Of course, the banker / farm owner was very thankful that I was there and knew just what to do.

The banker / farm owner was like most Mennonites are, very tight with his money. A cow was a valuable commodity, and having a veterinarian come out to the farm to perform the procedure would have been quite costly. One would think that this owner would have been happy to reward me with a small amount of money, but that never happened. What I received was a thank you and the question "How did you know how to do that?" The reason I knew what to do was because I had watched a veterinarian do the procedure on one of our cows at our farm.

After earning some money doing farm work, I wanted to find another dairy heifer for a 4-H project. So, I talked my father into taking me to another livestock sale in a town about twenty-five miles from our farm. My plan was to purchase a heifer, show her in 4-H dairy shows, raise her, breed her to a good bull, and sell her calves for profit. But Dad saw my plan as a fund raising opportunity for him to gain some finances and was willing to take me to this livestock sale. At this sale, there was this half-grown, good conformation Milking Shorthorn heifer calf that was perfect for me if she didn't sell for too much money. I was looking for a Holstein, Brown Swiss, Guernsey, Jersey, or an Ayrshire heifer. But a Milking Shorthorn was a duel type of animal, good for milking or for raising beef calves. As I was waiting for this red heifer to come into the sale ring, a long-legged, lanky, grayish-black Appaloosa filly with a white blanket marking over her hindquarters came through the sale ring. She had just been weaned from her mother and looked scared. She seemed to need a friend, and I thought if she sold cheap enough, I could afford to buy both her and the heifer calf. My father was supportive of me buying both. It meant more profit for him when he sold the animals. It so happened that she did sell cheap enough that I could buy her along with the red heifer calf I was planning on purchasing. I took that filly and calf home, cared for them continually, and became their surrogate mother. Wherever I went, that filly was always right behind me. She followed me everywhere, just like that old pet sow did. I never needed to use a halter or lead rope on her. I would just walk wherever I wanted her to go, and she would be right behind me. When I showed this filly at 4-H horse shows, she would follow me through the crowds of people without a halter on her or a lead rope. This filly would stick right behind me, no matter how large the crowd was or how tightly they were packed around us.

Unfortunately, my fund raising plan worked only as far as the raising of the heifer calf, the training of the colt, and the end of the 4-H shows. When the shows were over, my father sold those animals out from under me while I was in school and kept the funds for himself.

Along with all of the other animals we had on the farm, we had sheep for a short period. Sheep have to be one of the least intelligent animals God created. I am not sure why God created them that way. The Bible refers to people as sheep, telling us just how intelligent we really are. If one sheep fell off of a cliff, all of the other sheep would follow it over the cliff to their demise. But at times, it can be an advantage for sheep to follow one another. If you can get just one sheep to go in the right direction, nothing will prevent the entire flock from following it.

Three miles from our farm was a fenced county park, with a large river that ran through the middle of the park. Each year, my father would negotiate the price of the park's grazing rights, and we put a number of our sheep into one side of that park for the summer grazing season. Every year, a problem developed when a band of

Gypsies spent a week camping in the park. Each grazing season while the Gypsies were spending their week camping in the park, one of our sheep would disappear. It vanished, and no one seemed to know what happened to it. Of course, the Gypsies would always deny taking the sheep, but they always ate mutton while they were camped in the park. When my father would approach them about our lost sheep, they would deny knowing anything about it and would even invite our family to join them in their camp for a meal. Of course, lamb was always on the menu. My father cordially declined their invitations to eat what was probably our own sheep. Because Gypsies had a reputation of taking things that didn't belong to them, the first time we were in their camp, my sister became very fearful that the Gypsies would go to our farm and steal things. On the way home, our mother assured her that everything would be just fine and told her about an old wives' tale from the old country. She told my sister that if you put a broom across the door opening, Gypsies would not cross over the broom. When we got home, our mother put a broom across the door opening to calm my sister's fears so she could go to sleep. After a few years, Dad needed money and sold our sheep. We no longer had sheep to put in the park for the summer. Amazingly, without sheep in the park, the Gypsies stopped coming to camp there anymore.

Along with the sheep, pigs, horses, goats, and dairy cattle we had on the farm from time to time, my family raised rabbits for meat. As they were growing up, the rabbits were like pets to my sister and me. We enjoyed going out to the rabbit hutch and playing with the rabbits we raised, especially the baby bunnies. We would take the rabbits out of their hutch, hold them, and let them hop around and eat grass. They were always so soft and cuddly. It was a sad day when it became butchering day for those rabbits we had played with and raised. My father would take some of the rabbit meat with him on his evening excursions. Surprisingly, we were able to keep some of the meat for our own consumption. Growing up on a farm teaches one that even cute little animals would one day grow up and have to become food for the table. It was a time when one didn't go to the grocery store. You raised what you ate. After the cute, soft, cuddly rabbits were butchered, it was meat to eat.

One of the few evenings my father was home, my parents invited a neighbor family over for an evening meal. The only meat that we had to serve was the rabbit we had butchered. I was young, and my mother did not want me to spill the beans, so to speak, by saying what kind of meat was being served. Believe it or not, fried rabbit meat looks and tastes a lot like fried chicken.

The evening was going very well, and everyone was enjoying the meal, especially the meat. Our guest's high school–aged boy was really indulging in eating the great-tasting meat. After partaking of a large amount of meat, this boy asked for the plate of the great-tasting fried chicken to be passed to him again. Wouldn't you know it … without thinking, I blurted out, "Chicken! It's not chicken. It's rabbit!" My announcement ended this boy's desire for any more of that great-tasting "fried chicken." It seems that all unusual kinds of meat taste like chicken.

At the same time that we were raising rabbits, we raised mink for their pelts. The same man who got my father involved in the immoral lifestyle he learned to love got him into the mink-raising business. He convinced my father that raising mink for their pelts was a profitable enterprise. You would think that after all of the failed schemes he got Dad involved in, my father would not have listened to his wild sales pitches. But mink pelts were thought to be valuable, because of the demand for mink coats and stoles. Mink are vicious little carnivores that will eat almost anything. If you valued your fingers, it was extremely important that you never stuck your fingers through the wires of their cages. Mink are quick, mean little critters that would get to your fingers before you could move them and bite them off. A young boy in the community lost the tip of one of his fingers to one of their mink. He had the tip of his finger sticking through the wires of a cage, and a mink got it.

Since mink are meat eaters, we would feed the mink ground-up horse meat or ground-up jackrabbit. My father and the man who got him into the mink business would go to horse sales and buy the cheap old swayback horses that otherwise would go to the glue factory or be made into dog food. The old horses were butchered and ground up into horse hamburger. The jackrabbits were bought at what were called jackrabbit drives. A jackrabbit drive functioned with the participants of the drive surrounding a one-mile square area. All of the participants would slowly walk toward the center of the surrounded area. The jackrabbits would be shot using shotguns for safety reasons and loaded into the bed of a large farm truck The participants would be paid ten cents for every jackrabbit they shot and put in the back of the truck. At that time, jackrabbits were so plentiful that they were a major problem for farmers. Crop production was being affected, so jackrabbit drives were a common occurrence. It was not unusual to drive a car one mile on a country road at night and count over thirty jackrabbits in front of the car's headlights.

Baby mink were cute and fun to play with. But to play with the baby mink, the babies and the mother had to be separated. I would tap on the mink's cage, and when the mother mink would run out of the wooden nest box attached to the end of the wire cage, I would slip a metal plate over the hole to prevent the mother mink from being able to get back into the wooden nest box. I would then open the lid to the nest and play with the baby mink. When I was finished playing with them, I would close the lid, lock it, and let the mother mink back into the nest box with her babies. Unfortunately, one day my family was forced out of the mink-raising business. It was a very hot day, and my family was away from home. When we returned home that evening, we found that all of the mink had died. An automated watering system had failed, and the mink overheated. So, my father skinned all of our mink and sold their pelts and cages. I am not sure why, but at about the same time, we got out of the rabbit-raising business as well.

Along with our dairy cattle, rabbits, mink, sheep, chickens, hogs, and geese ventures, when I was in high school, I bought and broke horses to ride. I would buy colts, tame them, and break them to ride. One time, I attended a horse sale with my father about twenty miles from our farm. While watching the horse sale progress, a white mare came into the sale ring. The auctioneer said that the lanky mare was "green broke." Being green broke could mean the mare was almost ready for riding and just needed some saddle time, or it could mean she had hardly had a saddle on her back. You never could fully believe horse traders when they talked about their horses. My father encouraged me to buy this mare because she sold so cheap. As I look back on the situation, I think my father thought it would be a quick, easy way for him to make some money. He would have me buy her, get her comfortable with a rider on her back, and then sell her for a big profit. Well, I bought that white, long-legged mare at the horse sale. I should have known better when my father encouraged me to buy her.

After I got the mare home, I put a saddle on her back, cinched her up, and walked her into the middle of a plowed field. I used the plowed field in case she wanted to buck and I got bucked off. Landing on a plowed field would be less painful.

Also, in a plowed field, the horse would wear out faster bucking in the loose soil. Dad held the horse until I climbed on her back and was ready for what she might do. When my father released her, this mare just stood there, bracing her legs stiff, and would not move a muscle. No matter what I did, I couldn't get her to move. I could hit her, kick her in the ribs, or poke her, and she would just stand there. So I climbed out of the saddle, unsaddled her, and put her into our pasture with my other horses for one week. I thought she was probably just scared because of the new surroundings. After a week of being around the place, I thought she would feel more comfortable and cooperative. When the week was up, I caught the mare, saddled her up, and took her back into the middle of the plowed field and climbed on her back. This time was very different. She was definitely more comfortable with the situation but not more cooperative. My bottom no sooner hit the saddle than that old mare put me into orbit. There was more than a foot of space between my bottom and the saddle on each of her bucks. I rode her for a bit, but she knew how to buck, and I went flying through the air, landing on my tush.

The way this so-called green broke mare bucked made me think she had bucking experience in rodeos. As soon as I was off of her back, she stopped bucking and just stood there until I picked myself up off of the plowed field, walked over to her, unsaddled her, and led her back to the pasture. This was no common green broke mare. So, my father sold her to a rodeo string, and the last I knew, she was bucking in rodeos. Of course, the money I received from her sale Dad kept for his use.

All of his life, my father looked for ways he could make easy money. Early in his married life, he made money by trapping wild animals, skinning them, and selling their pelts. He would also hunt coyotes because coyotes were considered major pests to farmers and ranchers. Coyotes had a bounty placed on their heads. Their ears and tail were worth two dollars. So, my father would hunt coyotes and take their ears and tails into the county courthouse to receive the two-dollar bounty for every pair of coyote ears and tail that he brought in.

Not long after my parents were married, my father and mother were driving to attend an important wedding. A skunk ran across the road in front of their car and into a driveway culvert. Good skunk skins were profitable, and Dad saw dollar bills in that skunk's pelt. But my mother only saw an old, smelly skunk that was preventing them from getting to the important wedding on time. My father assured her that he was just going to take a look at the skunk and would be careful not to get dirty or sprayed. As usual, my father did as he pleased. He stopped the car, got out, and walked over to the culvert where the skunk had entered.

Dad thought he would only take a look at the skunk and determine if the skunk's pelt was worth the effort to come back later.

My father, being dressed in his "Sunday go to meeting" suit, knelt down and looked into the end of the culvert for the skunk. The skunk was there and took exception to my father's presence. The skunk, feeling threatened, proceeded to raise its tail and spray him with its noxious odor. That, of course, prevented the trip to the very important wedding.

When Mom told me the story, she said they hung my dad's suit out on the wash line for over a month. They were hoping the skunk smell would eventually fade out of the suit. But skunk scent is a very powerful odor that lingers for a very long time. The skunk scent never faded out of the suit, and my parents had to dispose of that suit by burying it. My parents did not know that a combination of hydrogen peroxide, baking soda, and dish soap could help neutralize the odor of skunk spray.

You would think that my father would have learned his lesson from that skunk incident, but no, not him. Six years later, a neighbor family was blessed with the birth of twin boys, but unfortunately, one of the boys did not survive. Our family was driving the two-mile distance to their farm to formally express our sympathy. When we were about a quarter of a mile from their farm, a skunk ran across the road and into a plowed field. Oh, yeah, my father stopped the car, jumped out, and chased after that skunk. It was wobbling over the large clods in the plowed field, giving my father the chance of catching up to it. When he got close to the skunk, the skunk felt threatened by his close proximity to it. That frightened skunk raised its tails and fired its noxious spray at him. Of course, that skunk was accurate with its potent spray, and my father got hit full force. When Dad got back to the car, he smelled so bad that we had to have the car windows rolled down and our heads out of the windows. He also was not able to go into the neighbor's house to express his empathy for their situation. I believe that particular incident, with that specific skunk, convinced my father to end his trapping of wild animals for profit ventures.

When we arrived at the neighbor's place, the man was neutering a couple of cats. He placed the cats in a gunny sack, closed the gunny sack around the cat's tail, held the gunny sack–covered cat tail so the cat hung down while he castrated the cat through two small holes in the sack. Performing the procedure this way prevented the cat's claws from sinking into the holder's skin during the procedure. Of course the cats were not happy about what was happening to them, but they survived the ordeal.

When Dad trapped wild animals, he sometimes caught rare animals like albinos. When this happened, he would donate these unusual animals to a museum. Examples of what he donated to museums are an albino cottontail rabbit and a kangaroo mouse. The albino rabbit he caught alive gave birth to four stillborn normal-looking cottontail rabbit babies. The albino mother rabbit and her babies, however, did not survive the ordeal, and she and her babies were donated to a local museum. The museum curator stuffed and mounted the animal skins in lifelike poses for the museum.

Wild animals can be major problems for farmers and ranchers. Our closest neighbor raised turkeys for Thanksgiving dinners and collected their eggs for hatching. The turkey pens would need to be moved periodically from one location to a new location. When my neighbor would move his turkey pen, I would help him move the turkeys to the new location. Turkeys are extremely stupid birds. Turkeys may even be more unintelligent than sheep.

When herding the turkeys into their new location, it never seemed to fail that they would almost get to the new location and then fly back to the area where the old pen had been located. One time, as the birds were flying back to their old pen area, I had a stick in my hand and swung the stick at some flying turkeys. I happened to hit one turkey just below its head. That turkey swung around the stick, making a complete circle, while in flight. This wounded turkey fell to the ground motionless. I thought I had killed that poor turkey, but a few minutes later, it revived and staggered around. Eventually, we would get all of those turkeys moved to their new location. I would have appreciated if the neighbor had paid me for my help, but that never happened. It probably was just as well because my father would have taken what I would have been paid. Coyotes would often cause our neighbor lots of problems by killing his turkeys. So he would put poison in the dead turkey's carcasses and place them in areas where the coyotes would find and eat them. That was an effective way of controlling the coyote population, but unfortunately, sometimes our farm dogs would find those poisoned turkey carcasses and consume some of the poisoned meat themselves. We would find their lifeless bodies after they returned home. We lost a number of farm dogs that way.

One day, what appeared to be a German shepherd dog followed the car my mother was driving to our farm. We didn't want that dog to stay, but she decided our farm was the perfect place for her. The milk that she received along with our cats every morning and evening was a powerful incentive for her to stay. This German shepherd–looking dog had an unusual, wild look in its eyes. We thought that some city slicker who no longer wanted their dog must have dumped their dog off in the country to fend for itself. This type of thing happened every once in a while. Not too long after this German shepherd–looking dog arrived, she gave birth to five pups that looked just like their mother. They had those same unusual, wild yellowish eyes.

At the time this dog arrived at our farm, we had about sixteen Guinea fowl. Guineas are gray feathered birds with white spots speckled all over their feathers. They are originally from Africa and are great watch birds. These birds are as good as any watchdog for warning of something unusual happening around them. When disturbed, these Guinea foul would screech loudly, warning that something was not quite right. At night, the Guineas would roost in low tree limbs. As the German shepherd–looking pups grew, the Guinea fowl started to disappear.

One day my father threw a ham bone out for the dogs to gnaw on. This mother dog picked up the ham bone and carried it out into a plowed field. She met a coyote, dropped the ham bone for the coyote, and returned to the farmyard. When that happened, we realized why the pups and the mother dog had such an unusual, wild look to them. They were hybrids, part coyote and part dog. The wild part of the hybrids would take over at night, and they jumped and snatched the Guinea fowl from the low tree limbs. By the time we figured out why the Guinea fowl were disappearing, only three Guinea fowl were left. These hybrids had to be destroyed. The wild part of them was too strong for them to be kept as farm dogs. With my father usually gone and his lack of concern for what was happening, it was up to me to put one rifle bullet into the brain of each of those coyote/dog hybrids. With the hybrids gone, the remaining Guineas survived.

At the time my parents moved to their farm, a nudist camp was located three-fourths of a mile away from the farm. This was an unusual situation for a Mennonite community to deal with. When I was about three years old, the nudist camp shut down and moved away. My mother told me that she was extremely happy when that camp moved out of the area. She said that I was a venturesome and inquisitive youngster, and she was concerned, as I grew older, that during my daily excursions around the farm, I would probably sneak over to the camp to see what it was all about. I cannot say that would not have happened if the camp hadn't moved before I was old enough to think about going to see what was going on there. My mother's concern was probably well founded.

To get my father more involved in my life, Mom would tell him that he needed to do things with me. So, to pacify her, he would once in a while take me along fishing, hunting, or when he was helping neighbors. A few times we went pole fishing in the river close to our farm. Other times, it was hand fishing (noodling) or hunting coyotes, ducks, geese, pheasants, quail, or rabbits. I never got into hand fishing because it was against the law. I, however, loved pole fishing. I could pole fish for hours. I would use sod worms that I dug up for bait to catch crawdads at the park's dam near our farm. I then used the crawdads I caught for bait to catch channel catfish and flathead catfish in the river. When I fished pasture ponds, I would listen for a leopard frog to squeal. A squealing leopard frog meant that a garter snake or some other nonvenomous snake had caught it out in the grassy area. I would follow the sound of the squealing frog, catch the snake, and take the frog out of the snake's mouth. I would then use the frog for bait to catch channel catfish. These fish I caught were meat for my mother and I to eat when our food supply was low.

On some summer evenings, after my mother and I finished milking the cows and doing the chores, I would talk her into taking me to an undeveloped pond near our home. I would go into our pasture, locate a wet area, and dig up long sod worms to use for bait. We would drive the five miles to this undeveloped pond and fish for bluegill. I would bait my hook with a worm and throw the baited hook near a patch of moss floating in the water. As the baited hook dropped into the water, a bluegill would strike the worm-baited hook, and the plastic float (bobber) would disappear below the surface of the water. When that happened, I would set the fishhook in the fish's mouth with a small jerk of my fishing pole and reel the fish into the bank. When the fish were large enough to be keepers, I would take the fish off of the hook and place it on a metal fish stringer. If the fish were too small, it was released so the small fish could grow larger for a later time. When we had caught enough keepers for a meal, we would take the fish home and butcher the fish for eating. To butcher the fish, I would use a quick kill method to humanely kill the fish for flaying by breaking their spine so it wouldn't suffer during the butchering process. I would flay it, sliding a butcher knife under the scaly skin to remove a nice piece of meat. My mother would make a flour batter, roll the fish meat in the batter, and fry the fish in a cast iron frying pan. Those bluegill were the best-tasting fish to me. Probably because of hunger. That pond had a very large population of good-sized bluegill that were fun to catch and very good to eat. Ironically, that pond belonged to the man who got my father involved in his immoral evening activities.

My mother was a fantastic cook. She could make almost anything taste great. The exceptions were cooked spinach, beets, pineapple, coconut, and cooked cabbage. Those things were always nasty tasting to me. If mom was incapable of making them taste good, no one could make them taste good.

When my mother was able to secure the ingredients, she would make ethnic dishes for us to eat. The ethnic dishes were so good! She would make *knepp* (made of one-quarter by one-quarter homemade noodles, potato wedges, bacon pieces, and a milk or cream sauce), *dunn kuchen* (a dessert-type dish made of flat dough like pizza dough, covered with sugar and cream and baked), *mak* kuchen (a jelly roll or ice-cream roll–type of dish with ground-up poppy seed and sugar instead of jelly or ice cream), *kaeivei* (a type of coffee cake topped with cream and sugar icing and candy corn), *bohne beroggi* (a brown-bean-filled sweet roll covered with a sweet milk or cream sauce), case beroggi (a homemade dry cheese inside a boiled and then pan fried pie dough–like wrap), kraut beroggi (a sauerkraut-filled fried pie dough wrap, boiled and then panfried), and what we called flap jacks, which were thin pancakes similar to crepes. The dunn kuchen my mother made we called "Jake S. Kuchen." The reason we called it that was because a family that lived near where my mother grew up made this dish often. Until I was old enough to know better, I thought it was called by a different name; because it was said so fast, it sounded like that. The dough looked like the imprint of someone who sat down on it. These were the ethnic foods we enjoyed frequently before my sister left home.

Things were what I considered good at that time, as far as having enough to eat. When my sister was in high school, my mother baked homemade bread and cinnamon rolls every Saturday night. At that time, my brother-in-law was dating my sister. He would make sure they were back at our house by nine o'clock each Saturday night, because that was the time the cinnamon rolls came out of the oven. My brother-in-law-to-be enjoyed those cinnamon rolls with their gooey caramel-like bottoms.

When we had butchered beef or chicken, we would eat fried steak or fried chicken after the milking and chores were done. My brother-in-law-to-be knew how to estimate the right time to bring my sister home from a date. They would arrive in time to eat steak, fried chicken, or fresh baked cinnamon rolls with my mother and me.

After my sister graduated from high school and moved out of the house, things changed drastically. My sister was fortunate that she did not have to face the really tough times my mother and I faced. I am extremely happy that she was able to escape those tough times At this time, the ways my father had obtained money were drying up. My father found that borrowing money was much more difficult to do since he had mortgaged or sold almost everything we had. There were times when my mother and I did not have anything to eat except the milk from the few dairy cows we had left. The wintertime was especially difficult because it was too cold to go catch bluegill, and with Dad gone, my hunting had to be done on foot, and the game wasn't as plentiful in my limited hunting area.

My father had sold most of the remaining cows, so milk was in short supply. Sometimes we would have a little flour for my mother to mix with the milk to make what we called milk gravy. At times, we would have a little homemade bread to pour the milk gravy over. On a few occasions, my mother would have secretly saved a little money to buy pork n' beans, macaroni, and Velveeta cheese. When this happened, we would have what I considered a gourmet meal of macaroni and cheese with pork n' beans for supper. I was always a big eater when food was available. I think I ate a lot of food during those times, and even today, because there were so many times when we didn't have much to eat, if anything at all. I would eat three regular-sized platefuls of macaroni and cheese and one can of pork n' beans by myself, at one meal. Sometimes Mom would make a pancake mix out of flour and milk. When this happened, we would have pancakes with an egg I could scrounge up from a chicken that was still left running around the farm. That did not happen too often though. Chickens didn't last long, so eggs were not available.

To this day, some sixty years later, I find it difficult to see someone not finish everything on their plate. That bothers me greatly. When my wife cannot finish eating everything on her plate, I will finish it for her, whether I am still hungry or not. I know just how hungry a person can feel when food is not available. To this day, seeing food go to waste is difficult for me . I have to bite my tongue, so to speak, not to say something to those who do not eat everything they have ordered at restaurants.

When times were what I considered good, we would have some meat from animals we had butchered, shot during hunting, or caught while fishing. However, a large amount of the time, it was only milk, maybe milk gravy, or nothing. The lack of available meat to eat was due to my father having sold all of the animals that would have produced future meals, and money wasn't available for us to purchase any meat. Even though sometimes we did not have food to eat, we were conditioned not to tell anyone, and we feared what my father would do to us if we did. We may not have always had a lot to eat, but we had enough to survive. I am extremely thankful to God that He provided whatever we had to eat. Most of the time, we had milk to drink. God never promised us easy sailing or good times in life, but He did promise that He would provide for us, and He always did.

Jesus said, in Matthew 6:25–26, "Therefore I say unto you, Take no thought for your life, what ye shall eat, or what ye shall drink; nor yet for your body, what ye shall put on. Is not the life more than meat, and the body than raiment? Behold the fowls of the air: for they sow not, neither do they reap, nor gather into barns; yet your heavenly Father feedeth them. Are ye not much better than they?" Sometimes it was tough, and you wondered if God would provide, but He always did. He took care of my mother and me during those tough times, and I became more of a person who can look beneath the appearance of things and empathize with others because I experienced it myself.

My mother was not only a talented cook; she was a great seamstress, barber, and pianist. She would cut hair for a couple of neighboring ladies for extra money to buy groceries and pay bills. When I was really young, she would take me over to my maternal grandparents' home, and when I fell asleep, my grandmother would hold me while Mom would cut my hair. As a young kid, I never liked getting my hair cut, so this was the easiest way to get the job done.

Mother's sewing talent was evident when she would sew clothes for my sister. My sister loved shopping for clothes, so our mother would take her shopping. They would not have the money to buy the clothing my sister liked. They were only able to look at the beautiful clothes. However, when my sister would see an article of clothing that she really liked, our mother would go to a fabric store and purchase enough fabric to make the clothing item. She would take the fabric home, make her own pattern like the dress my sister saw, and sew it for her. The dresses mom made looked just like the dresses my sister saw in the stores. Mom was very talented that way. She just made her own patterns and created many beautiful clothes for my sister. Mother sacrificed for us children, and my sister was always well dressed. There were times when Mom would sew clothing and hide them for special occasions. When the special occasion arrived, our mother often forgot that she had hidden the clothing. When found, my sister would receive those items of clothing, unwrapped, in a brown paper sack, with an explanation of why she had made them. Sometimes it would be six months or more before our mother would find them. Mom's sewing talents were such that she even sewed me a few shirts to wear, and she created many patchwork quilts as well.

When my mother and sister would go shopping for fabric or just to see what was available, I would beg Mom to let me stay home by myself. I would convince her that I would be careful and fine by myself. I would promise to clean the whole house if I didn't have to go shopping with them. That bargaining chip was a big concession on my part. Mom was under the impression that I stayed inside the house while they were gone, but that never happened. So, as long as nothing happened when they went shopping, I was able to stay home by myself. Cleaning the house only took me a couple of hours, and I had the rest of the day to do as I pleased.

When my mother and sister left on their shopping trips, my father would leave as well, if he wasn't already gone by then. Being alone was just fine with me. I had a bird egg collection and spent most of the time my mother and sister were shopping on searching for and gathering different kinds of bird eggs for my collection. My bird egg collection was quite extensive. I would find bird nests in tall trees, lower trees and shrubs, and on the ground. I would collect only one egg from the nest if I didn't already have one of that kind. To preserve the egg shell, I would poke a small hole in each end of the egg shell with a needle. Then I would blow through one small hole, forcing out the inside contents of the egg through the small hole in the opposite end of the egg shell, leaving only the shell left. I collected over seventy-five different kinds of bird eggs from chicken hawk–size eggs to the tiny wren-sized eggs. In 4-H woodworking, I made a large glass-covered wooden box to display my bird egg collection. I would take my collection to show-and-tell assignments at school and 4-H presentations. One day, while my mother and sister were shopping and I was out searching for bird eggs, I spotted a red star bird nest. My collection did not have a red star egg in it. This nest was hanging on a tree limb about fifteen feet off of the ground. A red star bird nest was very similar in size and shape as a Baltimore oriole nest. This red star nest hung down in a sack-type nest near the end of a limb. I climbed up the tree trunk and slithered out on the branch to get close to the nest. Unfortunately, the branch was very flexible and bent down as I crept along the limb toward the nest. When I got close enough to reach the nest and gathered one egg, the branch had bent down so much that I could not slide back to the tree trunk. My only option was to drop the fifteen feet to the ground. I was worried that I might hurt myself or break the egg as I dropped to the ground from that height. I had no choice but to drop to the ground and was fortunate that I did not break the egg or hurt myself in any way. I kept my mouth shut about that incident, and my mother did not find out about how close I was to getting injured. I think of that collection often and wonder what happened to it after I went off to college. I suspect that Dad may have sold it or given it to another child. He did that with everything else. Another day while my mother and sister were shopping, I took my BB gun outside to target practice. It was a used gun when I got it, but it still somewhat worked. While shooting BB pellets at things, a chicken a long way away from me walked into my view. Even though the BB gun was not very accurate, I peppered that chicken's backside with a BB pellet. The chicken just clucked and ran off. I was far enough away from the chicken that the BB pellet did not penetrate the feathers, and the chicken was not injured in any way.

Later that day, I saw another chicken, so I peppered it with a BB pellet too. But this time the chicken didn't run away. It fell to the ground lifeless. I guess I was too close to the chicken, and the BB pellet penetrated the feathers and skin. It must have hit a vital spot, because the chicken died. There I was with a dead chicken on my hands and wondering what I should do so Mom and especially Dad would not find out what happened. I was scared what my father might do to me, and I knew that those dreaded shopping trips would be in my future. At first, I considered butchering the chicken and putting its carcass in the freezer to be eaten at a later date. So I quickly went to check the freezer for other frozen chickens, but the freezer was basically empty, and there weren't any chickens in there. I was left with a dilemma. If I butchered the chicken and put it in the freezer, there would be only that one chicken in the freezer, which shouldn't have been there. My mother would be sure to find out what I had done, and then Dad would probably find out too. So, butchering the chicken was out of the question. What could I do to prevent Mom and Dad from finding out what happened? I sure did not want to have to go along shopping, and I definitely didn't want to face my father's wrath. Throwing away good meat that could be eaten since we often didn't have very much to eat was extremely tough to do. But all I could think of to solve my problem was to carry that dead chicken far out into a plowed field, dig a hole, and bury it. Maybe some coyote would find it and eat it, and if remnants of that chicken were found, everyone would think a coyote caught and killed it. Burying that chicken was wasteful though. While I was carrying that dead bird out into the field to bury it, all I could think of was how good that chicken would have tasted. As I saw it, the only solution to my problem was to bury that chicken. So, that is what I did! But when I was hungry, it came back to haunt me. I never told anyone about what had happened, and I never shot at another chicken again. Maybe this chicken experience caused me not to enjoy hunting animals like my father did. But telling some of the hunting and fishing stories has always been fun, and quite often, incredible things happened on those outings.

Hunting was always an activity that my father enjoyed and indulged in. Hunting was so much a part of his life that elk hunting in Idaho was my parents' honeymoon trip. Mom never was into hunting, so the honeymoon trip was only for my father's benefit. She stayed in a cabin the entire time Dad and some of their friends went out hunting during the day.

The following accounts are three of those incredible hunting stories. One time, my brother-in-law came out to the farm to do some hunting. My father took my brother-in-law and me out to hunt pheasants in the area around our farm. When we arrived at a shelter belt (a number of rows of trees to provide a wind break), Dad instructed my brother-in-law and me to start walking through the trees, beginning at one end of the shelter belt. We were to walk through the shelter belt while my father drove to the opposite end of the shelter belt to shoot the birds as they ran out ahead of us. When my brother-in-law and I were about halfway through the wind break (a half mile away from my father), a pheasant flew out the side of shelter belt and down the roadway toward where Dad was located. He was a very good shot with a shotgun and knew just when to shoot the flying bird as it was flying toward him. Dad had won many dressed turkeys at shooting events before. I am sure that my father told this story many times. When he shot at the pheasant, he, of course, hit it, and incredibly, the pheasant landed in the back of the pickup truck parked on the roadway.

My father enjoyed entertaining people by taking them hunting.

One day, he took five friends, my brother-in-law, and me duck hunting in our sandhill pasture. There were many ponds in the pasture and lots of ducks on the ponds. You could hunt ducks all day in the pasture, doing what is called "pond jumping." One could shoot up a couple of boxes of shotgun shells and never even leave the pasture. This particular time, all eight of us surrounded a pond about two acres in size before the season opened at six in the morning. The ducks were so plentiful on the pond we surrounded that when one duck would try to land on the water, it would knock a couple of other ducks under the water. Each hunter had three shells in their gun, and when the season opened, all eight hunters stood up and shot three times. That meant twenty-four shots were fired. Ducks fell like leaves out of a tree, and when we gathered up all of the ducks that had been shot, there was a total of seventy-two ducks. That meant nine ducks per hunter or three ducks per shot had been harvested. That number of ducks was well above the daily limit for the eight of us. In a matter of minutes, our duck hunting that day was over. We did not want the duck meat to go to waste, so we put all seventy-two ducks in the front seat of our pickup truck so they were not easily visible, leaving the seven of us to ride in the back bed of the pickup the few miles to our farm.

It took a very long time to butcher all of those ducks, well into the afternoon that day. All of my father's friends took as many ducks as they wanted, my brother-in-law took as many as he wanted, and there were plenty of ducks left. As usual, Mom and I were low on the totem pole. But we were allowed to keep one duck for us to eat. We were actually grateful for that one duck. My father took the remaining ducks with him when he left home that afternoon. I do not know where he distributed the ducks or to whom he gave them. But I am confident that he enjoyed giving them away and recounting the story.

Another time, my father, his brother, a friend, my brother-in-law, and my sister were deer hunting in our sandhill pasture. Everyone positioned themselves to wait for the deer to move and come by them. My sister was to walk through a wooded area next to the pasture in hopes of jumping up some deer, causing them to run toward the other hunters. She hadn't walked far when she jumped up an animal, but it wasn't a deer. It was a mountain lion. My sister was too scared to shoot the mountain lion, for fear she would only wound it and it would attack her. The mountain lion was a bit shaken too since they were only a few feet away from each other. My sister said that it felt like five minutes when it was probably only a few seconds before the mountain lion ran away. The mountain lion ran past where my brother-in-law was located, who verified the fact that it was an actual mountain lion. For years, the fish and game commission had denied that mountain lions were in Kansas. But I know for a fact that mountain lions have been in Kansas since at least 1965. One afternoon, as I was riding home on the school bus, we approached a country bridge, and a full-grown mountain lion was standing on the bridge. When the bus approached the bridge, the mountain lion slowly walked off of the bridge and down into a wooded area.

My father hunted pheasants and quail each year, and he would travel to western Kansas during pheasant-hunting season to hunt the birds. He did this annual hunting trip even though we never had the money for him to make the trip. He would charge motel rooms to his account, and we would later receive the motel room bills through the mail. My mother and I were expected to find ways to pay off these motel bills. Dad made no effort to pay for these bills himself, so it was up to my mother to pay these bills out of her hard-earned money. Dad would pay for all of the expenses of the people he took with him, and one can only guess who those people were. One thing I do know: it was never one of my family members. As usual, my father would justify these hunting trips by claiming they had to do with his undercover work. His unpaid bills probably caused me to never want to owe anyone anything. It was always difficult for my mother and I to come up with the money to cover his debts. Like most farms, we had a round, galvanized metal grain bin. One time, when this grain bin was half-full of corn kernels from corn we had harvested, an eventful thing happened. My father hadn't sold the corn yet, because he was waiting for a higher grain price before selling any of it, and it was work to remove it from the grain bin. It was at a time when money was very tight for Mom and me, so we decided to load some of that corn into our pickup truck and haul it to town to secure enough money to buy groceries and pay utility bills. Even though we knew that Dad would probably be upset with us for selling some of the corn, we were hungry, utility bills needed to be paid, and the corn was available to solve the problems we were facing.

When a person enters a grain bin with any kind of grain in it, things can happen to them. While we were scooping that corn into an auger system to carry the corn kernels from just inside the door of the grain bin out into the bed of the pickup truck, a mouse came out of the corn and started running around the inside of the grain bin. You wouldn't think that a little ole mouse could cause a problem, but it was looking for an escape hole. Not finding one right away, my pant leg must have looked really inviting, because that mouse made a direct beeline to my pant leg and went up inside it. Quick thinking on my part saved me a lot of anguish, discomfort, and misery. Using both hands, I clamped my pant leg to my leg just above my knee, preventing the mouse from climbing any higher. While I was preventing the mouse from climbing any higher, I shook that mouse out of my pant leg. It must have been quite a sight watching me jumping around, shaking my leg while standing in a pile of corn.

My mother was too scared of mice to even come close to me. Mice gave her the heebie-jeebies. So, she was of no help to me. She just stood there, not knowing how to help me and not really wanting that mouse to get too close to her. I am confident that she was extremely thankful that mouse didn't choose her pant leg for its escape. As I was kicking my foot into the air, the mouse went flying out of my pant leg toward the open door. To our delight, the mouse kindly exited the grain bin. I do not consider mice as cute and cuddly animals. My experience with that mouse did not cause my heart to have any softer feelings for mice. In fact, I welcomed nonvenomous snakes to come into our farmyard because they ate those nasty little critters. I do not know what my father's reaction was or if he even realized that we had taken some of the corn and sold it that day.

Harvest time was always an enjoyable time of the year, especially when it was wheat harvest time. My sister and I would crawl up into the back of our farm truck and play in the harvested wheat kernels. We enjoyed making wheat gum, which we could chew for hours. One does not want to eat too many of those kernels of freshly harvested wheat though. One's body isn't used to that much fresh wheat bran, which would affect one's stomach and bowels, sending one scampering toward the bathroom or the outhouse, whichever was closest. My father was not much of a farmer, and during harvest time he generally was elsewhere, doing whatever he was doing. He would hire custom wheat cutters, or one of my uncles would harvest the wheat for us. That way, he did not have to be around during harvest time.

As I got older, I worked for farmers in the area and would plow, disc, springtooth, and harrow their fields; drive grain trucks; cultivate row crops; combine wheat and other grains; and bale hay for wages. You may wonder how I learned to do all of these different farm tasks since I had no one to teach me. My learning experiences came from on-the-job training. I taught myself by just doing these tasks on my own. If a problem arose, I solved it myself. Being self-reliant was basically all I ever knew, and it has always been difficult for me to ask anyone for help. I have always been the helper.

I was in great demand because of my work ethic. I worked at a fast pace and made sure the job was completed as well as it could be done. When I took on a task, I didn't stop until it was completed. Sadly, most of the money I earned was taken by my father for his evening activities or used for paying our utility bills. Because my father took the money I earned, I was never able to put any money into a savings account for myself. What money I was able to keep was spent on purchasing and feeding 4-H animals.

The 4-H organization was very beneficial for my sister and me. We were active in our local club, presiding over meetings as officers. We showed dairy cattle and other livestock at local town and county fairs. Our mother made sure that we were able to attend all of the 4-H club meetings. She even served as a 4-H club leader, making my father a 4-H club leader in name only. Mom did all of the work, but my father was always there for the accolades.

I showed my woodworking projects, dairy cattle, hogs, and horses at the local and county fairs. A neighboring carpenter taught me woodworking skills, and I even showed some of my woodworking projects and livestock at the state fair. I would stay at the state fair with my animals twenty-four hours a day for the ten days of the fair. I would begin my stay with one dollar in my pocket that I could use to survive. One dollar didn't buy much, so I had to become innovative. There were these cranes, and you could spend ten cents to pick up items worth ten cents to five dollars. When I picked up the items with the cranes, I would sell the items back to the vendor for what money I could get. When I needed money to eat, I would go to the cranes to make enough money to be able to buy something to eat. I survived off of those cranes for ten days. Sometimes I sold back so many items the vendor would not allow me to play anymore, especially if they were worth five dollars. When that happened, I would go to a crane the vendor wasn't paying any attention to. I became so knowledgeable of what items were worth that at times I had to dicker with the vendor for the proper amount I would receive. So, how did I know which cranes to play? I would first watch to see someone pick up an item at a particular crane. I would watch that crane for five more times while people lost their money on it. The cranes followed set patterns, and when the cranes were positioning themselves to be able to pick up a valuable item, I played them. If the crane pattern was not set properly, I never used that crane. When my son was young and my family attended the state fair, I told my son how to play the cranes for money, and he was able to come out ahead money wise. It is amazing how hunger can teach one to be innovative.

I was fortunate to win the showmanship award for showing hogs at the county fair for four straight years. Because of my swine-showing abilities, a local hog farmer asked me to show his breeding stock at the Kansas State Fair and the American Royal Livestock Show. I was very successful showing swine, dairy cattle, and horses. During my first county fair, my Holstein heifer won Grand Champion. My sister and I won many purple and blue ribbons, which was helpful for our feeling of self-worth. My father helped clip the hair of my sister's and my dairy cattle for showing one time. After that, I was on my own. I would prepare my sister's and my show animals for the fairs, haul them to the fairs, and care for them while they were there. It was always a special time to stay at the fairgrounds with the livestock. I would be there twenty-four hours a day caring for the animals' needs.

During the last day of the county fairs, there would be a livestock sale. At these sales, 4-Hers could sell their animals for a premium price. I would sell my two market hogs for much more than it cost me to raise them. Unfortunately, my father was always there to collect the check I received for my prize money and from the sale of my 4-H hogs. He would take my money and leave me with the expenses (purchase price, feed costs, etc.) to pay for out of other money I earned working for farmers.

I enjoyed judging dairy cattle in 4-H. My mother would take me each Saturday morning to different dairy farms in the area to practice judging dairy cattle with other 4-Hers. I became very proficient and competent in judging dairy cattle. As a thirteen-year-old eighth-grader-to-be, I made the county dairy-judging team, which represented our county at the Kansas State Fair Dairy-Judging Contest. That year, our county judging team won the state fair's dairy-judging contest. This team consisted of a freshman-in-college-to-be, a senior-to-be, a junior-to-be, and little old me. By winning the Kansas State Dairy-Judging Contest, we earned the right to represent the state of Kansas at the National Dairy-Judging Contest in Waterloo, Iowa.

At these dairy-judging events and contests, the contestants had to give what was called "oral reasons" for why we placed a class of four dairy cattle in the order we did. These oral reasons for placing the dairy cattle as we did had to be given to the official judge of the contest, which was quite intimidating. A predetermined group of cows was chosen as the group to be the class of cows we gave reasons on. We had to try to convince the official judge that the way we placed the four animals was more correct than the way he placed them, if we placed them differently than he had. God blessed me with a quick memory. To help me in my reasons giving, I would picture the class of the four dairy cattle in my mind. I would use that mental picture of the animals as I gave my reasons for why I placed the class as I did. Fifty points was a perfect score for giving reasons. From having to give so many oral reasons at the 4-H judging events, I learned to stand before someone and try to convince them that I was correct even if I wasn't. At the National Dairy-Judging Contest, I was fortunate to place the predetermined group of cows correctly and received a score of all fifty points. It was almost unheard of to receive a perfect score of fifty points on oral reason giving, especially at the national contest. As a thirteen-year-old kid, it was quite an honor to have received a perfect score on giving oral reasons at the national contest and placing in the top twenty judges.

Being proficient at things like this without my father's support helped me to become very independent. When my father found out that we had won the state contest, he bragged about my achievement to his friends but never to me. I assume that he received the desired recognition by telling other people about his son's judging accomplishments. However, I do not believe my father even knew how I did at the national contest. He never asked me about it, and I never told him. When I was in my middle twenties, my dairy-judging experiences paid off. I served as the official dairy cattle judge at different county fairs. I have never known an official dairy judge to be someone other than a university professor in a dairy science department. But here I was being paid for my judging work and shown respect for being the official judge.

You may wonder how I was selected to be an official judge at these county fairs. During my first year of teaching school in a small western Kansas town, some 4-H people learned that I knew something about judging dairy cattle and other livestock. So, they asked me to work with their 4-H children on learning how to judge the conformation of these animals. After that one year of working with the 4-H children and teaching school in that community, I accepted a teaching position in the town where my wife grew up, fifteen miles from where I grew up. The 4-H leader of the community where I had taught that one year contacted me to see if I would be willing to substitute judge that year for their county dairy cattle show, because they were in need of an official dairy judge and unable to locate one. I was a bit surprised by their request but consented to do the judging for them. They must have been satisfied with my work because they asked me to judge their 4-H dairy cattle shows for the next three years. Word must have gotten around about my judging ability, because another county fair and a local city fair contacted me to judge their dairy cattle shows. I judged these shows for three years as well. I was asked to judge a fourth year but had to decline the offer because of other commitments. I enjoyed judging these shows, and the money I received help my wife and me financially.

I have my mother to thank for my dairy-judging accomplishments. She was the one who encouraged me and took me to all of those judging events and contests. As I write this narrative, I am realizing just how successful I actually became. Even with all my achievements, I never realized just how successful I was until I sat down and put my life's story on paper. For some reason, I never looked at myself as skilled or talented. Maybe that was because I always felt rejected and inferior to others.

Our county 4-H judging team made our appearance at the National Dairy-Judging Contest. One evening, we attended the evening entertainment provided for us. One of those evening entertainment groups was the Lennon Sisters from the *Lawrence Welk Show*, which I watched because it was one of my sister's favorite TV shows. As my team was walking back to our car after their performance, I saw this black limousine parked by the side door of the Hippodrome, Iowa's oldest entertainment arena. I told my teammates and our adult leader that it was probably the limousine for the Lennon Sisters. I tried to convince my teammates that we should go see if we could meet them. I had a big crush on Janet, the youngest sister, who was my age. No one on the team had the nerve to go see if we could meet them. But I did. I had felt rejected many times before in my life, so not being allowed to meet them would be no big deal to me. So, little ole me walked over to the door and opened it. I walked inside, and there they were, the four Lennon Sisters and their parents! I introduced myself as a big fan of theirs and a national judging participant. I explained to them how I enjoyed their performance and that I watched them perform on the *Lawrence Welk Show*.

Since I didn't come back out to join them, my team members eventually joined me inside. I had expected the Lennon Sisters to tell me to get lost, but they didn't. They were extremely nice to me, and we were able to talk to them for what seemed to be at least thirty minutes. We got their autographs, and talking with them was an experience that I never forgot. After meeting them, watching these sisters perform on the *Lawrence Welk Show* took on a whole new meaning for me. I am not sure why I had the nerve to do things like that. It probably had to do with my lack of fear of rejection. I was used to it. With my father not being there for me, the feeling of rejection was normal, and I was driven to be successful and prove myself as worthwhile on my own. As I grew up, Dad told me that I would not amount to a hill of beans. At the time, I was not sure if he was just joking or serious about what he was saying. Whichever it was, it helped drive me to become a successful person.

When I was a senior in high school, I was almost able to return to the national dairy-judging contest, only this time on my high school Future Farmers of America dairy-judging team. My FFA judging team lost by only one point from winning the right to represent Kansas at the national contest. One of the team members dropped eighty points in the state contest. If he had dropped seventy-eight points, I would have been able to return to the national contest. And, of course, being a senior, the next year meant I would be out of school and FFA.

During my sophomore year in high school, my Future Farmers of America teacher took some of us students to a swine-judging contest. This contest was in a city located one hundred miles from the town my high school was located in. To my surprise, I won the judging contest. The winner of the contest was awarded eighty dollars to be spent on a pig at the futurity pig sale that evening. I had eighty dollars to spend but no way to get the pig home if I bought one. I called home to see if my father could drive the hundred miles to get the pig and me if I bought one. As usual, he was nowhere to be found, and even if he could have been found, he probably would not have made the effort to come and get me and the pig. So, using the eighty dollars I won was out of the question, and I went home with my classmates and FFA teacher. If I could have stayed at the event, I would have bought a breeding gilt with my winnings. She would have provided me with an opportunity to raise some litters of pigs and make some money from their sales at weaning time, as long as my father didn't take the money. Instead of being able to use eighty dollars, I lost the opportunity. As I think back on events like that, a feeling of disappointment comes over me that my father did not care about me and the successes I achieved.

Another Saturday, during my senior year of high school, my Future Farmers of America teacher took some of us students to a grassland identification contest. We had to identify many different types of grasses and weeds. I had never tried to identify weeds or grasses before. My quick memory paid off again. I studied the different types of weeds and grasses as we drove the two hours to the contest. To my surprise, I won the identification contest. I also won other judging contest like poultry and beef cattle. Poultry was not that much fun to judge except for "candling eggs" (checking to make sure the inside of the egg was good and edible). At these poultry-judging contests, you had to hold the live chicken and feel the chicken's "back end orifice" to determine if she was a productive egg layer. That was before we had hand sanitizing gels, so hand washing sinks were very important to me. I won these contests but received very little recognition for winning. I do not think that my father ever knew that I won all these contests.

At the end of my senior year of high school, I received the FFA chapter's individual award for leadership, personal growth, and career success through agricultural education. I do not know if anyone other than me and my FFA teacher knew that all of that happened. None of it was ever printed in the local newspaper. I know that the FFA teacher reported all of these things to the local newspaper, but it never found its way to the printed page. I am confident that my father's reputation had a lot to do with that.

Even though my father did not seem to care a lot about my activities, one day when I was young, my father did me a huge favor without really knowing what he had done for me. While my family was waiting in our car to pick up my grandma at the railroad station in a town fifteen miles from our farm, a drunken man came up to our car window. This drunk asked my father for a dime. He claimed that he needed the dime to get a cup of coffee at the diner across the street. Being young and naive, I thought the request was legit and my father should have gone ahead and given him the dime for the coffee. But my father, being a worldly individual, wouldn't give the man the dime he requested. Instead he offered to take the man to the diner across the street and buy him a cup of coffee. The man wanted nothing to do with going to get a cup of coffee. He just wanted the dime for more booze. When that drunk staggered away, I asked my father why he didn't give the man a dime for the coffee. Dad just turned to me and told me that the man was an alcoholic and I could become one too if I drank alcoholic beverages. Of course, I never wanted to be like that drunk man, and I always wanted to be an athlete, so I never drank alcoholic beverages, used illegal drugs, or used tobacco products.

My father did, however, drink alcoholic beverages and could have been at the point of being an alcoholic himself. I am told that a doctor once asked him if he was an alcoholic because his liver was in such bad shape. My mother said that there were times he would come home early in the morning under the influence of alcohol. But he never appeared intoxicated or inebriated around me. My father may have known that my genetic makeup could make me susceptible to becoming an alcoholic, and that was why he told me that I could become an alcoholic like that drunk man if I drank alcoholic beverages.

CHAPTER 7

DOUBLE-DEALING

Deception allowed my father to live two separate lives. He lived the life of a wealthy, single, womanizing man out in the world and what appeared to be a somewhat normal, married family man to some people of the Mennonite community. Because my father possessed a very likable personality, many people just assumed that he was an OK guy, or they just looked away from the egregious situation. Dad wasn't what some perceived him to be, and he was what others believed him to be. With his lack of concern for his family, one may wonder why he didn't just leave his family and never return. The answer to that question is quite simple. Being considered a wealthy big shot was important to him. Since his mother and uncles were wealthy, he expected to inherit land, money, and a monthly oil check when they passed away. If he left his family, inheriting anything from his mother and uncles would have been out of the question. His extended family did not know about his deceptive, dishonest, immoral life. They only knew that he was irresponsible and gone from home too much. To my father, the prospect of inheriting cash, an oil income, and land was worth waiting for and would allow him to continue to fund the life he chose to live. I am convinced if it had not been for this inheritance, he would have deserted us years ago.

Because of my father's chosen life, he was around a lot of very worldly, immoral people. In the mid-1950s, he told us that the next biggest problem our society would be facing would be illegal drug use. Living in our small Mennonite community, we had not even heard of illegal drugs, let alone the use of them. The only drugs I had heard about were over-the-counter pain medicine like aspirin and antibiotics like penicillin and sulfa drugs. So it was hard for me to wrap my mind around what illegal drugs actually were. To help me grasp what illegal drugs were, Dad made the claim that during his undercover work, he had been drugged himself. He told us of times that people had put drugs into whatever he had been drinking. He said that he would become lightheaded and groggy, and when he realized that he had been drugged, he would go into the restroom, where he would pass out for a period of time. He told me never to get involved in drug use because if I did, bad things would happen to me. By that time in my life, I had already experienced tough times, and I did not want to have to face any more bad things. So I chose never to get involved with any illegal drugs. As it turned out, my father knew what he was talking about. Drugs, both legal and illegal, have become a major problem for our society. The early 1960s ushered in an increase in drug use and disrespect for authority. Our society has never recovered from that period. Disrespect and addiction to alcohol, tobacco products, and drugs are still major problems for our society. I am confident that my father, at some time, had firsthand experience with illegal drugs but not because he worked undercover as he claimed.

My father joined a bowling league in the large city forty miles from our farm. He used the excuse of needing to do this because of his undercover work . He claimed to be bowling with certain people he needed to watch and gather information from and about. He stated that his work was centered out of a particular bowling alley. This, of course, gave him the perfect excuse to socialize with people at the bowling alley at least two nights every week. It also gave him an excuse to be at that bowling alley in case someone saw him there and told us about it. I remember Dad saying that he used the auto dealership's name he worked for to sponsor bowling teams at this bowling alley to assist with his undercover work. Since my father's passing, I have been told that he sponsored coed bowling teams, a women's bowling team, and little kid bowling teams using the dealership's name but financing the bowling teams himself. The kids on the bowling teams called him "Uncle Harv" and would nickel and dime him to death. Sponsoring these bowling teams and providing the children money whenever they wanted it, of course, authenticated him as a wealthy bigwig. Finding out that he paid for all of these teams' expenses along with buying multiple women new cars, furniture, and jewelry, I understand why he was always in need of cash and why he took my mother's and my hard-earned money for his use.

One story I've been told had to do with him challenging another bowling team consisting of people he worked with at a local auto dealership. He challenged his coworkers with the wager of the losing team buying the winning team steak dinners. His coworkers accepted his challenge, and the event took place. The problem my dad had was that he did not inform his bowling team about the wager. After his bowling team lost the match, his team members went home, leaving him with the entire bill for the winning team members' steak dinners and those of their wives and families. I was told that the bill for those steak dinners cost Dad around two hundred dollars. Two hundred dollars was a lot of money in the mid-1960s.

There were many times when I questioned my father's honesty about why he was gone so much. I even considered crawling into the trunk or hiding in the back seat of the car before my father left for whatever he was doing. I wanted to see for myself if he was telling us the truth or just lying to us. I would always talk myself out of trying to do that because of the fear of what he would do to me if and when he found me in the back seat or trunk of the car. He had an extremely violent temper. He had put me out of the car on that dark country road and left me there when I was four years old, and he had physically abused my mother and sister. I could just imagine what he would do to me if he found me hiding in the back seat or trunk of the car.

When I was in high school, I was able to drive myself places, and one evening, I decided to drive to the bowling alley where my father claimed his undercover work was centered. I wanted to see for myself if he was actually bowling on a team or just lying to us. When I arrived at the bowling alley and walked inside, I saw him bowling with a coed team consisting of three men and two women. Thus, his claim of using the bowling alley as a center of operation for his undercover work seemed plausible. However, I found out later in life that he was having a special relationship with one of those women on that bowling team. Later in life, Dad told me this lady's husband was in prison for some reason. Dad used the situation and his money to get what he was after.

Another part of my father's double-dealing lifestyle had to do with the woman who lived in a larger city, fifteen miles from our home. He claimed that she and the man who got him into the Mexican gold mine and the oil speculation business were business partners of his in Oklahoma and southeastern Kansas oil wells. He maintained that they had to travel together to southeast Kansas and Oklahoma one evening each week to take care of the oil business. He said that he at times had to leave his car at or near this woman's house until they returned. Along with this claim, when my sister questioned him about seeing his unattended car parked on a side street near this woman's house, he justified it by saying it was parked there because he was helping the woman's father to build custom cabinets in her house for extra money. Maybe it was true that he was working there for pay, but maybe he wasn't. I do not know the truth in this matter. He may have actually been helping this woman's father build cabinets in her house.

The day after my Holstein heifer calf won the Grand Champion ribbon at the county fair—it was very unusual for a heifer calf to beat mature cows as Grand Champion—my father brought a group of adults and children through the dairy barn to see my heifer calf. At the time, I was working with my calf, keeping her fed, watered, and clean. I was spreading out a bale of wheat straw for my calf to lay down on and stay clean. My father talked to this group of people about this heifer calf and how unusual it was for a heifer calf to win Grand Champion. What was hurtful to me was that he intentionally refused to take notice of me or acknowledge that I was even present. I knew that my father wanted recognition for my Grand Champion calf, but I did not understand why he wouldn't acknowledge me or introduce me to this group of people. After they left the building, an empty, hollow feeling came over me, and I felt insignificant, unimportant, and miserable, but that was par for the course, so to speak. I felt that way most of the time. I didn't understand why I deserved to be ignored or treated that way. Ten years later, it all made sense to me. I found out that this group of people he had brought to see the Grand Champion Holstein heifer consisted of the woman he claimed to be partners with him in the oil speculation business, her parents, and her children. During my growing-up years, my father attended this woman's children's activities and sporting events instead of attending mine.

My mother was often suspicious of my father's excuses and yet afraid of what he might do if she pushed the issue too far. One evening, my mother had me get into our pickup truck and told me that we were going to go to the larger city fifteen miles from our farm. I assumed we were going to see my sister, her husband, and their children. But when we arrived in that city, my mother drove past a house that I was unfamiliar with. There wasn't a car in the driveway, and the garage door was closed. My mother parked the pickup truck on a side street, where she could still see the house, and we waited to see if my father would show up there. This house belonged to the woman who my father claimed was an oil business partner. After waiting about an hour, surprisingly, my father backed his car out of her driveway. We didn't see him drive his car into the driveway, so how did he get his car in the driveway? When he reached the street, he saw us parked on the side street and drove around the block to where we were parked. Needless to say, he was not happy to see us and sternly asked what we were doing there. When asked what he was doing there, he claimed that they had just returned from doing oil business in Oklahoma and southern Kansas. When my mother questioned him about his car being in her driveway when no car was there earlier, he said that he parked his car in her garage to keep people from starting rumors about his car being at her place. I do not know the discussion my parents had when he got home, but I am confident it wasn't pleasant. It could have been one of the times my father was abusive to my mother.

There was something to my father's Oklahoma connection even though the oil business was only an excuse for him to be out and about enjoying himself. My father claimed to often go coyote hunting with some friends who lived in Oklahoma. I have no idea how he got to know these people or who he took hunting with him. We were told that he got to know these people through his so-called oil business. He said that some of these people owned the land his oil wells were located on.

One day, while embellishing his Oklahoma coyote-hunting stories to my brother-in-law's parents, my brother-in-law's father asked to be taken along on one of those coyote hunts. Without considering the ramifications of what that situation would be, as he usually did, my father promised to take him coyote hunting in Oklahoma. I do not believe he had any intention of taking them coyote hunting, but after being pressed on when he would be taking them, he made arrangements for them to go on a hunt with him. When my father planned my brother-in-law's parents' hunting trip, my sister and brother-in-law wanted to go along too. The number of people going on this hunting trip continued to grow. My mother, hearing about the hunting trip to Oklahoma, expected to go along as well. There were more people going along to hunt coyotes than could fit into one car. The need for a second car gave the opportunity for my mother and I to go along as well. My sister, brother-in-law, and his parents drove in one car, which provided room in the car my father was driving for both Mom and me to go along. So, because of his embellished coyote-hunting stories, my dad was forced to take my sister, brother-in-law, his parents, my mother, and me along with him to hunt coyotes in Oklahoma.

After the coyote hunt was over, my mother demanded my father show her the oil wells that he claimed to be a part owner of. These phantom wells were supposed to be located in that same area of Oklahoma. While we were hunting, it rained, and the dirt roads became rather muddy, making them less than desirable to drive on them. My father tried to use these muddy roads as an excuse to not show us the oil wells he owned. But because of my mother's insistence, my father pointed out some oil wells as those he owned while we were driving along the interstate. These oil wells were not far from the interstate highway. They were actually less than one quarter of a mile away.

Mom kept insisting on seeing them close-up. So, to pacify her, Dad drove about twelve miles to the first interstate interchange and back through the country roads to where those oil wells were located. We stopped at one oil well, which was set way back into a field. The dirt driveway into the field where the oil well was located was far too muddy to drive the car any closer or to walk to the well itself. We were not able to see the name of the oil company on the faint, weather-beaten company sign and verify what my father claimed. It was a touch-and-go situation for him, but Mom, no doubt, still had questions about his honesty.

One time, my father invited these Oklahoma friends to come to Kansas to hunt coyotes. During that hunt, my father gave me a walkie-talkie and told me to walk through an eighty-acre prairie covered with big bluestem grass taller than I was. I couldn't see anything around me because the grass was so thick and tall. I had to use my hands to push grass out of my way so I could squeeze through it. I could hear the coyote-hunting dogs barking as they were chasing a coyote, but my vision was obscured by the thick grass. So, to see where the coyote would go, I hustled as fast as I could through the tall, thick grass to the bank of a creek at one end of the acreage. When I reached the bank of the creek, I walked into a very dangerous situation. The coyote came up the creek bank exactly where I was standing. Both that coyote and I became extremely nervous with each others presence. It was me in front of him and the dogs in hot pursuit close behind him. We both stood there, looking at each other no more than eight feet apart, wondering what our best option was. The coyote was scared of the dogs behind him, I was scared of the coyote in front of me, and neither one of us knew what to do for a few seconds. I knew how dangerous the situation was for me. Cornered coyotes can become vicious in tight situations, and I was just an unarmed kid with a walkie-talkie in my hand. Fortunately for me, the coyote must have thought I was too tough and chose to run away from me instead of through me.

Oklahoma had other drawing powers for my father. The man who got him involved in the Mexican gold mine took him fishing in a large lake in the northeastern part of the state. They would always bring home very large, live flathead catfish to show off to the community people. At times, my father would take other people along with him. They would check trotlines on mud flats in the middle of the lake. If they didn't catch any big flathead catfish over thirty pounds, my father and his friend would secretly buy live, large flathead catfish at a local bait shop and bring them home to show people the fish they claimed to have caught. Dad told me of a time when his friend and he took some others from the community along fishing. When they didn't catch any large fish on the trotline, they went to the bait shop, bought a few large fish, and late that night took them out into the lake and hooked them on their trotline. When they took the other men out to check their trotline, it looked like they caught big flathead catfish, and their reputation of being big-time fishermen was still intact.

I witnessed firsthand Dad buying large fish, bringing them home alive, and passing them off as fish he had caught. One time he needed to get big fish for some reason and couldn't find a suitable person to go with him to get the fish from Oklahoma. So, my mother and I were his only option. He took us along, and at around midnight, we went out onto the lake to check an existing trotline located on a mud flat. The unusual thing about this situation was that we had not placed the trotline there, we had no bait to rebait the hooks, and we had to check that trotline after midnight. He claimed that he had someone place that trotline in the lake for him. I am not sure that he actually had someone place the hooked line there for him. I had the feeling that we were simply raiding someones trotline. Another time when he took my sister and brother-in-law along with him to catch large catfish at this particular lake, they had a similar experience. They checked for hooked fish on a trotline that they hadn't set. They checked this trotline around midnight and three in the morning but never checked it for fish again.

The time my mother and I went with him, we didn't catch any big flathead catfish either. So, in the morning, Dad went to the local bait shop and bought two sixty-pound fish to take back home alive and show them off as his catch, proving that he was the "great white fisherman" of central Kansas. His dishonesty bothered me greatly, and I did not want to become like him. The only attribute he possessed that I have chosen to emulate is his giving nature. But the difference between his giving nature and mine is that I never gave at the expense of my family.

I would, at times, witness my father actually catching large flathead catfish that weighed from thirty to sixty pounds in the small river near our farm with his hands. When he would catch some of those large fish, he would show them off to the community and have a fish fry for his extended family, or he would take the fish with him when he left at night. We seldom had any of those fish to eat unless it was at a family fish fry. I am told that when he worked as a car salesman, one time he took a used car from the dealership's lot, lined the trunk with plastic, filled the trunk with water, and placed three large flathead catfish in the water-filled trunk. He then drove around town, showing off the large fish he had caught. When he was through building up his ego, we never knew where those large fish ended up.

One day, after showing off his big catch and not being able to butcher it or keep it alive until he left for the evening, my father took an eighty-pound flathead catfish over to my sister's house for her to butcher. He needed some place to dispose of the big fish, so he just dumped the fish off on her driveway and made no effort to assist her in cleaning it (skinning and gutting it). Dad left my sister with her two little boys to butcher that very large fish by themselves. As he drove away, my sister thought, *I can't believe this is actually happening to me.* My girly-girl sister never got involved in butchering anything, and butchering an eighty-pound catfish is a substantial task to be taken on by even experienced people. Because that fish was so good to eat, my sister was determined to salvage its meat. She did not want that amount of meat to go to waste, and it was one of the very few times Dad ever gave her anything. So, butchering that fish became an on-the-job training experience for her and must have been quite a sight to witness.

When the small river, located not far from our farm, was on the rise after heavy rains, my father would set up limb lines and fish traps. Limb lines were legal, but fish traps were not. Sometimes he would catch freshwater eel along with channel catfish, flathead catfish, large carp, and bigmouth buffalo. You may think that freshwater eel were uncommon in central Kansas rivers, but they were very common in the river near our farm. You might turn your nose up at the thought of eating one of those freshwater eels, but, believe it or not, they taste just like catfish without any bones. Along with keeping up his great white fisherman reputation, in the fall and winter months, Dad worked at sustaining his great white hunter reputation. When it snowed, my father would take me along with him to shoot cottontail rabbits. We would drive the dirt roads around our farm, looking for humps in the snow on wheat fields. Those bumps under the snow were cottontail rabbits waiting out the snowstorms. My father would take the cottontail rabbits we shot home, dress them (skin and gut them), and prepare them for eating. I do not recall that he left any rabbit meat for us to eat when he left for the evening.

Being considered by many to be the great white fisherman and the great white hunter served my father well since he was never considered to be a great farmer. His ability to do physical labor became limited one day while he was getting bales of alfalfa hay off of my uncle's haystack. Because of my father's lack of integrity, he could never be trusted to do the right thing. I am not sure that my uncle even knew that Dad was taking hay bales from his haystack. While climbing down from the haystack, Dad fell, injuring his lower back. His back injury was so severe that he was unable to walk. No one was home at my uncle's place at the time. There was no one to help him but me. I was too small to be of much assistance to him, yet I helped him crawl to the pickup truck's cab, opened the door for him, and stabilized him as he slid into the driver's seat to drive the two and a half miles home. His severely injured lower back needed to be surgically repaired. My father's lower back vertebrae discs were crushed, and the doctor had to fuse his vertebrate together using two big, long metal bolts. Dad almost died during that surgical procedure. His heart stopped beating, and he had to be revived.

While he was in the hospital, people went to see him. One afternoon, when my sister and mother arrived at the hospital, three unfamiliar women were visiting him. They thought that the situation was a bit unusual since one of the women was sitting on the side of his bed. But there were only two chairs in the room to accommodate visitors. So, the side of the bed was the only option for a third person. These three women were very rude and disrespectful to my sister and mother. These unpleasant females made snide remarks about what my sister and mother were wearing, even though they were dressed just fine. Of course, my sister and mother didn't have the money to dress sophisticated, and this situation was definitely awkward and tense to say the least. My father excused the women's insolent behavior by saying that one of the women was a person he was investigating in his undercover work.

Being such a worldly man, my father's spiritual life was never anything to look up to, and it deteriorated as the years went by. When I was young, my father attended church assemblies with us. But as years went by, faith in God and Jesus Christ was no longer of any importance to him, and his actions and language were not in line with living a godly life. Biblical faith and his lifestyle were not compatible. He always seemed to be uncomfortable in the worship assemblies. With a lifestyle like his, one couldn't help but be uncomfortable in a spiritual setting. He would have us sit in the balcony or the basement of the church building, where he could sleep through the worship assembly. His sleeping in the church assemblies was not surprising, since he never got home until just before dawn. After moving out of the community, his attendance at assemblies stopped completely. His mother no longer knew if he was attending church assemblies. All I remember is that he appeared to hate to go to the church assemblies and attended only to appease his mother. He didn't want to lose his inheritance.

When I was in college, one time my father had me meet him in a bar located in the large city forty miles from where we lived. I was uncomfortable doing that, and when my mother found out about his frequenting this establishment, she confronted him about it. As usual, he had a plausible story to get her off of his back, so to speak. He claimed that the owner of the establishment owed him money and gave him part ownership in the bar as payment. The problem with his story was that even though he was supposedly a part owner of this business, no money was realized by my family.

CHAPTER 8

THE EXTENDED FAMILY

Extended families have different roles and interact in different ways. Our extended families have provided my sister and me with a sense of stability that we did not experience in our immediate family. We were expected to eat Sunday dinners (lunch to some people) with grandparents, uncles, aunts, and cousins. After the Sunday-morning worship assemblies, we would alternate eating meals between our grandparents' homes. My father's mother would make more conventional meals, but there would also be some unusual dishes served. Tripe (pig stomach lining) and pickled pigs' feet were some of those unusual dishes. When we ate with my mother's side of the family, we had more ethnic foods like knepp, dunn kuchen, kaeivei, mak kuchen, bohne beroggi, case beroggi, kraut beroggi, and dried green beans and ham, which I learned to love. My maternal grandmother could really cook, and my mother learned from her. As I got older, my mother's family, which had seven children, grew in numbers. As the family number increased and they became older, my maternal grandparents were unable to continue the Sunday dinners as often. At that point, it became Sunday dinner at my grandma's home every Sunday noon with his siblings and their children.

Meals shared with Grandma, uncles, and cousins were special

events to us. Other memorable events with our grandma were when she would take my sister and me along with her to pick gooseberries and mulberries and dig horseradish roots. Those activities were not always the most enjoyable. But the rewards were great. My sister loved eating those gooseberries we picked. She would pick them and eat them before they reached the bucket. I, on the other hand, couldn't stand those gross-tasting things. Gooseberries are so sour that I couldn't even eat the gooseberry pie or jam that my grandma would make. When our grandma took me to pick mulberries, she would lay old quilts under the mulberry trees to catch any ripe berries if they fell to the ground. After having to pick berries for a while, she agreed to allow me to climb up into the trees to shake the branches so the ripe mulberries would fall down onto the quilts, making gathering mulberries much easier than handpicking each one like we did gooseberries. After that initial time of shaking the branches, Grandma like the ease of gathering the berries that way and had whoever she took with her climb into the tree and shake its branches.

Our grandmother would make mulberry pie for us to eat, which was a big reward for helping her gather the berries. Her mulberry pie was great, but you didn't want to eat too much of that fresh mulberry pie in one sitting. If you did, it would have the same effect on your body as the freshly harvested wheat kernels had.

Digging wild horseradish roots out of the country ditches was hard work, and I do not remember my sister going along to dig those horseradish roots too often. It was very physical labor, digging up those roots with a shovel. Since there wasn't anything to eat off of branches, my sister used her brainpower to get out of participating in that physical activity. Since I was of the male gender, there was no getting out of helping dig those roots. The horseradish my grandmother made was extremely strong flavored, with a good bite to it. Her horseradish would easily open one's sinuses, even when you were stuffed up with a bad cold. After eating that horseradish, regular radishes were calm in comparison. I loved radishes and ate them like candy.

My grandma was a very resourceful woman. She would make a salve from beeswax and anise extract. This salve was used to help heal wounds by drawing an infection out of a wound. My grandma passed away in the early 1990s, but twenty-seven years later, I still have plenty of her homemade salve (three jars) on hand. I use it every time I am injured and the wound becomes infected. While the salve is on the wound, you can feel the infection being drawn out. Sometimes there is even a little discomfort while the infection is being extracted from the infected wound. I actually have the instructions for how my grandma made her very effective salve.

I have already mentioned an ethnic dish called mak kuchen made out of poppy seeds. Making this ethnic dish involves a complicated process, and you just can't go to the store and get the tools and equipment it takes to plant, grow, harvest, clean, and dry the poppy seeds. To grow the poppy plants for theirs seeds, one needed to know how to prepare the soil properly, plant the seed for maximum production, cultivate the plants, harvest the seed, and store the seeds properly, because they could mold easily.

My grandfather was a very resourceful and innovative man. He invented a poppy seed cleaner that looked like a long, wooden box with a wire cage at the end. The poppy seed cleaner had a fan at one end of the box and blew air over the poppy seeds, which were spread out on the bottom of the box. This fan-blown air would clean the chaff from the seeds and dry them so they wouldn't mold and have to be discarded. It was a unique machine, and people of the community would bring their poppy seeds to have my grandfather clean and dry their seeds for them. I wish I could have acquired that poppy seed cleaner. But I wasn't financially able to buy it at the extended family's estate sale after my grandparents passed away. I was, however, able to obtain his homemade poppy seed planter. This planter was made out of 16-gauge wire for its handle, wood for its wheels, and a baking soda can for the seed-holding and planting mechanism. He placed strategic nail holes in the baking soda can so the right amount of poppy seeds would drop out as the planter was rolled along the ground.

As a young boy, I remember going to my maternal grandparents' home and watching them clean the poppy seeds they grew for the mak kuchen (poppy seed roll) they made.

I would also watch my grandfather shave his whiskers. He used his single-edge razor to cut the whiskers and the shaving brush to soften his whiskers by applying soap to his face. Fortunately, I was able to purchase his shaving brush at the extended family's estate sale. I wanted his single-edged razor too, but it was far too expensive for me to purchase.

I have since given my son his shaving brush and an old manually operated hair clipper that was used to cut my hair as a child. This manual hair clipper was used before my grandparents got an electric hair clipper. At the estate sale, my sister acquired the old wooden stool that we would sit on to have our haircut when we got older.

My maternal grandparents also had a very large strawberry patch, and when my mother would go over to their place to pick strawberries, my sister and I would go along with her. By example, my sister taught me well about how to get out of doing something I really didn't want to do. I didn't enjoy bending over and picking strawberries, so I would offer to use my grandfather's old, manually operated, push rotary blade lawn mower to mow his lawn. It was a lot of work to push that rotary blade mower around cutting the grass, but I enjoyed doing that much more than picking strawberries. Physical labor never deterred me from anything.

The only problem I encountered mowing his grass was if the grass had grown too tall. Cutting tall grass with that rotary push mower was no fun, but neither was picking strawberries.

After dark, while we were at our maternal grandparents' house, my sister and I would catch fireflies. We would put one firefly on each fingernail. Glowing fireflies on all of one's fingernails looked awesome, especially when you moved your hands around quickly in the dark. I also enjoyed picking cicadas off of his tree trunks, throwing them into the air, and listening to them screech as they flew away.

My children always referred to my maternal grandmother as the grandma who could cook and to my paternal grandmother as the grandma with the flowers. Grandma with the flowers earned her name because every time we stopped to see her, she would go outside and cut a rose for each of my children to have. We never left either of my grandmothers' homes without something to take with us.

My sister and I spent a considerable amount of time with my father's family because they lived so close to us. His family would harvest alfalfa hay and butcher hogs together. Those days were long, and the work was difficult. When my cousins and I got old enough to work, we worked until my uncle told us that the job was finished. We would often eat on the run, as we called it, until the job was finished. Because of my uncle, I developed a great work ethic, and to this day, I will work until a job is finished or someone stops me. During these family workdays, large meals were prepared for the entire family, and when the job was finished, we ate very well.

My father's brother believed in doing things his way, just like my father. He always made his bales of alfalfa hay weigh one hundred pounds. If the bales of hay were lighter than that, he would adjust the baler so each bale came out weighing one hundred pounds. My cousins and I worked stacking those hay bales on the hay rack, loading the bales of hay on to the bale elevator that would carry the bales of hay up into the barn's hayloft, or stacking the bales in the barn's hayloft. We did this physical labor at a young age, even before we could lift the hundred-pound bales. To accomplish the task, we would drag the bales where they needed to go and position them where they needed to be set. We were handling those bales of hay as young as nine years old. Of course, that demanding work was hard for us to do, but working that hard developed the work ethic that I have to this day. You can tell me that I can't do something, and I will show you that I can. I didn't understand back then that you get what you expect and demand out of people. As I got older, I realized that my uncle instilled that work ethic in me. It is something that I have used in my teaching and coaching profession.

The extended family's hog-butchering events were always interesting days. The family would gather at one farm at around five thirty in the morning. The hog would be shot, with one well-placed 22-rifle bullet into its brain. That way, the hog died instantly and didn't suffer. One time I even had to do the shooting. After the well-placed shot, the hog's throat would then be cut, so the blood could drain out of its body. Its carcass would be hoisted above a fifty-gallon barrel filled with scalding-hot water. A wire fence stretcher was used to raise and lower the hog's carcass into the scalding water. The scalding process made it easier to scrape the hair off of the hog's hide. The hog would be pulled up out of the scalding water and its hide scraped clean of all hair. The hog's abdomen would be cut open with a knife, and its internal organs would be removed. The heart, liver, and intestines were always saved. Once the internal organs were removed, the head would be separated from the carcass. The carcass would then be sawed in half, cutting it down the middle of its spine.

The women would take the head, heart, liver, and intestines to be cleaned, while the carcass was cut up into hams, pork chops, and so on. The ears, snout, jowls, and other edible parts of the head were removed and used in grandma's pickled pigs' feet dish. One never wanted to watch the women clean out the hog intestines. The intestines were used for the sausage casings. Eating the sausage wasn't bad, if you didn't see where the casings came from and what they looked like before they were cleaned. The intestines were turned inside out and scrubbed clean with brushes, soap, and water.

Cracklings and hog brains were always a part of the butchering-day meal, but they were not something I could stomach. Fried hog fat and hog brains just weren't appetizing to me. I considered everything else as edible. My grandma's pickled pig feet dish was made from all of the leftover meat parts cut from the hog's feet, head, tail, ears, jowls, stomach lining (tripe), and so on. Nothing went to waste. Someone might think that eating my grandma's pickled pigs' feet was a bit unusual. But what I considered as real unusual was that my sister and grandma would chew on the yellow, scaly legs and feet of butchered chickens. I enjoyed the pickled pigs' feet, but I never understood how anyone could enjoy chewing on those scaly yellow chicken's feet.

One day, my father's extended family was out in our sandhill pasture fixing the pasture fence so cattle could be placed in the pasture for the summer grazing season. Before everyone arrived for this fence-fixing event, a cousin and I went riding with my uncle in his pickup truck. My uncle had a very heavy lead foot. He drove us into the middle of our 640-acre sandhill pasture. As we were looking at the windmill and stock tank located there, my uncle noticed an unidentified pickup truck in a wooded section of the pasture, about a quarter of a mile from where we were. He assumed that the pickup truck belonged to a deer poacher who frequently cut the fence wires to access the pasture for his illegal deer hunting. My uncle was not going to allow a poacher trespassing on our family's property, so we traveled at a very high rate of speed over the hills of sand. On our way to the possible deer poacher's pickup, the speedometer reached seventy miles per hour. We went airborne many times and covered the quarter of a mile distance in a very short period of time.

When we arrived where the would-be deer poacher was, we saw that the deer poacher turned out to be just another uncle, cutting limbs off of trees so he could drive his pickup truck through the wooded area. The uncle I was riding with had a large metal toolbox stretched across the back of his pickup. This toolbox had two closed, locked lids when we started our high-speed, airborne adventure. Upon arriving where my other uncle was cutting limbs, those locked toolbox lids were no longer closed. Needless to say, an amusement park ride cannot hold a candle to the excitement I felt during my uncle's pickup ride through our sandhill pasture.

Since my sister and I did not have many close friends, working and playing with our cousins at our grandparents' homes or at the family workdays were very special for us. Now and then, we were able to go over to our cousins' homes, and occasionally, they would be able come to our house. Working and playing with them in these situations was always a highlight in our day. My sister and I also enjoyed family outings with my father's family. The extended family would sometimes go to a river where the children would swim, the men would hand fish (noodle), and the women would sit on the riverbank, watch the children swim, and prepare a picnic lunch. At times, the extended family would have a picnic in a park a few miles from where we lived.

One day, some of my cousins came to our farm. We climbed up into the barn's hayloft to play in the bales of hay, making tunnels to crawl through. When we were finished playing in the hay, I told my cousins to grab me and act like they were hurting me. If they did that, they would see just how protective of me my dog was. We stood in the second-floor hayloft of the barn near a hayloft open door. When my cousins grabbed me, I yelled, "Help!" and my dog ran to the barn and jumped as high as he could, trying to make it into the second-floor hayloft to protect me. About a foot below the second floor was an open window, and my dog jumped through it, missing the second floor by only one foot. After that happened, my dog would not allow any of my cousins to crawl down the ladder until I went down and assured him that I was OK. As long as my dog was with me, I did not have to worry about anything. He definitely was my protector.

Another day, while I was visiting my cousins at their farm, they showed me that cats always land on their feet. I had heard that cats would land on their feet when dropped or falling from high places, but I had never witnessed it happening until my visit at my cousins' farm. They decided to prove the theory for me by dropping a cat out of their barn's hayloft door. This was a drop of only about ten feet. One of my cousins held the cat in the hayloft while another cousin went down to the ground to retrieve the cat to test the theory again. From that little experiment, I can verify that cats always land on their feet. They may twist and turn in the air, but they have the ability to always land on their feet.

In the summertime evenings, when these cousins came over to our house, we would go out into our sandhill pasture and catch large bullfrogs in the ponds located in the pasture. The 640-acre pasture had many small ponds on it where we would find those large bullfrogs. We would catch around thirty large frogs each evening with our hands, using flashlights to blind them. We would take the frogs home, butcher them, and fry their legs in a cast iron skillet. The one thing I remember most about frying bullfrog legs was that they would often jump out of the skillet while being fried. My mother would prepare them for frying by rolling them in a flour batter, but she would have nothing to do with frying those jumpy frog legs and never even got close to them while they were in the frying pan. Frog legs are very tasty, and it is true that frog legs taste a lot like chicken, only salty chicken.

These same cousins, who were one and two years younger than I, led what I considered sheltered lives. I felt that they were not experiencing social opportunities that they should be experiencing at their age. They never got out much on Friday or Saturday nights. So, when I was a senior in high school, I would pick up my three cousins and take them along with me to drag Main Street in this larger town fifteen miles from my home. We would spend the evening driving up and down Main Street, checking out and meeting the girls who were also dragging Main Street. Gas was inexpensive because of the gas wars. Gas was fifteen cents a gallon. My car would make twenty-five miles to a gallon, so dragging Main was a relatively inexpensive form of entertainment. We were always good boys and never did anything that could be considered bad or immoral.

One evening when we went to drag Main, a girl I knew from 4-H asked me to drag Main Street with her. So, I let my cousins drive my car for a few minutes. It was at a time when local boys in one town did not want boys from other towns dragging Main in their town. While I was riding with this girl, a group of boys chased my cousins out of town. When they returned to get me, they told me what had happened to them. So, my car was now a marked, out-of-town vehicle.

One evening while I was dragging Main Street by myself, my brother-in-law saw me and stopped to talk to me. He had a friend of his with him. My Mustang was new and interesting, so my brother-in-law and his friend decided to hop into my car and ride with me for a few minutes. My brother-in-law's friend had a really tough guy reputation from his high school days. Most people considered him the toughest guy in town.

When we came to one end of the street, I attempted to turn around and drive back down Main Street. Since my car was marked as an out-of-town car to the boys who were dragging Main Street that evening, five cars loaded with boys surrounded my car. The boys got out of their cars and yelled for me to get out of town, but when this tough guy heard the boys telling us to get out of town, he jumped out of the car's back seat and informed the boys that they were going to have a very difficult time running him out of his own town. He used a few expletives to get their undivided attention. When the boys realized who they had upset by their demands, they all quickly got back into their vehicles and left the scene. My brother-in-law's friend told me that if anyone ever bothered me again, to just let him know. He would take care of it, but he had already been very convincing, and I never had to worry about anybody trying to beat us up or run us out of town again. If my cousins and I were in my Mustang, we were safe dragging Main Street anytime we wished.

My cousins and I did other things together besides dragging Main Street for entertainment. A few times, my cousins and I were able to hunt and fish together. Hunting and fishing had always been a way of life for my father's family. When they hunted and fished, they ate everything they caught or killed. Food was never wasted. Hunting and fishing, for my father's family, was a food-gathering activity as well as entertainment, family time, and a time of enjoyment for all who participated. Hunting and fishing stories were embellished, fun to share, and relived at family gatherings.

My father's family learned how to hand fish when it was legal in Kansas. I am told that even my grandma was really good at hand fishing. The family would hand fish for the food the large fish provided them. Once hand fishing became illegal, my grandmother stopped the practice. But even after it became illegal, my father continued his hand fishing ways.

When my sister and I were young, our father had us walk the bank of the river in the local county park. This was after dark, so he could hand fish under the cover of darkness. When he caught fish small enough to throw up on the riverbank, my sister and I had to pick them up and put them in a gunnysack. We carried this gunnysack along the riverbank, which was a mile long. When the fish were too big to throw up on the bank of the river, we had to carry the sack to the edge of the water, so our father could put the fish into the gunnysack. Our mother had to drive the pickup truck to the opposite end of the park and wait for us.

A humorous incident happened when my father took two other Mennonite men hand fishing with him. Ironically, these Mennonite men chose to become law-abiding Mennonite preachers. They parked their pickup truck on a country road about a half mile from the river and walked to the river to hand fish for big flathead catfish. After they had caught three large flathead catfish (all around thirty pounds each), they started walking back to their truck. Each man had to carry a thirty-pound fish back to their pickup truck through a full-grown alfalfa field.

About halfway through the field, they noticed what appeared to be a man leaning on the hood of their pickup. They assumed this man had to be a game warden waiting for them to return to their vehicle so he could ticket them for their illegal activity. It was around two o'clock in the wee hours of the morning, and to prevent being seen by this game warden, they hid themselves in the alfalfa field and waited for the game warden to get tired of waiting for them to return and leave. But this game warden did not leave, and they lay four hours in that alfalfa field until the sun came up. When it was light enough to see, they realized it wasn't a game warden leaning on the hood of their pickup. It was only a well-placed fence post in front of their pickup that looked like a man leaning against its hood. This hand fishing experience must have been traumatic for these men because it became these future preachers' last hand fishing adventure. But it was not Dad's last hand fishing venture. He took many people hand fishing with him. When my sister got married, some of her husband's relatives also liked to hand fish. When they would come out to our farm, Dad would take them hand fishing in the river not far from our farm.

My father and his younger brother were ten years apart in age. These brothers were different in many ways, yet very similar in other ways. They had an interesting relationship. There were times when they were close and times their relationship was very volatile. My uncle, rightfully so, did not approve of the way my father treated us and spent his money, and my uncle was very verbal about it. My sister recalls a time when my father's family called a family meeting at our grandma's house to address the family's concerns about my sister's and my welfare. The family felt that we were growing up without proper supervision because our father was away from home so much. They thought the family needed to address their concerns with my father. I was too young to remember this family meeting. During this family meeting, one of our aunts stayed with my sister and me and explained to us that the family had concerns about our lack of male supervision. Not realizing that our father was doing anything wrong and having been told of the importance of not saying anything to anyone concerning what our father told us he was doing, my sister defended her father and reassured our aunt that we would grow up just fine.

My father would often complain that his brother had a terrible temper and broke laws that could put him in jail. But my father had just as volatile and severe a temper, and he broke just as many civil laws that could have landed him in jail as well. These brothers had a reputation within the community. And yet when the community people would speak to me about them, only good things were shared.

During my father's car salesman years, he would purchase a car for someone, finance the car through the dealership, and never make payments on the car. He would do this so that he would achieve the company's monthly sales quota, which meant more money in his pocket through commissions. Dad learned how to play the system. Soon after the new models came out during my senior year in high school, Dad purchased a car for me to drive. This car was a 1964 silver Ford Mustang Fastback with a four on the floor, and six months after I got that 1964 Mustang to drive, my father sold it for $600 more than he paid for it. This meant that he received the extra commission money for the sale of the car, and when he paid off the car loan, he pocketed a $600 profit. After he sold that car, he then purchased a honey-gold 1964 and a half Ford Mustang for me to drive, which he also never paid for.

CHAPTER 9

THE SECONDARY YEARS

My secondary education years provided new experiences. Some of those experiences were positive in nature, but others were very negative. When I entered high school, I was determined to study hard and do well in my classes. Each day, I sat in the first two rows of the classrooms. I had a desire to please my teachers and learn as much as I could. I was hoping to put past treatment behind me. One day in my algebra class, I experienced something that affected me immensely and soured my outlook on life again. Each day, my algebra teacher would ask the class questions to be answered orally. We were to raise our hand to answer his questions. So, I always raised my hand and waited to be called on to answer the questions. I did this to let my teacher know that I was interested in learning what was being presented in the class. My classmates wouldn't attempt to answer the questions, and since no one else raised their hand to answer the questions, the teacher had to call on me.

After a few weeks of school, as usual, I raised my hand to answer a question. My teacher's reaction to my hand being raised changed my approach to learning. In front of the entire class, he told me not to raise my hand anymore. He told me that he wanted other students to have to answer his questions. His response took me by surprise, and I took his comment as a put-down. Having been snubbed and rejected by my peers in the past caused me to see this teacher's comment as slap in the face, a dart to the heart, so to speak. I had experienced many rejections in my life, and his statement made me feel foolish in front of my peers. That situation was such an embarrassment to me that from that day on, I sat in the back row of his classroom and never answered another question the rest of the school year. I lost my desire for learning. If this teacher would have only approached me privately and told me that he liked my willingness to answer his questions, but his goal was to get the other students to participate more in answering his questions, I would not have felt the rejection and embarrassment I did. A teacher can have a detrimental effect on a student. I never forgot that experience. During my teaching career, I made every effort not to be a detriment to any of my students.

One of my positive experiences happened in my biology class. I thoroughly enjoyed this class and was pleasantly surprised when my Biology I and II teacher asked me if I would be willing to be his classroom aide. I have no earthly idea why my biology teacher chose me. I never dreamed that any teacher would ever consider me to be acceptable as their classroom aide. Being chosen as an aide for any classroom was quite an honor. I was totally blown away that someone, let alone a teacher, wanted little ole me as his handpicked aide. That was a huge, positive, ego-building experience for me, and I am confident that my teacher never realized just what he did for me by choosing me for his classroom aide.

My duties as a classroom aide involved pickling (preserving) snakes, stuffing animals and birds, and doing whatever the biology teacher needed done during the sixth hour of my school day. One day, after euthanizing and preserving snakes for display, I asked my teacher if he wanted me to catch a bull snake and king snake to add to his collection of kinds of snakes in Kansas. He was pleased that I would do that for him. So, when I went to get our cows for milking that evening, I kept my eyes open for suitable snakes in the pasture grass. I found and caught both a bull snake and king snake that evening and planned to take them to school the next morning to add them to the biology classroom's snake display.

After doing the milking, meal preparation, and eating supper, my

FORGED IN FIRE

mother usually took a bath instead of a shower. Thinking that my mother would take a bath, I put the two snakes in a large gunnysack, tied the opening of the sack shut securely, and placed the sack of snakes on our concrete shower floor, planning to take them to school the next morning. Unfortunately, I chose the wrong evening to put a gunnysack of snakes in the shower. My mother, for some reason, chose to take a shower that evening instead of a bath. Finding a gunnysack in the shower, with something moving inside it, my mother untied and opened the gunnysack to see what it contained. Let's just say I never brought snakes into the house again. My mother ordered me to take the snakes out to the dairy barn until morning.

The next day, I took the snakes to school and thought it would be neat to lead one of the snakes into the classroom like you would a dog on a leash. I made a leash from baling twine, looped it around the three-foot-long bull snake's head, and had him crawl on the concrete walkway leading to the classroom, up the stairs, through the doorway, and into the classroom. The snake cooperated perfectly and slithered up the stairs and into the classroom, just as a dog would.

Now, at that time of day, there was a freshman English class with a female teacher using the biology classroom. There were two doors to exit the room, and the snake and I eliminated one by entering through it. That left just one door for the more than twenty-five students to exit through at the same time. As the students exited the classroom, it appeared that they forced the doorway to widen. The female teacher climbed up on the teacher desk, and there seemed to be a considerable amount of excitement as the room emptied and the teacher ascended to the desktop. The snake and I exited the room the same way we entered and went into the storeroom for my euthanizing duties. I was expecting some repercussions from my practical joke, but the next day my biology teacher just chuckled as he told me that it would probably be best I not do anything like that again. Of course, I promised him that I wouldn't lead any more snakes into the freshman English classrooms again. I am sure that my biology teacher had to calm the waters, so to speak. Surprisingly, I never reaped any undesirable consequences from that situation, and no one else even mentioned the snake incident to me.

Many years later, just before he passed away, I understand that this former biology teacher recounted that snake-leading incident. I

133

am told that he said it was the most amusing and unparalleled thing he had witnessed during his entire teaching career.

That biology classroom had a wire cage that housed two small garter snakes. This cage was located on a countertop near the teacher's desk. It so happened that a few days after my leading that bull snake into this classroom, the two little garter snakes escaped their cage and were somewhere in the classroom. My biology teacher informed me that it would be best not to excite that same freshman English class or the female teacher with another snake incident. According to him, that particular class and teacher didn't need to be traumatized again. He instructed me to casually look like I was taking inventory as I searched through the classroom shelves and cabinets in my effort to locate the two missing snakes. I counted and recorded the number of books and each item that was situated on the shelves and in the cabinets as I searched for the two elusive snakes.

Before I began my search, I told my biology teacher that I was sure we would find the Houdini snakes coiled around the coils located on the back of the refrigerator. This refrigerator was positioned very close to the teacher's desk. I was not to move the refrigerator while the teacher and students were in the classroom. I was to wait until that class period was over and the students and teacher had exited the room. I was to just appear like I was taking inventory, as I left no stone unturned in my probing through the shelves and cabinets.

After the class period ended and the students and teacher left the room, I checked the refrigerator coils. Sure enough, I found the missing snakes wrapped around the refrigerator coils. The students and the teacher never knew what I was doing that day or that they had been in the presence of two escaped snakes. I also enjoyed my high school agriculture classes. During my four years in those classes, I built a number of projects. One of those projects was a hog-farrowing crate for a sow I had purchased at the local sale barn. The sow was definitely pregnant, so it was imperative that I build that farrowing crate before she was ready to birth her piglets. My plans were to make a profit after I raised her piglets to feeder pig size. I arranged to sell the piglets to a local farmer for finishing. My sow farrowed as planned, and the piglets grew into feeder pig size, ready to be sold. However, my father beat me to it. He sold the feeder pigs to the farmer and the sow at the local sale barn before I got home from school one day. My hope of building a bank account went out the door again. As usual, my father kept the money, and my bank account remained basically empty. I had already covered the feed bills and other costs with my hard-earned money from baling hay and other farmwork before they were sold.

When I was a sophomore in high school, a freshman girl had her friend ask me if I would ride with her on the school bus to a varsity football game. I was shocked and flattered that a girl in the community would want to associate with me and ride with her since many peers were not always kind. I agreed to that arrangement and was looking forward to the bus ride with her. But the very next day, her brother and his friends, who were in my class, approached me and started to verbally mistreat me for agreeing to the bus trip with his sister. I would have liked to have ridden with her, but the threat of future mistreatment caused me to step aside and not go through with the bus ride together. I wish I had been stronger at that time and stood up to this bullying. The next day, one of her brother's friends asked this girl to go with him and not with me.

I played both basketball and football in high school and college. My father seldom attended my games to watch me play. He was usually somewhere else more important to him. His lack of concern for me and my activities reinforced my feelings of inadequacy and inferiority. Later in life, I found out what it was that was so much more important to him. He was attending the games of the children of the women he was seeing. Finding out that attending the activities of other women's children was more important to him than attending his own son's activities hurt immensely.

Even without my father's support, playing sports was therapeutic for me. When playing football, I preferred playing on defense, because I could release all of the frustrations that had accumulated that day. It was a major release for me to deck or nail the ball carrier or quarterback. It felt fantastic, exhilarating, and satisfying when the offensive players had to pick themselves up off of the grass and hobble back to the huddle. It was especially uplifting when the ball carrier had to remove the blades of grass and mud from the facemask of his helmet or spit grass and dirt out of his mouth after I had tackled him. Football allowed me to be aggressive in an acceptable way, and it became an important emotional release for me. Playing on offense was OK, but you couldn't hit people like you could on defense.

I played the last three quarters of my final high school football game with a broken nose. I broke my nose on a downfield block and was knocked out for a short time. When the coaches got me to the sideline, the head coach instructed the assistant coach to get smelling salts, wake me up, and get me back into the game. The smelling salts did their job and woke me up almost immediately. But my nose was still bleeding, so they stuffed cotton balls in both nostrils to keep the blood from running out of my nose. I played the rest of my final high school football game that way. When I would make contact with someone, the cotton balls would shoot out of my nose, and I would have to search the playing field grass to find the cotton balls and stuff them back into my nostrils before the next play. I not only had a broken nose, I had a concussion. That was my first concussion. Today, the possibility of a lawsuit would have prevented my reentering that game.

A few months later, my second concussion happened. My biology class was on a field trip to the sandhills area. How that concussion occurred was quite unusual. A classmate found a box turtle, picked it up, and, just for fun, threw the turtle at me. It was thrown from a short distance, and when he saw that the turtle would actually hit me, he yelled my name. Upon hearing my name, I turned my head toward him. The turtle hit my forehead with a force so hard that the turtle's shell was crushed. That left the turtle in very bad shape and me with my second concussion. For a long time after receiving that concussion, every time I moved my head quickly, I became extremely dizzy. I am not sure if the turtle was thrown just for fun or for meanness.

When we returned to school from the field trip, I didn't feel well. My head hurt, and I got dizzy when my head moved. I tried to remain in school, but I was not able to concentrate or focus. It so happened that I had driven our pickup truck to school that day. So, I left school, drove home, and did an incredibly stupid thing. Not knowing that going to sleep after a concussion is a definite no-no, I lay down and went to sleep. What saved me was the amount of time between the concussion and the time I went to sleep. It was more than a two-hour period from when I got hit with that turtle and when I went to sleep.

My third and final concussion happened during one of my college football practices. It was a scrimmage situation, and I was playing the defensive end position. Near the end of practice, the offensive team ran a pass play. The quarterback dropped back into the passing pocket, and as I rushed the passer, I was hit with a strong forearm shiver to the front of my helmet. It was directly over the area where I had been hit with the turtle, which had caused my second concussion. The team doctor informed me that my third concussion was severe enough that if it happened again, I might not wake up from it. So that third concussion ended my football career.

While in high school, on basketball and football game days, I would walk over to my grandma's house after school. I would eat a pregame meal and wait until it was time for me to walk back to the athletic bus on away games or to the dressing room on home games. We lived eight and one-quarter miles away from town, so if I rode the bus home after school, I would not have had time to get back to the school before the bus left for the games, and I would not have had a way to get back to town.

My grandmother was always happy to have me come to her house, fix my pregame meal, and wait until it was time to report for the game or the bus ride. I had the same pregame meal before every football and basketball game for four years. My pregame meal consisted of three grilled hamburgers, without bread or anything else on them, and one large can of Del Monte peaches.

Having learned how to handle bullies in the sixth grade proved beneficial to me when I was in high school and college. In one of my high school basketball games, I had to guard an all-state player. This player would throw his elbow into my chest. Catching an elbow in my sternum did not feel good, and the officials would not call a foul against this great player. So, I took things into my own hands. As I was playing defense on this player, after he threw his elbow into my chest for the third time, I pinched the back of his leg with my fingernails. He jumped and yelled, "Ouch." The official looked at us, but I was in a great post guarding position, appearing as if nothing happened. The official knew something had taken place, but he didn't know what. After the official looked away, I informed that player that if he elbowed me again, I would pinch him harder the next time. That player must have believed me because he kept his elbows to himself.

A similar thing happened to me in a college basketball practice. When I was a freshman, an upper-class player deliberately elbowed me every time I got near him. I got tired of his elbows making contact with me. One time, when I got close to him, I nailed his shoulder with my elbow as hard as I could before he was able to elbow me. That surprised him and knocked him back a bit. When I got close to him again, I inform him that I would elbow him harder if he ever elbowed me again. That player believed me as well. I never had a problem with him again.

The high school I attended held an intra-school basketball tournament when I was a senior. There was a freshman team, sophomore team, junior team, senior team, and Future Farmers of America team. I had to make a decision on which team I would play with, and I chose to play with the FFA team. The reason I chose to play with the FFA team was because the senior team members were never really nice to me, and there were no seniors on the FFA team.

As I was dressing for the game, between the FFA and seniors, my FFA team members expressed their surprise that I was going to play in that game. They informed me that the senior players had put the word out that if I played in that game, they would gang up on me and beat me up. I told my teammates to tell the seniors to go ahead and give it their best shot. It was not going to be as easy as they thought. My biggest problem was not getting beat up after the game. The biggest problem I had was what to wear to play in the game. I didn't have a pair of shorts to wear. I didn't have an extra pair of jeans to cut off the pant legs for jean shorts. I didn't have the money to go buy shorts, so all I had left was to wear my swimsuit to play in the game. My team won the game, and after the game, I was prepared to face a group of upset senior boys. But the seniors must have believed it wouldn't be an easy task to beat me up because no one tried.

During my high school senior year, my father drove a school bus. When he drove his afternoon route taking students home, he would scan the wheat fields for migrating geese. When it was goose-hunting season, he would locate the wheat field where the migrating geese were feeding on the green blades of the wheat plants. After his bus route was finished and my football practice was over, he would want to go back to hunt the geese he had located.

So, Dad would pick me up from football practice and tell me I was going to go help him hunt geese. My father was not one to argue with because of his violet temper. He would drop me off on one end of the field the geese occupied and have me walk slowly toward them.

I would walk a few steps and then sit down for a while. I would repeat this procedure to appear like a predator sneaking up on them. That is the way a fox, a coyote, or some other predator would attempt to secure a goose dinner.

My father would drive to the opposite side of the field and walk down a deep drainage ditch to get opposite me, putting the geese between us. As I moved toward the squawking geese, they would slowly walk away from me and toward where my father was waiting. When the geese moved close enough to him, he would stand up and shoot at the geese. I never had the chance to fire even one shot at a goose all season. I never had a gun, and they would fly up too far away from me to even be able to shoot at them.

During that hunting season, I endured having to walk in mud-covered shoes and sit in many muddy wheat fields while my father shot thirty-two geese. He would take the geese home, dress them, and take them with him when he left for the evening. You would think that my mother and I would have gotten at least one goose to eat, but I cannot remember eating even one of those thirty-two geese. If my memory fails me and we got a goose to eat, it was only one.

Before and after graduating from high school, I worked in the summertime for a roofing company owned by my brother-in-law and his father. I helped shingle many roofs, and when my parents' house needed the shingles replaced, I replaced them. My father had no desire to help with replacing his shingles or pay me for my labor. However, my two young nephews came to help me as much as they could.

While I was shingling, I heard my mother in her bathroom, and I told my youngest nephew to look down the roof vent pipe to see Grandma sitting on the toilet stool. My oldest nephew thought something could be up, so he stayed away from the pipe. But my youngest nephew's curiosity got the best of him. He put his head close to the vent pipe opening so he could see down the pipe. Vent pipes do not smell good, and just as he looked down into the vent pipe, my mother flushed the toilet stool. The flushing toilet sent a foul-smelling odor up the vent pipe and into my nephew's face. Needless to say, he jumped back quickly and wasn't happy that he got pranked.

After that prank, my youngest nephew kept pestering me. I warned him that he had pestered me enough, and it was time to stop, or I would turn him upside down and stick his head in a mud puddle.

He didn't think I could do that to him and didn't stop pestering me. So, I caught him, picked him up, and held him upside down. I lowered him down into a mud puddle until his very blond hair had a muddy ring around the top of his head to about ear level. His older brother laughed so hard because he had warned his little brother to stop pestering me. He knew that I would put up with his pestering only so long, and then I would take action.

My nephews often took the brunt of my practical jokes. One day, my sister and I were working at our mother's house and her elder son called to inform his mother that it was time for him to be picked up from a church activity. When the phone rang, my sister said it must be her son. Since I was closer to the phone, I told her I would go ahead and answer it. I picked up the phone and said, "Murphy's Mule Barn." My nephew hung up immediately. He tried calling three more times, and each time, he would hang up when I would say, "Murphy's Mule Barn." The fifth time he called, he figured it out and asked if it was me who was answering with "Murphy's Mule Barn."

When this same nephew was in high school, I called my sister's house. He answered the phone. I thought it was a good time to prank him. I said that I was from the local police department and would like to talk to him about being behind a drugstore. I said it was reported that he was seen in the alley behind the drugstore that had been robbed the evening before. Of course, he was quick to explain that it couldn't have been him, because he was not in that alley at any time that evening. I had him worried until he realized that it actually could be me pranking him again. My nephews remember me for the unsought excitement I caused them to experience, and over fifty years later, they still talk about all the things I did to them at their immediate family gatherings.

Another time that I played a practical joke on my older nephew was when he was carrying shingles up a ladder to his father and me while we were shingling a garage. He was working really hard carrying those shingles up the ladder. I saw him tiring from the physical labor and told him that there was a skyhook on the interior garage wall that would make his job of getting those shingles up onto the roof much easier. Anything that would make the shingle-carrying work easier definitely got his attention. For about thirty minutes, he searched for a skyhook to use to make things easier. He eventually realized that there was no such thing as a skyhook and that he was being pranked again.

I had many interesting things happen to me while I was shingling roofs of houses. One time I was nailing shingle tabs onto the ridge of a roof to finish up a job. When nailing ridge tabs over the ridge, you sit and move backward as you nail each tab onto the ridge. I was so focused on finishing the job that I shingled right off of the end of the roof peak. It was probably a fifteen-foot drop to the ground, but I didn't get hurt. I just picked myself up off of the ground and started to clean up the scraps of roofing materials. My brother-in-law noticed that I was no longer on the peak of the roof and went to see what had happened to me. But by the time he arrived to see if I had fallen off of the roof, I had hit the ground, gotten up, and had gone to the other side of the house.

Another time, we were working on a flat roof two and a half stories off of the ground. My nephew had played with the ladder, and when I stepped off of the roof onto the ladder to crawl down to get supplies, the ladder slipped out from under me, and I rode that ladder down the two and a half stories. Again, I was fortunate and didn't get hurt.

CHAPTER 10

ALTERNATIVE SERVICE

After my freshman year of college, I was drafted and spent two years in alternative service. The draft office where I registered was staffed with an elderly lady who had a tough reputation. Because of her stern and demanding reputation, every time I went into the draft office, I was as polite as one could be. I didn't want to be on this lady's bad side, since she could control my life. My being polite to this lady paid off big-time. This draft lady did not live up to the horror stories that I had heard about her. She must have taken a liking to my politeness, because she treated me extremely well each time I went into the draft office.

The day I reported to the draft office to travel to Kansas City by train for my induction physical, I again was extremely polite to her. There were seventeen of us reporting for our induction physicals that day. When we were ready to leave for Kansas City, the draft lady said, "Bob," and I replied, "Yes, ma'am." She said, "Here are the train tickets and hotel room reservations for all seventeen of you. You will check everyone on the train and into the hotel in Kansas City." I replied, "Ma'am, I think someone else would do better at this than me." She replied, "Bob," forcefully, and I said, "Yes, ma'am." She said, "You will take care of these tickets and reservations." I looked at

her and said, "Yes, ma'am. I'd be more than happy to do that, ma'am."
She smiled and handed me the tickets and reservations.

I checked everyone onto the train and into the hotel when we
reached Kansas City. Now, wouldn't you know that the hotel we
were staying at was located at Twelfth and Vine. Twelfth and Vine
didn't mean anything to me, being a Mennonite farm boy from central
Kansas. Later that night, the young man I roomed with wanted to
go out and see the sights of the city around our hotel. I thought there
wouldn't be any harm in just looking around the area, so we went
outside the hotel to look around. It didn't take us long to realize
that Twelfth and Vine was not a normal street in Kansas City. As
we walked along the street, skimpy-clad girls came out of the bars
and strip joints, grabbed our arms, and tried to drag us inside their
establishments. I didn't drink alcoholic beverages and was under the
age for legally entering that kind of establishment, so I did not allow
those young ladies to drag me into those bars. That was an eye-
opening experience for me, to say the least.

The next day, we went to the induction physical facility. That was
quite an experience as well. The examination people lined everyone
up in straight lines, walked by each of us, and checked our private
parts. Then they had us bend over and spread our cheeks to check
for hemorrhoids. I had physicals every fall for high school and college
sports for five straight years, but this physical was not like any physical
I had ever experienced.

I was assigned to a hospital in Nebraska and spent the next two
years of my life working as a surgery technician. The hospital must
have felt comfortable with me, because they taught me how to be
a surgery technician. I learned how to assist doctors with all the
different types of surgeries.

During those two years, I would work all day in the surgery
department of that hospital and then be on call for surgeries every
hour of the night. After two years of spending each day in the
surgery room, many nights on call, patching up drunk drivers, their
passengers, and their victims and delivering babies all hours of the
night, I wanted nothing to do with the medical field. The financial
rewards in the medical field were not enough for me to choose that
profession for my life's work. I wanted a better life for myself than
the life I experienced in the medical field.

Before the hospital accepted me into the surgery department, they had me watch a surgery, to see if I was suitable for the surgery position. I had to be able to handle seeing and working with some very difficult situations. I was confident that I could handle any type of surgery since I grew up on a farm and had faced similar types of situations growing up.

The surgery that I observed first was a leg amputation. I stood in the surgery room, watching the leg being severed, and when the amputation was complete, the scrub nurse tossed me the amputated leg. The scrub nurse did that without thinking about it being my first surgery. I caught the leg with the leg stump facing me. The blood vessels had hemostats clamped on them, and they were dangling from the bloody cut end of the leg. Raw flesh and cut bone were in my face, so to speak. Fortunately, that experience didn't faze me one bit. My farm boy experiences had prepared me to be able to stomach situations like that. I had seen many other gross things.

Since I didn't pass out, they must have thought I was suitable for the position, because I spent the next two years assisting with operations. Sometimes I even assisted the doctors with the actual surgeries. I had assisted in so many surgeries that I knew how to perform many different types of surgeries myself.

The first surgery case I assisted with was a doctor performing a hemorrhoidectomy (the surgical removal of hemorrhoids, an enlarged, swollen, and inflamed cluster of tissue inside the rectum or at its opening). I believe the nurses in the surgery department had me assist with this particular surgery because it was assisting an almost ninety-year-old doctor who had unconventional ways. I had used electric soldering irons, claw hammers, and other conventional tools many times in life. I used soldering irons, both electrical and nonelectrical, to solder things like copper water pipe couplings to prevent water leaks. But I had never experienced an electric soldering iron being used as I did that particular day. This old doctor used only an electric soldering iron, a hemostat, and a scalpel to perform that hemorrhoid operation.

The electric soldering iron was an easy surgical instrument to sterilize. All I had to do to sterilize that soldering iron was plug it into an electrical outlet and let it heat up. As I acted a bit confused because of this doctor's unconventional ways, the surgery personnel chuckled.

I believe they assigned me this particular situation to see how I would handle it. The interesting thing about this doctor's primitive methods was that his patients healed faster and with less pain than any of the other doctors' hemorrhoidectomy patients did.

There was just one time that I nearly passed out because of the situation I faced. One evening, two young boys decided to drink alcoholic beverages and drive. These two drunken boys were driving down a country road, and at the top of a hill, they hit a car driven by a young man who was driving his date home. This happened around midnight. The four youngsters were all brought to the emergency room of the hospital, and being on call, I was assigned to care for one of the drunk boys. This boy's nose had been almost completely severed off his face. Only a small strip of skin kept his nose attached to his head. As I held his head, his nose hung off the side of his face, and he was vomiting up secondhand blood mixed with alcohol. The odor of that alcohol and blood mixture was almost more than I could take. Because of the odor, I became lightheaded. It was a good thing I was sitting down at the time. We reattached this young boy's nose, and as far as I know, he is still living and doing fine today.

Opening large black bags in an emergency room and looking inside will happen only once. No one ever wants to see what is inside that body bag again. As an eighteen-year-old kid, experiences like these I have just described influenced my decision-making and sped up my maturing process.

I am convinced that all young people need to see similar situations to what I experienced firsthand. If they saw the pain, agony, and trauma people endured because of poor decisions like the young boys made, there would be a whole lot less drinking and driving or riding with anyone who has consumed alcoholic beverages or illegal drugs.

The doctors who performed surgeries in the hospital I was assigned to took a liking to me and exposed me to more than what the normal surgery tech people might experience. I am confident that the doctors expected me to go back to college and seek a life in the medical field. They had me witness unusual surgery situations. I witnessed such things as ovarian cyst operations, called "chocolate cysts," that contained teeth and hair as long as any I have seen on anyone's head. The fluid inside the cyst was chocolate in color. I asked the doctors why teeth and hair grew inside those ovarian cysts, and their reply was that the medical field hadn't figured that out yet. I witnessed and assisted with lung cancer operations and drunk driver accident victims that convinced me that I had made the best choices of never using tobacco products, illegal drugs, or alcoholic beverages. I am convinced that my surgical tech experiences were God's way of showing me that I had made the correct decisions.

Those two years of being a part of life and death helped me mature quickly. I learned the true value of human life and the importance of showing compassion to others. One of the many experiences that has stuck with me over the years was when an unwed teenage girl gave birth and bled to death. When the doctor realized that she was what they called a bleeder, fifty seven pints of blood were pumped into her, in the attempt to save her life. That teenage girl had left her boyfriend and family behind to raise her baby girl. That was as tough a situation as one can imagine. And even tougher was having to tell the family that the doctor and medical staff did everything they could to save her yet lost her. Informing family members that their loved one did not survive in spite of all the efforts made to save their life has to be the toughest part of being a medical doctor. It is a heart-wrenching experience just to witness it, let alone being the person to do it. People expect doctors to be able to handle everything they face, and when things do not work out as expected, they want to sue, not realizing that it is just as hard on the doctor as it is for them, or maybe even harder. With what I have experienced, I have compassion for doctors when they do everything they can do and things still go wrong.

During my service time, I had to be frugal with what money I was given during those two years. I received a total of $130 a month to live on. That included paying for my meals, the room I rented, gas when I needed it, and a car payment. When my father refused to make car payments for me, I paid $100 a month for the car payment and twenty dollars for the room rent. I had ten dollars left for food and for gas. My father refused to help me financially, and my mother was not financially able to help. I never told anyone just how tough things were for me at this time in my life. I had grown up not being able to share what was happening to me, and I did not tell anyone about the situation I was facing. I had experienced times in my life when food was not available, and those times helped me get through these trials.

I would eat breakfast at the hospital when I had the money,

because a bowl of oatmeal cost me one dollar. I didn't have enough money for many breakfasts, noon meals, or evening meals, so I would buy a gallon of milk and a box of cereal when I could afford it and have that for my evening meals. The first few months I was there, my grandma sent me care packages of nonperishable food items. I learned to appreciate such items as cans of Spam. Those nonperishable food items were greatly appreciated. I think God was preparing me for this experience through the times in my life when we didn't have things to eat except milk. I weighed 195 pounds when I started my service, and two years later, I weighed 170 pounds.

When the local dairy farmers heard that I had grown up on a dairy farm, they had me come out to their farms and milk their cows for them when they needed to be out of town and when I was able to do it for them. If I wasn't scheduled to work in the surgery department and not on call for surgeries, I would be able to do the milking and feed their livestock on Friday night, Saturday morning and evening, and Sunday morning and evening. They would pay me to do this for them, and I would make a little extra money. At times, I would be able to go to their farms and help them with field work or cut and split firewood for their basement heating stoves. This didn't happen too often, but it happened often enough to help me survive. Sometimes, people invited me over to their homes for meals after Sunday morning or evening worship assemblies, which was a huge help for my need of nourishment.

Home-cooked meals at this time in my life were impressive, beautiful, and elaborate to me. While I was serving as a surgery technician, a folk singing group performed in a large city near where I was stationed. I saved enough money to attend their performance. After their performance, to my surprise, I was selected to go back stage and meet the performers. To this day, I have no earthly idea why I was selected to go back stage to meet them. These performers were very personable and talked with a small group of us for a considerable amount of time after their performance. I was able to get their autographs, and after meeting and talking to them, their songs meant more to me.

While I was serving those two years as a surgery tech in Nebraska, something that I thought would never happen did. My father was arrested for theft. He was working as a salesman in the furniture department of a major local retail store, selling new furniture. Sometimes when he sold new furniture, he would take trade-ins. When he sold the used trade-in furniture, he pocketed some of the money he received. Eventually, his unethical practice caught up with him, and he was arrested for theft and jailed. He needed $250 for bail, which he didn't have, and, of course, my mom didn't have the money either. My mother called me to see if I could help with the bail money, but I was in Nebraska with no extra money of my own. So, my father had Mom ask my sister for the bail money. It just so happened she had $250 in savings and gave my mother the money so that she could bail Dad out of jail. Of course, my father had no intention of paying my sister back for the money he received from her. He never even thanked her for what she did for him.

Since my father would not pay my sister back, Mother took it upon herself to reimburse my sister. She paid my sister twenty-five a month out of her check before my father could get his hands on it, until the $250 debt was paid in full. Looking back at this situation, I believe it would have been beneficial for my father to have spent some quality time in jail.

Needless to say, my father lost his job at the retail store. I am not sure what all happened after he was bailed out of jail. No one seems to know. All that my sister, mother, and I knew was that the retail store dropped the charges against him. I assume he had to make restitution to the store for the charges being dropped. This was another situation that lent itself to my not wanting to be considered to be like my father.

My being so far away from home was agonizing for my mother. She was concerned that I would find some girl up north to marry who wouldn't be a good spouse for me. She thought that this girl who worked for the same grocery store as she did would be perfect for me. One weekend while I was still in service, I was able to return home for a visit. My mother needed to go to the grocery store, and she had me go along with her in hopes that I would meet this girl she approved of. She told me that there was a cute girl my age who worked there. I was questioning in my mind Mom's opinion of cute. What she considered cute and I considered cute often didn't match. When she was ready to pay for the groceries, we went through the checkout counter manned by this beautiful young woman. I couldn't believe it. Mom was actually right that this girl was cute, and she definitely got my attention. My mother introduced me to her, but I had to return to Nebraska two days later, so there wasn't much time to pursue her. I did, however, ask her if she would like to go see a movie together the next evening, and she consented. The next day, I returned to Nebraska and lost contact with her. After my service time ended, I returned home. The evening I returned home, I got into my car and did what most young people did for entertainment. Dragging Main Street was still the popular form of entertainment, and as I was driving down Main Street, this little blue Ford Falcon came cruising by in the opposite direction. A female arm stuck out of the driver's window and waved at me. I thought, *I better check this chick out*, so I drove around the block to see who she was.

The young woman behind the waving arm turned out to be the checkout girl at the grocery store. I asked her if she wanted to "drag Main" with me that evening, and she accepted the invitation. We drove up and down Main Street together for a few hours before she had to go home. She was impressive, and I decided to explore the possibility of dating this young woman. I thought if I acted too eager to ask for a date, she would probably act a bit indifferent about going out together. So, I waited a few days before I called her. I thought after a few days, if she was truly interested, she'd be anxious to go out to see a movie together. Sure enough, when I called, she sounded anxious to go out together. We started dating that summer. That fall, she went back to college in Arkansas, and I went back to college where I had attended before going to service. We kept in touch through letter writing that school year. I amused her with the little artistic ability I possessed. I periodically sent her my Snoopy cartoon drawings along with my letters.

CHAPTER 11

THE COLLEGE YEARS

During the summer, after my senior year of high school and during my first year of college, I was offered the position of managing a hog farm. A local hog farmer who was called to active military duty with the National Guard contacted me about this managerial opportunity. This farmer needed someone he could trust to run his entire hog operation while he was away from the farm. I had worked with a relative of this hog farmer, and he suggested that this hog farmer contact me for the position. He knew my work ethic and the type of person I was. This hog farmer also knew who I was from my 4-H hog-showing days. He knew who my father was and had heard stories about him, so he had to be somewhat skeptical about hiring me. But based on his relative's recommendation, he took a chance on me, contacted me about his need and how I could be of assistance to him, and offered me the position.

I knew that I could handle the managerial position, but I was a bit surprised by the offer since I was only eighteen years old and entering my first year of college. I was honored that someone would trust me with his entire hog operation while he was away. I accepted the position, and the monthly pay I received was very beneficial to a college student who had never had a chance to put anything away in a savings account.

While this farmer was away from his farm, my responsibilities were taking care of his entire hog farming operation, from birth through finishing and the breeding stock. His operation was extensive and kept me busy while I was a full-time college student. I would spend one to two hours every morning and evening and all day Saturday at the farm. I rotated sixty-six sows through a twenty-two-crate farrowing house, which I kept full most of the time. During my time there, sows birthed an average of fourteen piglets per litter, with some sows birthing up to as many as twenty-two piglets. When that happened, I had to farm out some of those piglets to sows that only birthed nine to twelve piglets. Most of the sows only had fourteen to sixteen "dinner plates," so turning over some of the piglets to other sows to raise was necessary. Adopting out piglets to other mothers is not an easy thing to do. A sow usually will not accept a piglet that is not her own and may even kill it. To get the adoptive mother to accept the piglets, I would take the newborn piglet and rub the adoptive sow's manure all over it so it smelled like her own piglets. My method worked like a charm, and I never lost a single piglet. The farmer told me that my pig per litter ratio was where his own had been, so he was happy with my work.

After the piglets were weaned, I moved them to a nursery barn, and from there to a finishing building. I chose some of the pigs for breeding stock replacement with the owner's approval. The owner had me show his breeding stock at the Kansas State Fair and the American Royal Livestock Show. From the exposure his breeding stock received at these shows, buyers would come to the farm and buy his breeding stock at premium prices.

One day while I was out working at this hog farm, feeding, castrating, vaccinating, ear notching, and doing the general work around the farm, a truck from the local feed store drove up to the nursery barn's feed bin. That was not unusual when an order had been placed for feed to be delivered. I had informed the farmer's wife that the bin was getting near empty and feed needed to be ordered. So, feed being delivered to the farm was to be expected. However, it was the manager of the feed store driving the feed truck, which was a bit unusual. The manager got out of the truck and set up the truck grain auger system to transfer the grain from the feed store's grain truck into the nursery's barn's feed bin. He started the auger's system to fill the feed bin, and about thirty minutes later, the grain auger was turned off. It appeared that the manager had finished transferring the feed into the grain bin. He put the auger system away and left the farm.

Later that day, I walked by the nursery barn's feed bin and tapped on the metal bin to see just how full the grain bin had become. When I tapped on the metal bin, it didn't sound like a bin with feed in it. I thought that was a little strange. The feed store manager surely wouldn't try to cheat this farmer by charging him for feed that was not delivered. But to make sure that feed was actually delivered, I climbed up to the top of that feed bin and opened the bin lid to look inside and see just how full the feed bin actually was. To my surprise, the bin was still almost empty. I could hardly believe that the feed store was trying to defraud this farmer. The feed store manager thought that since the owner was gone, no one would realize that he was charging for feed that was never delivered.

I contacted the owner through his wife, and he came home from his assignment to deal with the situation. I am not sure how many other farmers this manager tried to defraud in this manner, but I am confident that this wasn't the only dishonest situation he was involved with. The farmer got law enforcement officials involved, and because of what he tried to do, the manager of the feed store lost his job. Beyond that, I do not know what happened to him. It wasn't long after the incident that the feed store closed its doors. The farmer was very pleased with how I took care of his operation. I saved him a boatload of money in that one situation. When I worked outside of my home community, I felt appreciated for who I was and what I was capable of doing, but when I worked in my home community, I never felt understood or valued.

During the first two months of college, a number of the male students would go to the gymnasium each evening and play pickup basketball games. I loved playing basketball, so almost every evening, after I completed my work at the hog farm, I would go to the gym and play ball. The guys who I played with hated playing against me because I knew how to use my bony elbows and butt to box out on shots and aggressively rebound missed shots. I was what they considered an aggressive player. These boys talked me into going out for the college basketball team. Even though I didn't think I was a good enough player to make the college team, they thought I was. So, I gave it a shot, thinking it would be great if I made the team. If I didn't make the team, I would play in the college's intramural league.

After going through a two-week tryout period, I felt very fortunate to have been selected for the college team. Players were cut that I thought were pretty good players. Due to my father's lack of interest in watching me play the game, I assumed I wasn't a very good ball player.

I had entered college as a pre-veterinary medicine major, but when I went back to college, after my service time, veterinary medicine seemed way too much like the medical lifestyle that I had decided was not for me, and I did not continue down that path.

That summer, after I had returned from my service experience, I secured a job in my home area at a major university's experimental farm and saved enough money to pay for the first semester back at school. But for my second semester, I had to find a way to finance it. The only way I could come up with the money was to secure a loan. I thought that maybe I could get a student loan at a local bank, but that didn't work out for me. So, I went to my great-uncle and asked if he would loan me the money for my second semester. I promised that I would pay him back with interest if that was what he desired. My great-uncle was a very wealthy and a generous man. This generous great-uncle felt sorry for me because of what I faced during my growing-up years. I am not sure why he trusted me to pay him back because he had dealt with my father many times.

When I went to give my great-uncle the first payment for the money he loaned me, he informed me that he didn't need money and that I did not need to pay him back the money I owed him. At hearing this, I was surprised and relieved. I thanked him dearly for what he was doing for me. I didn't know if he realized just what he had done for me. He was just giving me that money for the semester's expenses. I believe that my great-uncle was testing me to see if I was like my father and would just take the money without any intention of paying him back. My father had borrowed money from him three times and had never made any attempt to pay him back for the loans he had been given. Since I took the responsibility of paying him the money I owed him seriously, he just gave the money to me. I am told that he expressed how proud he was that I was taking responsibility for repaying his loan. Since I made the effort to repay the loan, this great-uncle, who I would tell about the "Boo" as a very young child, made the decision to pay for my complete education. He talked with his sister, my grandma, and she explained how wonderful it was for him to do what he did for me. She convinced him it would be a kind gesture to do it for others of the family as well. So, later that year, this great-uncle decided to pay for all of his great-nieces' and nephews' and their children's education if they attended a certain college.

Well, for me, that was a no-brainer. Since I was a penniless kid with the desire to go to college, I attended my great-uncle's college choice with a new outlook on learning. For the first time in my life, I didn't have to worry about where the money I needed would come from. I looked for a course of study that was suitable to me and as far from the medical field as I could get. I always loved working with my hands and found industrial education classes interesting and enjoyable. So, I changed my major course of study to the field of industrial education.

During my second year of college, much to my displeasure, my father sold my honey-gold 1964 Ford Mustang out from under me. I had struggled and sacrificed to paid for that car during my service time. For almost two years of my life, I had suffered and lived frugally to pay for that car, and I didn't want it taken from me, but my father said it was a done deal and there wasn't anything I could do about it. So that I still had wheels in college, my father had me drive the dealership's used cars in hopes that I would sell some of them for him. But college kids generally do not have a lot of excess funds, and his scheme didn't work out as he planned.

About six months after he took my car and supposedly sold it, he came to my college late one evening and told me to go with him to get my car back. He asked me if I still had the extra set of keys for the car, which I did. He stated that he and I were going to repossess my car, because the people to whom he supposedly sold the car hadn't paid him for it. The idea of getting my car back was appealing to me. So, I went with him to repossess my car. We drove to a house in a city about forty miles away. When we arrived, it was very late in the evening, and everything was dark inside the house. The car was parked in the driveway, and my father told me to hurry, get into the car, and drive it quickly back to my college. He acted very nervous about this situation of repossessing my car, and I wondered why he just didn't go to the door and get the other set of keys they had. He informed me that it would not be a good idea to ask for the keys. I had the second set of keys, so repossessing my car was not a problem, and I was extremely happy to get my car back. But I was also concerned that the people who supposedly bought my car would report it stolen. My father assured me that would not happen because the title of the car was still in my name, and he had the title. Later in life, I found out that we picked up my car at a woman's house who he was having a special relationship with. My father had lied to me again; this person hadn't bought the car at all. He had just given it to her to drive.

After finding out the real situation concerning the supposed sale of my car, I felt an inner pain caused by the fact that my father could just take the car I had sacrificed for and worked hard to pay for, just to give it to someone he wanted to impress. if,I had a choice to make. I could harbor hard feelings and dwell on the emotional pain I felt, or I could choose to put the situation behind me and move on with my life. I chose to move on with my life.

After my second year of college, I got sidetracked again. The young checkout girl who took my fancy captivated me, and we were married. I was looking for a wife who was a sound Christian woman, a helpmate who would have the same moral values I had. I did not want to experience in my marriage what my mother experienced in her marriage to my father. The good-looking checkout girl fit the bill.

The summer before my wife and I married, I was offered the opportunity to spend a year in Switzerland in a 4-H exchange program. I informed my wife-to-be about the opportunity I was offered. She was not excited about me spending a year overseas and delaying our marriage. But she said that the choice was mine to make, and the experience would be a once-in-a-lifetime opportunity. My choices were marriage to this sweet girl or Switzerland. The choice was easy for me to make. I chose marrying my sweetheart. That free trip to Switzerland couldn't hold a candle to her.

When I gave my wife-to-be her diamond ring, I was somewhat concerned. My father told me that he had a number of diamonds, and I could chose the one I liked. I was more than a little surprised by his offer. He had never given me anything before. I went ahead and chose a good-sized diamond from a number of diamonds he had in his possession. I had no idea where and how he got possession of them, and that caused me major concern. Had it been legally obtained or obtained by unscrupulous means? Later in life, I found out that my father frequently patronized a particular jewelry store, purchasing jewelry for women. These diamonds he possessed could have been purchased at this particular jewelry store. They could have been payment for a debt he was owed, or they could have been unscrupulously obtained.

Before we married, I told my wife-to-be that my father claimed to work undercover for the KBI and that marrying me could put her life in danger. I told her of the events my family and I had faced over the years and that her life could be in danger if she married me. This revelation scared her quite a bit. But I was fortunate she still said yes! We were married in August 1969, and this year we are celebrating fifty years of marriage.

I had two years of college left, and my wife had only one year left. So, we decided to spend our first year of marriage in Arkansas, while my wife finished her senior year of college. I worked as a surgery tech again at a hospital in a city in central Arkansas. Health care in Arkansas was much different from health care in Nebraska. After one of the doctors in Arkansas realized how much I knew about surgery, he had me doing things that I was not qualified to do. I closed (sewed people shut), while this doctor watched me to make sure I did it right. I was extremely nervous about actually closing incisions. Up until then, I only clamped the bleeding vessels with hemostats, held them while the doctor tied off the cut vessels with suture, and cut the excess sutures. In Nebraska, I was only expected to assist the doctors, not to do their work.

I cleaned the surgery rooms after each surgery, making sure each room was as sterile as possible, in both Arkansas and Nebraska. But the main difference between the two situations was cleanliness. In Nebraska, if a fly or bug got into a surgery room, a panic set in, and the entire surgery room had to be scrubbed down with disinfectants. In Arkansas, a flyswatter was used to swat the flies, and bugs were stepped on. The surgery rooms were not scrubbed down like they should have been unless I did it. I did not like the idea of the surgery rooms not being sterile or as clean as I thought they should be. So, I would scrub the rooms down and disinfect them after each surgery. One doctor in Arkansas had me hold his money roll while he performed surgeries. This doctor obviously trusted me with his huge money roll. That money roll was so large that I couldn't touch my two thumbs and middle fingers together around the money roll. This money roll had more than dollar bills in it. In fact, there was more than tens, twenties, and fifties in that roll. I always made sure the roll of money was in that doctor's field of vision at all times. I did not want him or anyone else to ever think that I would take any of his money in case some of it came up missing. My father's reputation had caused me enough grief as I was growing up. I knew that taking any of that money would be theft and unacceptable to God. Another doctor took a liking to me, and when he found out that I knew how to ride horses, he took me out to his ranch in the foothills of Arkansas. We would ride his Arabian horses in the wooded foothills of his ranch. That ranch was located in the beautiful back-country of north central Arkansas.

I mentioned to the doctor that I had showed horses in competitions and broken them to lead and ride in my younger days. Of course, he was skeptical of my experience with horses and wanted to see my equine skills firsthand. The first time I went riding with this doctor at his ranch, he tested me on just how well I could function on a horse. He rode ahead of me on a narrow trail up and down the mountains, and after a period of riding, he had his horse leave the trail, going through the sapling trees. The saplings were so close together that the horse had a little trouble squeezing between the saplings with me on its back. I was a good enough horseman that those saplings could not scrape me off or cause me problems. So, I passed the test and was trusted with riding those Arabian horses whenever I chose to ride. Riding those horses helped make the time we spent in Arkansas much more enjoyable. In central Arkansas, squirrel meat and soup were considered a delicacy. As a kid, I hunted rabbits and squirrels in the wintertime, sometimes with my father but most of the time on my own. Hunting with my father never secured meat for us to eat. It only provided the goodies for other people. When meat was scarce for my mother and me, I would go out looking to harvest some for us to eat. Sometimes I was successful, and other times I was not. When I successfully shot a rabbit or squirrel, I would take the carcass home and butcher it. My mother would cut it up, roll the meat in flour, and fry it for us to eat. I was never a fan of the taste of squirrel meat, but, hey, it was food to eat, which we sometimes didn't have.

When my surgical coworkers in Arkansas found out that I wasn't a big fan of the taste of squirrel meat, they said that I needed to eat some of their squirrel soup because it was the best-tasting soup I would ever eat. These ladies claimed that there wasn't any soup that tasted better than their squirrel soup and I would simply love it. I have to say that I was more than a little bit skeptical of their claim. I knew what squirrel meat tasted like, and it would take everything short of a supernatural event to make it taste good to me.

Since I had eaten my mother's fried squirrel meat, I was confident that I could handle their squirrel soup. One day, they surprised me by making me some of that so-called great Arkansas squirrel soup. They gave me a bowl of their soup, and I ate it all, even though it tasted less than edible to me. I had a very difficult time downing it with a smile on my face, but I did not want to hurt their feelings, so I acted as if it was great. Eating that squirrel soup was not an easy task for me. As I was eating it, I was hoping that I would not throw it back up and that they would never make it for me again.

After my wife's graduation, we returned to Kansas, where I finished my college education. I received my bachelor of science degree in industrial education at a small Mennonite college. Because of my generous great-uncle, both my son and I finished college debt-free. Not having a role model or anyone to really encourage me, I never took my education too seriously until I was married and a junior in college. I had a very unique studying style. I couldn't study when things were quiet, so I studied with a basketball or football game on TV and another game on the radio, and I could tell you what was happening in both games and what I was studying. Quiet was a major distraction for me. I studied for my college tests by reading over my class notes just before I went to bed. During the night, I ran those notes over in my mind, and the next morning, I could tell you my notes word for word. I had a quick memory, but retention over a long period of time could be a problem. In high school, I would get on the school bus in the morning with thirty minutes to get to school. I would not have studied my thirty vocabulary words for my English class. So, I would give those vocabulary words to a classmate and then have him give them back to me. After hearing him spell the words and give their meanings, I could spell the words correctly and give their meanings as well. I would ace the vocabulary test that day. But the problem would come at the end of the semester when there would be over two hundred words to know, and you didn't know which words your teacher would select for the test. Memorizing all 240 words, their spelling and meanings, took a lot more effort.

Just before my graduation from college, I received the Thresher Award in Industrial Education. Thresher Awards are given each year to one senior in each area of study who had made an outstanding contribution in their academic fields. I was very pleased to have received that award, but I was even more pleased when my son received the Thresher Award in debate and forensics over thirty years later. Both of my children graduated from their respective colleges with honors. My daughter graduated summa cum laude, and my son cum laude. My daughter graduated from a church-affiliated university in Tennessee, and my son graduated from the same Mennonite college that I graduated from. My daughter got her bachelor of science degree and went on to get her nursing degree from a university in Tennessee. She went through her entire educational process receiving all A's except for one class. She received a B in a college calculus class while a sophomore in high school. She is presently a registered charge nurse, in charge of two clinic nurses at a major university's pediatric diabetic clinic. My son got his bachelor of science degree and went on to graduate from a school of preaching in Colorado. He is presently preaching for a Church of Christ in Minnesota. He has also graduated with a master of arts degree in New Testament studies from the same university that my daughter graduated from. He received the Award of Excellence as the outstanding student in the Graduate School of Theology. In May 2017, he received the Zondervan Student Award for outstanding achievement in the study of theology. God has truly blessed my wife and me.

During the first few years of marriage, my wife and I suffered through two miscarriages before our first child was born. Losing those two children was extremely hard on my wife. She had always dreamed of being a mother and thought that might not happen for her. It was a very difficult time for us, but God, in His time, blessed us with two wonderful children who have made us grandparents. We are now blessed with seven incredible grandchildren. My wife and I are extremely proud of the adults our two children have grown up to be. We couldn't have asked for anything better than that.

CHAPTER 12

LEFT ALONE

During the time that my sister's first son was a toddler and she was pregnant with her second son, she visited our mother at the farm at least one day a week. My sister enjoyed those visits, but she saw that Mom's personality was gradually changing. Our mother was either very fearful of something, or her mental stability was deteriorating. She would talk about our father constantly and how he must be working in something extremely dangerous, because she had heard another car drive by the farm and gunshots had been fired. She would then change the subject and talk about how mean one of the women at work was to her. She would talk about people who were trying to do harmful things to her, which went on for a few months. After I went off to college, our mother was afraid to be alone on the farm where she was most of the time, making her a very unhappy person. One can only imagine how awful she felt at that time in her life. She was an abused woman, both physically and emotionally. She was fearful of what could happen to her, felt deserted and forsaken by an unloving husband, and felt rejected by what appeared to be an uncaring community. She felt truly alone. Loneliness comes from the feeling that no one cares, not from actually being alone.

My sister saw her deteriorating day by day, and one Sunday in October, at our paternal grandmother's home, our father informed everyone that he was taking our mother to Colorado for their twenty-fifth wedding anniversary. One would think that it was a good thing for my father to do. But he also said that he was going to get a motel room in Colorado Springs, and then he would go hunting in the mountains. He would leave Mom in the motel room by herself for a week. I was in college and did not attend this family dinner, so I had no knowledge of my father's plan. This declaration that Dad made concerning our parents' so-called anniversary trip haunted my sister. Why was he going to take our mother to Colorado and leave her alone in a motel room for a week for a twenty-fifth wedding anniversary? If it was really a hunting trip, why wouldn't he just go on this hunting trip by himself? He had always gone on activities like this by himself in the past. My sister couldn't help wondering if he was actually planning something horribly evil.

My sister became fearful for mother's well-being, thinking of her staying in a motel room for five days by herself while our father was supposedly hunting. Dad never stayed in nice motels with the family, so my sister knew that the place he would have Mother stay would be a run-down, seedy place and not a place to spend a twenty-fifth wedding anniversary. My sister felt that she would be a terrible person if she ever shared what she thought our father was capable of doing to our mother. My sister had never seen Dad try to strangle Mother like I had. So this feeling she had of our father possibly harming our mother was almost unthinkable for her. My sister kept having a gnawing feeling inside concerning our parents' upcoming trip and what could possibly happen to our mother. Mom was also fearful and didn't want to go on this trip, but Dad was insistent.

My sister was torn inside. She did not think that she could talk about what she was feeling to anyone. She knew in her heart that Dad was not a man of integrity. She did not feel that he loved our mother, but was he really capable of doing the cruel and heartless things she was thinking? She could not remember a time that our father treated Mother with respect or said any caring words to her.

Early one morning, while Mother was sleeping, a vehicle drove by the farm again, slammed on its brakes, skidded to a stop at the end of our short driveway, and gunshots were fired through the yard. It was the third time this had happened. Later that day, Mother contacted the local sheriff's department, and the sheriff came out to talk with her. She informed him of what had happened in the past and the night before. After the sheriff finished talking with Mother, he drove away from the farm, wondering if what he had been told could actually be true. The sheriff saw a neighbor man working in a field, so he stopped and asked this neighbor if he knew my mother. This man acknowledged that he knew her. The sheriff then proceeded to ask this neighbor if he thought my mother could be believed in what she had told him, and the neighbor's reply was affirmative. After being told what Mother had said to the sheriff, the neighbor replied, "Whatever that woman says, you better believe every word of it." Unfortunately, the police department did not follow up on the situation Mom was facing.

While in my second month in college, Dad came home at his usual time and couldn't find Mother anywhere. It was just five days after my sister was told of the upcoming Colorado trip. When my father couldn't find Mother, he called my sister to see if she knew where Mom was. He stated that Mom was missing and he couldn't find her anywhere. Since my sister had no knowledge of where our mother could be, she told our father that she would be right there to help find Mom. My sister cannot express all of the thoughts that went through her mind as she drove to our parents' farm that morning. She was eight and a half months pregnant at the time, and not knowing what could have happened to Mom, she drove as fast as eighty miles an hour for the fifteen-mile drive. When she arrived at the farm, our father informed her that he had been told where our mother was. He stated that his brother had told him Mother was in a hospital's mental ward. Sometime that evening or early morning, while our mother was sleeping, she awakened to what sounded like gunshots again. This was the fourth time it happened. Our mother, being alone, became very fearful of what could happen to her. She grabbed a blanket and exited the house through the back door. She considered hiding in the concrete silo or the hayloft of the barn but thought it would be too easy to find her there. She eventually ran through the darkness to an old, abandoned car, located in a creek bed in our pasture. She felt if someone was actually trying to end her life, they would not find her out in that old, abandoned car. This was late October, and the temperatures became very cold after dark. Our mother spent the rest of the early-morning hours in that cold, old car, worrying about being found and killed. At daybreak, she saw the neighbor driving his pickup truck on the road by the pasture where she was hiding. So, Mother ran toward the road and waved to get the neighbor's attention. The neighbor saw her and stopped his vehicle to see what the problem was. Mother told him the story of what had happened to her. Not knowing what to do, the neighbor man asked if she wanted to go back to the farm, but she was fearful and not comfortable going back there. So, the neighbor took her to our father's younger brother's farm, and our father's younger brother contacted one of mother's brothers to help decide what needed to be done. They collectively made the decision to take our mother to the hospital.

Later that morning, his brother informed our father where Mother was located. Because Dad had not been around to ask what should be done, the decision had been made to take her to the hospital. Upon learning what had transpired, my father became extremely angry with his brother and brother-in-law for making the decision to take our mother to the hospital. Being alone and neglected by our father so much had caused Mother to suffer a nervous breakdown. She spent the next month in the hospital to recover. Later that day, my sister visited our mother in the hospital. She was feeling fine and could remember everything that happened to her in great detail. She was relieved to be in a place she considered safe and was happy to spend the next four weeks in the safety of the hospital.

Later that afternoon, my sister and father came to the college I was attending to inform me that Mother was in the hospital. When I was told of Mom's nervous breakdown, I was not surprised. I said that I was afraid something like that could happen to her, being alone on the farm so much. I knew that my mother had gone through a lot and shed tears for what had happened to her. My sister remembers that our father became extremely angry with me because I shed tears for her. The fact that he became so very angry with me hurt my sister, and she has never forgotten the look he had in his eyes at that time.

The so-called anniversary hunting trip was canceled, and when she got out of the hospital, our mother did not want to return to the farm and be alone again, fearing what could happen to her there. My father was required to attend Mother's sessions with her psychiatrist while she was in the hospital. Her doctor informed Dad that after Mother's release from the hospital, she was not to be left alone on the farm at night anymore. After my mother's release, my father did make a meaningless attempt to stay home more. But that lasted for a very short time, less than a week. My father's desire to regain his womanizing lifestyle caused him to take Mother to my sister's house each evening. Dad had to pick her up around midnight, and since he was picking her up much earlier than he wanted, this arrangement was not conducive to his desired lifestyle. In fact, it was a major impediment to Dad's nightlife, so he decided changes had to be made.

Having been told that he could not leave Mother alone on the farm, Dad decided it would be best if they sold the farm and moved into town. My mother's fear of being home alone at night caused her to agree with the sale of the farm. This decision was made quickly and quietly. Neither my sister nor I were ever consulted about the decision and were not aware of when the farm sale took place. After the farm sale was over, Mother informed my sister about the sale. I was away at college at the time of the sale and didn't learn about it until my sister told me. They held a farm sale to dispose of all of the farm equipment that was left, without my sister's or my knowledge. After I found out about our farm having been sold, I asked my mother why my sister and I were not consulted about it. She said that Dad didn't want us to know about it. My father had run up such a debt with his escapades that the money from the sale of the two-hundred-acre farm and the equipment only paid for the debt he had incurred over the years.

Once the farm was sold, my parents needed to buy a house in town. But after most of his debts were paid off with sale funds, my father had no interest in finding a house to purchase, so my sister went with Mother to look for a house to buy that would be suitable for them and that they could afford. When Mom and my sister found a house she liked, they went to the bank to secure a loan to purchase it. Unfortunately, my parents could not get a loan from any bank or loaning institution to buy the house. They did not have the money for a down payment or any collateral, so the institutions would not lend them the money to buy the house. The only option she had was for my mother to go to my father's wealthy uncle and request a loan from him to help with the purchase of this house. My great-uncle was well aware of my father's reputation and his irresponsibility in paying his bills. He had dealt with Dad before and required that he join Mother in the return visit. My great-uncle told my dad if it were not for my mother, he would not loan them the money. He made my father promise to make a payment from the family estate income, which was divided at the end of each year. My father agreed to his requirements, but after receiving the money and purchasing the house, Dad paid no attention to the promise he had made. In the seven years that he used this house as his home address, my father paid a total of $2,000 to his uncle, and that was during the first two years of the loan. Needless to say, my great-uncle was not happy with my father. He visited with his sister, my grandmother, many times regarding her son not paying his debt. Even though my mother was still living alone much of the time, she was living in a town with close neighbors, which helped her to feel more at ease. She was now living across town from her daughter's family and near the college I attended. Living that close to her children gave her some sense of security, and at the end of my first semester of college, which was only a month after my parents moved to town, I moved home to be around my mother at night, which helped her feel even more secure and comfortable.

CHAPTER 13

THE DECEPTION
EXPOSED

My father had always come home around four or five each morning. But as time went on, he stopped coming home on weekday mornings. He had taken a job driving a milk truck for a milk company in a large city twenty miles away. His milk route started early, about four thirty each morning, so his coming home at four or five in the morning didn't work any longer. He told Mother that he had rented a room in the larger city near the milk company he was working for, so he could make the milk route job work for him. From this time on, our father spent his weekdays and evenings somewhere other than his home.

Because of the new situation Mother found herself in, she became suspicious of what her husband was actually doing. To be able to handle the situation she was now facing, my mother went to a family practice doctor and expressed a desire to have a complete physical examination. With her husband being gone continually and not coming home weekdays, she expressed a desire to be tested for sexually transmitted diseases in case her suspicions were correct and her husband was being unfaithful to her. In the course of the visit, she asked the doctor how to find out if her husband was actually working for the KBI as an undercover agent. The doctor told her that he had some connections with the KBI and would check out the situation for her. On her next visit to the doctor's office, the doctor informed her that it was imperative for her physical and mental health that she get out of the relationship immediately. Maybe it was because of fear or maybe it was because of humiliation, but Mother could not bring herself to do it.

Mom would often lament over the fact that my father was hardly ever home. She questioned whether his work was actually the reason he was always gone from home. She was living a very lonely life again. She felt rejected and unwanted. One evening, when my wife and I went over to see her, she was depressed, unhappy, and dejected over a husband never being home. Who could blame her for feeling that way? She was physically and emotionally abused for thirty-two years of her life. I asked her if she really wanted to find out if what my father had been telling her was actually true. She said that she wanted to find out the truth about him, no matter where the results would lead. I told her that I would take her to find out where my father was staying and what he was doing. So, I loaded my wife and my mother into our car and drove to the larger city, twenty miles away, in hopes of locating where he was supposedly staying. The chance of finding where he was staying was very slim because he never gave my mother an address. Without too much to go on, I was going to give it my very best effort, for my mother.

I asked my mother for any information that would be helpful in finding him. She said that he had told her he rented a room in the north area of the city, so that he would have easy access to the milk company's truck that he drove on his milk route. I asked my mother if she knew where I could start looking for the place where he said he was staying. Since my father would never give her an address, she only knew of a general area to start looking for him. So, all we had to go on was a general location where he said he was staying. I planned to start looking near the bowling alley he frequented in that area of town. As I was driving to the bowling alley, I asked my mother if she knew where his milk route was located. She said she thought it was on the southwest side of the city. There was a small community just southwest of the city, so I changed my plans and started looking there. I thought that this small community would be the best option to start looking for my father. I drove to this very small town and stopped at the gas station located there. I thought by chance the man working in the gas station might be able to give me some information about my father. I stopped the car, told my mother and wife to stay in the car, and walked into the gas station. A man was standing behind the counter, and I asked if he could help me. He said, "I hope so." I asked the man if he knew my father. To my surprise, the man said that he knew him well. He claimed to see him on almost a daily basis. I couldn't believe it. The first place I stopped, someone knew him, and since this man knew my father, I thought there would be a good chance this man would know where my father might be living. Again, I was shocked that this man knew exactly where he was living. I really shouldn't have been so surprised because my father was a very social person. I asked him if he could give directions to where he was living. This man gave me the directions to a farm nearby.

As I drove to the farm, I realized that my father had been less than honest with my mother and unnecessarily caused her, my sister, and me to live our lives in fear for over twenty years. I knew that my father's deceptive scheme was about to be exposed. I followed the man's instructions and drove to the farm. I stopped on the road at the end of the driveway, turned off my headlights, and looked down the long driveway to the farmhouse. The lights were on in the house, and I realized that I had been to that very farm one time before.

Not long before this evening, my father had asked if I wanted to ride along on his milk route with him. I accepted his invitation, and for one day I rode with him. During our time together that day, my father told me that he had a boat he was not using. He informed me that I could use the boat for the summer if I wanted. My father said that the boat was stored in a garage on a farm nearby. After my father finished his milk route, we drove to this farm to see the boat. To my surprise, the old wooden boat was in usable condition. I was not expecting to see a usable boat. My father told me that an old farmer and his wife lived on this farm, and he rented the garage to store the boat. During the time that we were at the farm, my father acted very nervous. He kept looking at the house, and because of his nervousness, I thought that maybe this old couple actually owned the boat and he didn't want them to see me. He told me that he would bring the boat home sometime, and I could take it out for a spin. I figured it would be like all of the other promises my father made but never kept.

Now, as my mother, wife, and I sat on that rural road, looking at the house where my father was shacking up with a woman, I knew that I could not confront him by myself or with my mother and wife along. I was not sure how my father would react when his lie was exposed, especially with my mother along. I expected him to become very violent, and I was not willing to take the chance of him harming my wife or mother. I drove my mother and wife back to my mother's home. I knew that when my father returned home, my mother would not be able to remain silent about what we had found out, so I had my wife stay with my mother.

I called my sister, told her what had transpired, and asked her if she would go with me to confront my father about the lies he led us to believe for over twenty years. My sister agreed to go with me. So, I drove to her house, picked her up, and went back to the farm where my father was living. My sister and I walked to the house and knocked on the door. I was more than a little bit concerned about what might happen. After I knocked on the door, a woman opened the door, and we asked if our father was there. This woman said that he wasn't there at the time, but she expected him home any minute. My sister and I then asked if we could come in and talk to her. She said that we could, and we then quizzed the woman about our father's living arrangement. She explained that they had been living together for quite some time and that he only returned to his home on weekends to take care of what he said was business.

This woman claimed that Dad had told her our mother was in a mental institution and had been there for many years. He still was responsible for her care and needed to make sure her care was progressing fine. This woman also had her suspicions about my father and what he was doing. From the questions she asked us, I felt certain that she did not trust him either. Why should she? She basically snared him away from his wife for herself. With that history, if the pastures got a little greener somewhere else, so to speak, why wouldn't he dump her too? This women had questions about my father's attraction to Colorado. She asked us if we thought he might be having an affair with a woman living there. This woman's suspicions correlated with my father's planned anniversary trip, and things started to fall into place for my sister and me. We are convinced that our father planned on leaving our mother alone in some seedy motel for a week while he spent the week with this woman in Colorado. The woman, who Dad claimed to have been his partner in oil wells, had moved to Colorado a number of years earlier. My sister and I could not help thinking that it was actually possible that our father may have planned to terminate our mother's life while she was alone in that seedy motel. Otherwise, why would he take Mother along on that trip? With the type of person he was, who knows; maybe that was truly a part of his plan. With everything that had happened in the past, including gunshots and strangulation, our fears seemed well founded.

This visit with the woman he was now living with was very revealing. She informed us that she was taking care of our father and had been living as his wife. As we talked, she continued ironing his shirts. This mistress of his verified that all of his stories were nothing more than fabrications. Finding out that the person I was supposed to be able to trust had not been trustworthy was difficult for me to handle, even though I had suspicions about what he was telling us. I had a numb feeling inside, and this revelation hurt me greatly because our father had caused us to live with his falsehoods for all those years. I became angry, and it was probably a very good thing that Dad was not there at that moment. I am not sure how I would have reacted to him. Even though I feared what my father was capable of doing to us, if he had been there at that very moment, even though I am not a violent person, I do not know how I would have reacted. He callously put us in fear for our lives just so he could live the immoral life he desired, womanizing and spending the family's inheritance on his lustful entertainment.

Over the years, I learned to keep my feelings inside, and it is still very difficult for me to express my feelings to others as I am doing now in this book. As I saw it, my father had left us long ago, so I kept my feelings to myself and moved on with my life. I should have had a special feeling for my father, but I hadn't had a father during my growing-up years. He was never there for any of us, so I looked at him as just another person, with no special significance.

After talking to the woman, we returned to our mother's home and informed her how her husband had been unfaithful to her and had been pulling the wool over her eyes for years. Deep down inside, I do not believe it was a big shock to her. We discussed the situation with her and asked her what she wanted to do about it. She emphatically said that she wanted our father out of her house for good. With my father elsewhere most of the time, living alone would not be any different from how she had been living anyway. She knew her husband would never change his lifestyle and she would be far better without him in her life.

My sister and I were confident that when our father returned to the home where he was shacking up with the woman we confronted, she would address the situation with him. He would be told that my sister and I had been there and talked with his live-in promiscuous partner about the double life he was living. We were certain that as soon as our father found out that we had talked to his live-in mistress, he would return to our mother's home, and who knows what would happen. My sister and I had a deep concern for our mother's well-being. We did not want our mother to have to face our volatile father alone. We feared what he might do to her if she was there by herself and confronted him. I knew that he had attempted to strangle her at least three times before, so her being alone was out of the question. As we were discussing the possibilities of how we would proceed in protecting our mother, our father opened the front door and walked through the living room and into the kitchen where we were sitting at the kitchen table. This was only an hour or two after we returned to tell Mother about his infidelity. I saw that my mother feared him greatly because as he entered the kitchen, she moved quickly away from him to where my sister and I were sitting. Dad acted as if nothing was wrong, walked over to the stove, took a frying pan out of the bottom drawer of the stove, and acted like he was going to make something to eat.

My sister and I confronted him about the double life he was living and the pain he had put all of us through. Our statements about what he had put us through over the years and how we were affected didn't seem to concern him at all. He gave no excuse for what he was doing and did not apologize for what he had done to us. We asked Mother if she still wanted our father out of her house. She emphatically stated that he was no longer welcome in her home. So, we told our father that he would have to leave immediately and not return again. He reluctantly left the house without saying a word and returned to his mistress. To prevent him from returning at a later date and harming our mother when she was alone, we stayed with her that night and the next day changed all of the exterior door locks.

Eventually, my parents divorced, and since my father hadn't lived up to his agreement to pay off the house loan, my great-uncle threatened to take the home away from my family. Our father's siblings came to our rescue. They offered to help my sister and me pay our great-uncle the money he had loaned our parents. They told us we would need to use the family estate money each year to pay them back. My sister and I jumped at the chance to save the house for our mother and agreed to their terms. The debt balance was $11,000 of the $13,000 loan. Fortunately, the crop production was very good the next two years, and we were able to pay back the loan in that two-year period. Our father's relatives were instrumental in our being able to keep my mother's home and the inheritance that our great-uncle had given the family. Our uncles and aunts helping my sister and me this way was just one of the ways they showed that they cared about us. One of our aunts had given my sister the one and only birthday party she ever had. All of her classmates from school were invited to the party, and that party meant the world to my sister.

It is depressing to think about the amount of money that went through my father's hands over the years. Every year, the money from his family's estate crop production, the money made from the dairy farm, the oil well income, the money he obtained through mortgaging everything, most of the money my mother earned, and what I earned, he spent on himself and the women he was seeing. It is sad to think about his squandering all this money in light of the fact that we often didn't have enough money for food to eat or heat for our house. If my father had just lived a normal life, he could have become a very wealthy man.

At this same time, my father went to see my sister and informed her that he had made a seven-year mortgage on our one oil well. If my father had told my mother about his mortgaging the oil well, she didn't remember being told about it, and my sister and I had no knowledge of him mortgaging that oil well.

My father had signed a paper stating the oil income would pay off the loan, and if it didn't pay off the loan in the seven-year period, the oil well would become the property of the bank owner. The mortgage was just one week short of its duration when my father informed my sister of its existence. The banker was always more than happy to see my father come into the bank and ask for money. This bank owner fully expected to become the legal owner of the oil well. He knew that my father would never attempt to pay off the loan, and the mortgaged oil well would then be his. The amount of money left on the mortgage was $2,894.22 from a $12,000 loan. The oil checks had gone to pay for the debt for those seven years, which would have amounted to around $15,000, including interest. Of course, my father did not have the money to pay off the loan, or he wouldn't have come to us. Mother didn't have the money either. So that we could retain the monthly oil income, my sister and I had to come up with the $2,894.22 to pay off the loan.

The banker was not a happy camper when my sister and father walked into the bank the day we paid off the mortgage in full. He was shocked. My father's debts had never been paid off like that. He had to have his wife come to the bank and have her sign a document with him releasing the oil well back to us. He already had the oil well transferred into his ownership. I am thankful that our father remembered the loan's duration date and informed us of the loan's existence.

After my parents' divorce, my father's mother told him that he needed to marry his live-in mistress or move out if he still wanted to be considered a part of the family. My father could have never supported himself, so he had no choice but to get married. He thought this live-in woman was just what he needed for financial security. She had a great job, a nice savings account, and would have a nice pension after her retirement. My father felt that this woman would be able to support him, so he married her and spent the next twenty-some years living about an hour away from where my sister and I lived. Our limited relationship was merely tolerable and nothing more. He did invite us to his house for Thanksgiving and Christmas gatherings with our stepmother's family. So that my children knew who their grandfather was, my family attended many of those gatherings. These blended family get-togethers were never something my sister and I looked forward to attending. In fact, we were truly reluctant to attend those uncomfortable holiday events. They were meant to be cheery settings, but they only brought back many lonely and painful memories from past holidays. The gifts were abundant, unlike our Christmases growing up, and everyone went home with many presents. Our stepmother had four children and grandchildren from multiple marriages. Sometimes these holiday events made for a very large group, and the values and cultural differences made for an extremely awkward evening.

Soon after my paternal grandmother passed away, my father's wife retired from her job, and they moved two miles from the farm where I grew up. His mother left him money to buy this small farm. He stayed home, planted gardens, and raised livestock on that small farm. These activities were hard for my sister and I to watch him do. They were the things we longed for him to do when we were growing up. When Dad needed help with things, he would call and request our assistance. Even though our relationship with him was less than desirable, we always helped him. People may wonder why my sister and I would help him after all we had to endure because of him. My sister thinks that we would help our father with his needs because we secretly wanted a relationship with him that we never had, but the relationship we wanted never materialized. Maybe there is some truth in how she sees it.

My sister, who had a career in the health care field, felt an obligation to help with our father and stepmother's health care. I saw him as no different from any other sinful person, and I never held back helping other people based on their sinfulness. The Bible tells us in Ephesians 6:2 to "Honour thy father and mother; which is the first commandment with promise." This passage deals with the frame of mind of a child and what a child is to do concerning a parent. When a parent is like my father was, it is difficult to show honor to them since they are not a godly person. Yet the frame of mind of the child must be so that they recognize he or she is his or her parent. It does not mean that a child must tolerate abuse, reward evil, accept ungodly lifestyles, or give up hope of ever being treated nicely. It does mean that a child reacts to the situation in a godly manner. So, I helped my father when he needed help because he was my earthly father, and I would help any other person who needed my assistance as well.

Not only did our father not have a desirable relationship with his children, our father never developed a relationship with any of his grandchildren. He would make promises to them that he never intended to keep. He would promise to do things for them like take them fishing, but that would never happen. Not only did my sister and I feel rejected by our father, our children also felt rejected by their grandfather.

At this time in her life, our mother married again. Scriptural speaking, she was qualified to remarry, but my father was not. "He saith unto them, Moses because of the hardness of your hearts suffered you to put away your wives: but from the beginning it was not so. And I say unto you, Whosoever shall put away his wife, except it be for fornication, and shall marry another, committeth adultery: and whoso marrieth her which is put away doth commit adultery" (Matthew 19:8–9). My mother divorced my father because of my father's adultery. My mother was the innocent party in this divorce. The man my mother married was a wealthy widower who treated her well. She was able to do the things she had only dreamed about for years. Yet there were times when we knew the past still haunted her.

Time passed, and our parents aged. Our mother spent fourteen years living in a retirement home. Her husband passed away a few years after they moved into that retirement village. Before the move into the retirement village, our mother started demonstrating signs of dementia, forgetting where she had put things. The next ten years were challenging for her. Our mother would never admit that she was forgetting things or that her body was gradually deteriorating, even though she was well aware that she could no longer take proper care of herself.

At the age of ninety, she expressed a desire to move into the full health care part of the retirement facility, so that her every need would be provided for. She made the move, and the last five years of our mother's life were a carefree and happy time for her. She was always smiling and loved the food she was given. She played games such as Rook, Dominoes, and Bingo with other residents of the care facility where she was living.

My sister retired and spent a great deal of time with my mother, knowing I was occupied with caring for my wife, who at this time in her life faced serious medical issues and needed my assistance for her daily needs. My sister kept our mother informed about daily activities of both of our families. Either because of the dementia she was experiencing or by choice, our mother did not remember her years married to my father, nor was she sad about the past. My sister would read her some of the funny stories I had written about my life on the farm. They would laugh and have a great time talking about those incidents. One time they were laughing so loudly a nurse opened the door to make sure everyone was Okay.

One situation that brought about many laughs was when I delivered flowers to her for Mother's Day. She was concentrating on playing a game of dominoes and did not pay too much attention to the person who brought her the flowers. Without looking at me or losing her focus on the game, she thanked me and told me they were beautiful. Later that day, she asked the nurse who had brought the flowers. The nurse told her it was her son who brought the flowers to her. My mother became very stressed and made the nurse call me so she could apologize for not realizing who I was. She explained that she thought I was just a delivery boy. The minute my sister walked into her room, she told my sister what she had done. Upon hearing the story, my sister started laughing, which also caused our mother to laugh at the situation as well. So, after that incident, my sister would ask my mother if the delivery boy had been there. Our mother would laugh until the tears rolled down her face. She would reply, "Yes, he has been back to see me." When I would go to see her, I would walk into her room and say, "The delivery boy is here."

Another situation that I would tease my mother about had to do with fried chicken. My sister, her husband, my wife, and I took her out to eat for Sunday noon meals. She would always eat a chicken drumstick. One day, I filled my plate at the food bar and had a drumstick on it. When my sister went to fill our mother's plate, the drumsticks were all gone. I went back to the food bar for something, and when I returned, my drumstick was missing from my plate. My mother, however, had a half-eaten drumstick in her hand and a very big, guilty smile on her face.

My sister told me the only time she saw our mother sad during those years was when she informed Mom about my diagnosis of eye cancer. She would always ask my sister for the updates and was happy to hear things were going very well for me.

Our mother has now passed away. She passed away two days after my birthday. Even though my mother suffered from dementia, she always knew who my sister and I were. She was ninety-five years old when she fell and broke some bones. She developed pneumonia and was not able to recover from it. Our mother had been praying daily to go to her eternal home. She would question why she was still living at this old age. She lived ten years longer than her parents had and longer than all but one of her siblings. As my sister and I look back on our lives, we are so grateful for those peaceful years she had, and there is no adequate way to describe the love our mother had for us.

Watching my father age was quite different and very difficult for my sister in many ways. The last year of my father's life was inconceivable. My sister would visit him twice a week and tell me about those visits. While my sister was helping to care for him, when they were alone, he would share stories of his past that did not include us. Listening to these unfamiliar stories was heartbreaking for my sister. One of our father's stories was about the children of a friend of his. He stated that he did not know how many children his friend actually had because of his promiscuous life. While he was telling the story, my sister couldn't help thinking that he was actually talking about himself. My sister did say that one time our father said that he had some regrets. But hearing all his stories that didn't include us was extremely painful for my sister.

I am not sure why, but the times I visited my father, he and my stepmother portrayed everything as going extremely well for them, and they appeared to be living a happy life. But that was only a facade, an outward appearance that they maintained to conceal the less than pleasant life they were living together.

At the age of ninety-five, Dad landed in the hospital. He never totally recovered. He was no longer able to walk and was wheelchair bound. My sister requested that our stepmother consider having a home-care nursing situation to assist her. But our stepmother informed my sister in no uncertain terms that it would not happen. She would not be spending money for any home care. Soon after his return from the hospital, our father asked my sister to put him into a nursing home because his wife was mean and abusive to him. My sister made arrangements for him to go to a full-care facility and went to his home to discuss this situation with him and our stepmother. My sister was not expecting to face the reaction she received from our stepmother. She screamed at my sister, claiming that our father was mean to her and she was not going to use her money for his care. She also said, "You know how mean your father is. You know the terrible things he did to your mother." This statement of hers was puzzling, causing my sister to question and think carefully about what she had just said. Just how did our stepmother know what terrible things our father did to our mother? I doubt that our father told her about the terrible things he had done. So how did she come to know about them? It appears that the only way she would have known about them was through her involvement in the terrible things done to our mother. For her to have such firsthand knowledge about what was done to our mother makes my sister and me quite suspicious about her involvement.

From previous experience, my sister knew that they both had quick, abusive tempers and treated each other poorly. What my sister and I didn't know and still do not know is all of the terrible things our father did to our mother. We know of many terrible things, but not all! Before all this happened, we had no idea just how mean our stepmother could be. It didn't take long for my sister to learn our stepmother's true self. She was stunned by our stepmother's reaction, and my sister told our stepmother that she was only concerned about our father receiving proper health care since she was not physically able to properly care for him. When told of her inability to care for him, our stepmother looked at our father and asked him, "Do you think I will kill you?" Of course, our father replied, "No," which ended the conversation. Again, her question threw up red flags for us. Why was that particular question asked? What did caring for our father have to do with killing him?

A week later, my sister went to see our father again, and our stepmother stopped her on the back porch. She told my sister, "Your father will never ask you to take him to the nursing home again." She was correct about that. Our father never mentioned the full-care facility again. Everything that transpired in those two weeks brought back those gnawing, painful feelings for my sister. What did our stepmother hold over our father's head that he just accepted living in an inhumane condition? Just what caused him to change his mind, hand over all the financial business to her, and not talk about going into a health care facility again? My sister and I believe that our father did terrible things to our mother that we never knew about. And by our stepmother's questions and statements, we are convinced that more people than just our father planned the misery that our mother had to endure.

In the last year of our father's life, my sister repeatedly asked him if he thought he was dying. She stated that hospice care would be a good option, but he always said no. Then one day our stepmother called my sister and told her that she was unable to get Dad out of the bed. My sister went to their house and found our father in a fetal position at the foot of the bed, where he had laid for two days in very unsanitary conditions.

My sister called the ambulance, and they took him to the emergency room at the local hospital. While in the ER, a nurse asked if they had made arrangements for the nursing home. My sister replied, "No, but we need to do that." My father's wife screamed, "He is going home. He is not going to a nursing home!" She would not use her money or lose her house for him. My sister again told our stepmother that she was not able to care for him and he needed to go to the nursing home. They both would be healthier that way. At this point, our stepmother told my sister that if she forced this move, she would make my sister pay dearly for her interference, and my sister would regret getting involved.

Our father passed away in the hospital a few weeks after this emergency room incident happened. He passed away at ten o'clock in the morning, and we were not notified until noon. The funeral director did ask my sister and me to come to the funeral home the next afternoon to discuss our father's funeral service. My stepmother and her three daughters sat on one side of the table, while my sister and I sat on the opposite side of the table. There really wasn't what one would call a warm, fuzzy feeling in that room. The only input my sister and I had was in picking the scripture that the preacher would use for the funeral message. I believe this was because our stepmother and her daughters lacked enough biblical knowledge to be able to pick a scripture passage on the spur of the moment. When it came time to select the casket, our stepmother said she wanted to see the cheapest one they had. The funeral director went to a storage shed across the alley and brought back a brown tin casket. When our stepmother looked at the casket, she said, "That's good enough." Those were the last words my sister heard her say. As for me, I was not concerned about the casket that was used or about the funeral service. My father's funeral was just like any other person's funeral to me. I attend funerals for the living, not for the dead. I attended my father's funeral for my sister and my father's relatives.

My father's death was actually a big relief to my sister. Neither she nor I shed a tear. Even though my sister had taken care of all his and his wife's health care needs for his last twenty-five years, she felt no connection to him. That father-daughter relationship was gone. My sister had longed for the relationship she had with him the first five years of her life, but it was not to be. She realized that his wife's children felt closer to him and knew him better than his own children did.

Our father is gone, and the many secrets of his life have gone with him. How many half brothers and sisters do we actually have? How many women did he spend our inheritance on? Why were we never good enough for him? Why was his spiritual life not important to him? Those questions will never be answered.

I never really developed a relationship with my father and certainly had no desire to develop a relationship with my stepmother or her children. This woman knew what she had done. She knew that she had a big part in dismantling our family and did not concern herself about that fact. Because of the way my father spent money, I suspect that she thought there was money in his future through inheritance. I am confident that he had told her about his inheritance expectations, and he, no doubt, thought there was money in her future with her pension. As I see it, they both had selfish motives. Actions do have consequences, and I guess it could be said that they both faced the consequences of their actions.

CHAPTER 14

LIFE AFTER GRADUATION

After my graduation from a small Mennonite college, I began my teaching career as an industrial education teacher. Because I became a certified teacher, I could also coach high school sports. My first year of teaching was at a small, rural high school in a small, western Kansas town. That year, I coached basketball, football, and track.

My first day of teaching was a very eventful one and set the tone for the rest of that school year. During third hour of that day, I taught a drafting class to freshman students. Two of those students wanted to test the new teacher to see what they could get away with. Since these two students would not comply with my requests, I asked my principal if I had his permission to paddle a couple of boys who were disrespectful and uncooperative. He told me to go ahead and do it. He would support me 100 percent.

I took those two boys down into the shop room area and had them spread eagle with their hands on a shop table. Those boys were smiling at each other until I walked over to the wood rack and started looking through the pieces of lumber for a suitable paddle. The remaining students were watching through a large glass window to see if I would actually go through with it. The best piece of wood I found suitable for the punishment was a three-foot-long two-by-four. I did not want to hurt these students, so I gave them each one half a swat. The two boys looked at each other and smiled again. I knew that I would continue to have major problems with them if I didn't make the paddling a bit painful. So, I explained to them that the first swat was just the warm-up and they would receive the real one next. A very serious demeanor came over their faces as they anticipated the real swat. I gave them each one more swat, making sure that I hit only the soft area of their backsides. With that one swing, I lifted their heels up off of the floor. This punishment must have been effective since I never had another problem from them that school year. Word got around that it wasn't wise to mess with Mr. Graber. For the rest of that year, it was always "Yes, Mr. Graber, whatever you say, Mr. Graber," from every student in school. I enjoyed working with my students that year. My students didn't fear me, but they knew the limits of what was acceptable behavior in my classroom.

At the end of the school year, the two students who I had paddled on the first day of school told me just how effective that swat really was. After a track practice, the two students asked if I remembered paddling them on the first day of school. Of course I remembered and said that I did. They told me that the one swat I gave them stung so badly that they were unable to sit down for the rest of the school day without it stinging. I asked them what they did in their other classes that day. They explained that they asked each of their teachers to allow them to stand during their classes, and they ate their lunches standing up as well. From that conversation, I realized that to change student behavior, the punishment for the unacceptable behavior has to be severe enough so that the student does not want to face the punishment again. People may think that swatting these students was an unacceptable form of discipline. However, that one swat altered student behavior for those students as well as for the other students in school who heard about the incident.

Abuse is definitely unacceptable, but one well-placed swat is not abuse. It is definitely an attention grabber and a deterrent for other unacceptable behaviors. Those two students became what I considered friends. A few years later, as I was scouting a football team we were going to play the next week, one of these two students lived in that town, and when he saw me, he came over to sit with me and introduced his family to me. I am sure that he informed his children that I was the teacher who paddled his backside when he was a freshman in high school. Any discipline not severe enough to cause one not to want to face the discipline again is ineffective discipline. Disrespect and noncooperation will raise their ugly heads, and we've seen enough of that in our school systems. Proverbs 13:24 is correct: "He that spareth his rod hateth his son: but he that loveth him chasteneth him betimes." Parents and school administrators need to learn from this particular scripture passage.

I had one more discipline experience during my first year of teaching with two junior students. A few weeks after the paddling incident, two junior boys thought it would be funny to weld unacceptable words on the welding tables. When I found the words welded into the tables, I inquired about who needed a vocabulary education as far as acceptable and unacceptable word usage in my classes. To their credit, these two boys owned up to their actions. They did not want the entire class to pay a price for their inappropriate deeds.

I am quite sure that these two students thought a paddling was in their future. But instead, I gave them a handheld grinder and told them that during each day's class period, they would be hand grinding off the words they created on the welding tables. They would use the grinder until I could not see their handiwork any longer. Grinding off numerous metal welds is not an easy task to perform, especially when it has to be done to my satisfaction. It took those two students three days of hand grinding to get the welding tables to my specifications. These students told me that their arms got so tired they could barely lift them the rest of those school days. Again, the punishment for unacceptable behavior must be severe enough that they do not want to face it again. To this day, one of those students is one of my best friends.

I taught at this school for one year, and near the end of that school year, my wife's father suffered a debilitating heart attack. Her mother needed assistance with taking care of him, so my wife drove sixty miles each Monday and returned home each Friday evening until the end of the school year to assist her mother with her father's care.

About a month before the school year ended, a teaching opportunity opened in my wife's hometown, the same town where my mother was living. I applied for the position, and after my face-to-face interview, I was offered the teaching position. I accepted the teaching and coaching job contingent upon my being released on my continuing contract with my first school district. I requested a hardship release from the next year's contract with my present school district. I looked for a replacement for my position to assist the school district and found a teacher in my area. I was granted my release, and we were able to move back to my wife's home community and closer to my mother. My wife continued assisting her mother with the care of her father.

I taught at this new school for the next twenty-nine years and coached basketball for forty years. I coached football for only a few years at this second school. Cold weather and the verbal abuse I received from some of the other football coaches caused me to give up coaching football. I was ridiculed for my conservative Christian beliefs, and during coaches' meetings, I was asked where my Bible was. I loved coaching basketball and did not see any reason to subject myself to being mocked for my beliefs. Thus, I ended my football-coaching career.

At this second school, it was explained that I was not to touch a student during discipline procedures. I became innovative, and students were disciplined by having them clean the restrooms next to my classroom to my specifications. They scrubbed walls and floors, urinals and toilet stools until I said that they were clean enough. The restrooms were never clean enough the first or second time they asked me to check for cleanliness. After health issue scares in foreign countries, I had to change my discipline procedures. Student discipline changed to cleaning classroom hand-washing sinks with toothbrushes. During the school day, grease, oil, paint, stains, and more would somehow end up on the hand-wash sinks. A couple of days of scrubbing dried paint and stains off of a wash sink with a toothbrush corrected unacceptable behavior. The student would much rather behave in class and do their work than spend a few days scrubbing paint off of sinks with toothbrushes.

Students would often sit inappropriately in their classroom chairs. They would tip the chairs back, and if done often enough, the chair's welds would break. So, to prevent chairs from being destroyed and teach the students that there is a proper way to sit in a chair, the students would stand and hold their chair. Holding their chair during the time instructions were being given or during lectures could cause arms to become extremely tired. Again, the punishment must be severe enough to discourage unacceptable behavior. It is a proven fact that repetition is the best teacher, so chairs were held every time sitting in them was inappropriate. It did not take too long for students to sit properly in my classroom.

When students would talk in a foreign language to each other in class, I spoke to them in the Swiss-Deutsch dialect. They didn't appreciate getting instructions in a language they didn't understand, and I didn't appreciate their conversations in a language I didn't understand. I calmly would explain to them that when they spoke English in my class, I would give them instructions in English. Otherwise, they best learn my Swiss-Deutsch dialect. That was a very effective way to have all of my students speak only English in my classes.

The first few days of a school year are extremely important. Rules and regulations are established during those days. To grab my students' attention, on the first day of school, I used what my early grade school teachers taught me to do. I was able to use both hands equally well. I would put a piece of chalk in each hand and proceed to write my name on the chalkboard. What made me different from other teachers was that I wrote my name with both hands at the same time. That activity was a very effective way of getting my students' attention. They always wanted to know how I could write my name with both hands at the same time and make the handwriting look the same. Of course, they would then try to duplicate what I had just done. I had made it look relatively easy to do, but as they tried to accomplish the task, they realized that it was not as easy to do as I made it look.

My father's reputation has followed me throughout the years, and I face it even today. While I was teaching at this second school, a group of teachers from a school thirty miles away came to see our school and how we did things. One of those visiting teachers attended the same Mennonite church I attended as I grew up. He was a number of years older than I, and during his visit to the school where I taught, he refused to come into my classroom even though I taught the same classes he taught at his school. When asked by another teacher, who taught next door to me, why he would not come into my classroom, this visiting teacher stated that it was because I was the son of my father. He didn't really know me or what kind of person I was. He just concluded that since I was my father's son, I was just like him, and he wanted nothing to do with me. This rejection by this visiting teacher was par for the course throughout my life.

This same group of teachers came back for a second visit. This same man again visited the teacher who taught next door to me. My next-door teacher encouraged this visiting teacher to come into my classroom, because I had some pretty neat things happening in my room. He again refused. But this time my neighboring teacher explained to him that I was nothing like my father. He eventually convinced this visiting teacher to come into my classroom. After visiting with me and my classroom, I am confident that this teacher left with a different mindset about what I was like. Unfortunately, there are still so many other people from my home community who feel like this man first felt.

CHAPTER 15

OTHER FIRES
TO FACE

Life is hard, and trying times will undoubtedly come our way. What is really important is how we handle those times. We can face our problems head-on, we can sulk and blame others for the problems we face, or we can blame God. Blaming God and blaming others for the tough times we face are not good options. Facing our problems head-on with God's help is the only effective way to rise above those trying times.

Over the years, God prepared me to face difficult times through the tough times I faced because of my father. In 2011, my wife had back surgery. It was to be a very quick recovery period, and she was to be able to return to work in less than one week after the surgery. However, things didn't happen as expected. After the surgery, my wife developed a spinal leak and was admitted back into the hospital to stop the leak surgically. She had four more surgeries within a month just to try to stop the leak.

While in the hospital recovering from her last surgery, she developed blood clots in her legs. These blood clots moved from her legs to her lungs. This was a very serious situation. Blood clots moving to the lungs can cut off the airways and bring about sudden death. She was fortunate that the clots didn't close off any critical airways. But she had to have a wire filter put into her vein to prevent more clots from moving to her lungs and received a blood thinner to prevent more clotting and dissolve the existing clots. After the blood clot situation passed, she developed spinal meningitis. The spinal meningitis infection almost took her life. She was in the critical care unit of the hospital for five weeks. The spinal meningitis along with the blood clots, spinal leak surgeries, and anesthetics were very hard on her. The total time she was in the hospital for a surgery that was to have a short recovery time lasted from the first of June to the end of October that year. During that time, I became very familiar with the hospital reclining chairs. I slept in them each evening for those five months. The doctors encouraged me to place her in a full-care facility, because she would need constant help for a period of time. My wife wanted to go home, and I decided to take her home and care for her myself. For the first few weeks, I had to take care of all of her needs, but as time has gone by, she is now able to care for most of her daily needs. My wife has come a long way in her recovery yet still suffers some medical problems resulting from that back surgery, anesthesia, spinal meningitis, and all of the complications that followed.

Daily, she is dealing with back and leg pain, three leaky heart valves, abnormally low oxygen levels, blood pressure issues, cholesterol problems, partial heart artery blockage, partial neck vein blockage, and memory issues. Even though she is facing numerous health issues, I am thankful to God that she has recovered to the point she has.

In November 2015, after forty-two years of coaching basketball in the town where we lived, I had to give up coaching the game I loved. I was diagnosed with a melanoma on the back of one of my eyes and around my optic nerve. My local optometrist saved my life. During a routine yearly eye examination, he found the melanoma and referred me to an ophthalmologist, who diagnosed it as a melanoma. The ophthalmologist referred me to an eye specialist in Tennessee. My choices were to have my eye removed or to try a fairly new radiation procedure. I chose to try to save my eye. The eye specialist placed a radiation patch between the membrane layers of my eye at the back of my eyeball and around my optic nerve. I had to have that radioactive patch between the layers of my eye and around my optic nerve for one week. During that time, I was highly radioactive and had to stay away from people. My wife and I were able to stay in the Cancer Society's Lodge during that time. The radiation patch was so strong that I probably glowed green like the Hulk at night. At the end of that one week, the radiation patch was removed, and I was able to go home. Part of the cancer treatment had to be done during the basketball season each year, making it impossible for me to return to doing what I love to do, coaching basketball. I guess God thought I had coached it long enough and wanted me to see how I would handle the situation I was facing. Three years later, I coached my granddaughter's nine- and ten-year-old girls' recreation team. The team started out very inexperienced but by the end of the season was fairly proficient at the game. They finished the year as the recreation commission's tournament champions.

God has blessed me in so many ways. Since that eye radiation treatment, my melanoma has been reduced from the size of 3.8 to 0.0 cm. This happened in just one and a half years. The eye specialist told me that the radiation destroyed the cancer's defense mechanism, and my immune system was at work destroying what was left of the cancer cells. The radiation had also changed the cancer's DNA, so it was no longer able to send out cancer cells to other parts of my body.

The optometrist, ophthalmologist, and eye specialist have told me that they have never seen an eye respond to treatment as well as mine has. I had twenty-twenty vision in both eyes, with my glasses. Now, more than four years after the eye treatment, I have some radiation scarring on the back of my eyeball affecting the blood vessels located there. I am now having monthly eye injections to stop the radiation scarring and blood vessel deterioration. It seems to be helping, and my vision in that eye is improving. I am told that if cancer cells from my eye spread, the lungs and liver are the areas where the cancer would go. So, I have full abdominal body CT scans every six months to monitor any possible cancer development.

Since my cancer diagnosis, my CT scans, chest x-rays, and blood work have been normal. I, however, did develop a left lung problem. I experienced a severe pain in my left lung twice, a month apart. I have had numerous chest x-rays, a sonogram, another CT, and powerful antibiotics. The lung problem must have been a pneumonia-type infection both times because the powerful antibiotic did its job, and things have cleared up. A pulmonologist prescribed an inhaler to help prevent pneumonia from happening again. I also had to take pneumonia-prevention shots.

Unfortunately, about one month after my eye cancer procedure, my daughter-in-law was diagnosed with a cancerous brain tumor. It was four weeks after giving birth to her fifth son and our seventh grandchild. Two days after having an MRI that showed a tumor in her brain, the tumor was removed. She underwent radiation and has completed one and a half years of chemotherapy. Her outlook on life is exemplary. She faces each day feeling blessed that God has given her another day with her family and opportunities to bring others to Christ. She is an example and an inspiration to all who know her.

I have God to thank for the health improvements of my wife, my daughter-in-law, and myself. The prayers offered on our behalf and the God-given abilities of those who administered to us in our time of need have made a difference in the improvement of our physical health. God is truly a great, loving, and merciful heavenly Father.

CHAPTER 16

THE CHOICES
WE MAKE

Every person makes numerous daily decisions, and these decisions greatly affect the direction our lives will take and what kind of people we will become. The path we choose will forever affect the lives of others. The type of people we choose to associate with is often an indication of what our own character has become. The wrong choices in our affiliations can morally destroy us. So, the type of person we become is the direct result of the choices we make. I live my life by the choices I make, and my family is affected by them in either positive or negative ways. As I have stated, my father chose to live his life without concern for how his choices affected his family. He chose to associate with the type of people who took him down the path of moral debauchery, which taught him to enjoy a carnal, materialistic, and nonspiritual lifestyle. His selfish, immoral, and secular choices caused my mother, sister, and me physical and emotional pain.

We all face adversities, some more severe than others. When adversity comes our way, we can become bitter about what we have to face and use that difficult situation as an excuse to go down a wrong path in life, or we can rise above those hurtful situations, even when we have experienced a rough childhood with suffering and turmoil, as I did.

Unfortunately, when bad things happen in our lives, we often place the blame on other people and how they have treated us, on poor home lives, on tough situations we have previously faced, or most often on God. But God does not cause bad thing to happen to us. He is there with us, to help us through those tough situations when they happen to us. In spite of what we have had to face in the past, we are the only ones responsible for the choices we make in life. We are the ones who enslave ourselves, refusing to let go of the past and move on. Instead of making the necessary changes in our lives, we continue down the same path, trying to justify our sin.

Sin leads to spiritual death and a separation from God. He no longer hears our prayers. Isaiah 59:2 tells us, "But your iniquities have separated between you and your God, and your sins have hid his face from you, that he will not hear."

If you feel that you have had a tough home life, I totally understand your feelings because I also feel that my home life was tough. I know what childhood trauma and suffering can do to a person. But the choice of whether we are a victim or a conqueror is totally up to each of us.

No one can change their past. It is done and over with, but each and every person can change the present and their future by making good choices. In 1 Corinthians 6:11, Paul reminds us that we have the ability to change the direction of our lives no matter what our past was like. In verse 11, Paul points out their sinful past behaviors and then tells them, "And such were some of you." The word *were* is an important word here. These people had left their past behind and did not allow their past to define who they would become. These people made the choice to change the present and future direction of their lives.

Life changes require self-control. Proverbs 25:28 says, "He that hath no rule over his own spirit is like a city that is broken down, and without walls." Self-control involves managing behavior, thinking, and emotions. For our benefit, the Bible gives us examples of two men who made poor choices, but one of these men chose to repent and change the direction his life would take. We read that a man named Peter, while warming himself around a fire, cursed and denied knowing Jesus three times. The second man was with Jesus during His three-year earthly ministry. Yet this man named Judas betrayed

Jesus for thirty pieces of silver. The difference between the two men was not that one committed a more severe sin than the other. What was different was what each man did after he realized he had sinned. We see Peter weeping bitterly, repenting, and eventually preaching the first Gospel sermon in Jerusalem, on the day of Pentecost, recorded in Acts chapter 2 . Peter put his past behind him and chose to live a godly life. Judas, instead of repenting and changing his life, hung himself. The choices we make are so important.

In spite of one's background or what one has had to face and overcome in life, one does not have to feel unfortunate or deprived. Far too often, we choose to see ourselves as deprived and underprivileged instead of blessed. We need to stop looking at ourselves as disadvantaged, underprivileged, poverty-stricken, and deprived, no matter what we face or perceive others to have.

Our society has become so concerned with the privilege of others, whether it is skin tone privilege, gender privilege, financial privilege, or some other privilege. Many people perceive others to be more advantaged than they are because of something they see as beyond their control. They understand that privilege is advantage. But what they do not understand is privilege or advantage is freely available to each and every person. The real privilege in life is not a skin tone privilege, gender privilege, or financial privilege. The real privilege or advantage in life is in being a Christian, a follower of Jesus Christ. There is no privilege greater than being a true follower of Jesus Christ, obedient to God's plan of salvation, and living according to the scriptures. Christians are truly the advantaged people, and every person can choose to be privileged.

It is unfortunate that many people do not understand that every person is important. People often attempt to make others feel guilty or inferior and strive to divide us with skin tone, gender, financial position, and so on. There is only one race of people in our world. It is called the human race. And there are only two genders that God created. They are male and female.

We may not realize that being obsessed with skin tone, gender, financial status, or some other difference can actually be categorized as envy and covetousness, and they are not good qualities to possess. Envy is nothing less than having a feeling of ill will toward another person or group of people who are perceived to have more privilege or advantage than we do. Covetousness is simply a strong desire to have that which belongs to someone else. In other words, we want what we see or perceive someone else has; we want it for ourselves so they cannot have it.

The scriptures tell us in Hebrews 13:5, "Let your conversation (conduct, life, behavior) be without covetousness (desire for advantage or of having more); and be content (satisfied) with such things as ye have: for he hath said, I will never leave thee, nor forsake thee." 1 Timothy 6:7–8 says, "For we brought nothing into this world, and it is certain we can carry nothing out. And having food and raiment let us be therewith content." So, we need to stop concerning ourselves with privileges we see others having and start to live our lives as God wants us to live. It does absolutely no good for anyone to think of him or herself as a godly person and not live as God wants them to live. God has given each of us only one life to live. The question then is, how are we going to live it? What will consume our time, thinking, and energies? What are we doing with the one life God has given us to live?

Everyone is born with a sufficient knowledge of what is morally right and wrong. God has put His moral law in our minds by virtue of being created in God's image. Children inwardly know that certain things are wrong, like stealing, lying, and killing, but unless those unsavory things are reinforced as being wrong, as they grow, children will choose to disregard that inborn knowledge.

Children who are never held accountable for their choices and actions will go through their lives thinking that they are special; nothing is ever their fault; the world revolves around them; and they believe that the world owes them everything. They need to understand that it is always wrong to do a wrong thing and never wrong to do a right thing. When we do what is right, our influence attracts people to us and gives us the opportunity to impact their lives.

When adults marry and choose to have children, they have chosen the responsibilities and consequences that go along with raising children in a loving, caring environment. Regrettably, like my father, far too often, parents disregard those responsibilities and consequences.

When unmarried individuals choose to participate in activities that result in pregnancies, they have chosen the consequences and responsibilities that go along with their decisions. It is unfortunate that many adults selfishly shirk those responsibilities and ignore the consequences of their actions. In making those choices, they often do not value the sanctity of human life and are merely encouraging moral decay. When individuals choose to live unnatural, alternative lifestyles, they have chosen to face the consequences and responsibilities that go along with their choices.

We either choose to be right in God's eyes or unacceptable to Him. There is no middle ground or gray area in this. I made my choices and chose to follow Jesus Christ and His teachings and to live my life obedient to God's will. I did not allow my father, his actions, or my community's expectations of me to determine how my life progressed. The consequence of living a godly life was so much better than the consequence of living an ungodly life.

Each day, we are given another day to live to the fullest extent and influence the lives of others for the better. We can make a difference in the lives of those we come in contact with or we can be a self-absorbed person, seeing only what we want to see. All lives are equally important, and we need to strive to touch the hearts of people in positive ways. In so doing, we will put smiles on faces instead of frowns or feelings of sadness or misery and show that we truly care.

Everyone chooses how his/her day begins and progresses. No one should allow others to make this choice for them. Every morning, each of us should make a conscious effort to approach that day happy—never sad, miserable, dejected, dissatisfied, or feeling unfortunate. It is important that each of us wakes up each morning grateful for the blessings God has given us, no matter what kind of situation we are facing.

My sister and I have always felt that our home community never accepted us, but neither of us allowed that feeling of rejection to hinder or dictate the direction our lives would take. We could have felt that other children were more privileged or advantaged than we were because of the way our father treated us and lived his life. If we had felt that way, we would have been guilty of envy. Instead, we chose to use that feeling of rejection and others' expectations of us to motivate us. So, without actually intending to do so, it can be said that my home community helped me make the choices I made. They unknowingly nudged me to rebel against their treatment and expectations. I chose to prove them wrong, rather than prove them right. I dismissed the poor treatment, the criticism, and others' expectations. I chose to "fight the good fight of faith, lay hold on eternal life, whereunto thou art also called, and hast professed a good profession before many witnesses" (1 Timothy 6:12). A person either dwells on the situations they are forced to face in life or they rise above them. Each of us needs to heed the apostle Paul in Philippians 4:11: "Not that I speak in respect of want: for I have learned, in whatsoever state I am, therewith to be content." This doesn't mean that I do not work to improve my situation in life. I put my trust in the God of the Bible, and with His help, anything is possible.

I read somewhere that we all have the freedom to choose whatever we want to do or be, but we are never free from the consequences of our choices. This is so true! We have personal responsibilities for the choices we make. We can be forgiven for the bad things we do, but being forgiven does not mean we are free from the consequences that go with our choices. Our society has lost this concept of personal responsibility, personal accountability, and negative consequences for undesirable actions. Choices having consequences is a very important concept that needs to be taught to every generation's young people. We all need to learn to consider the possible consequences of our choices before we do anything. Are we doing the right thing, are we living each day as God wants us to live, and are our choices worth the consequences we will face?

When Dad made his choices in life, he never considered the consequences that would result. Because of his choices, my sister, mother, and I suffered.

My home life certainly was a far cry from exemplary. Granted, I had one parent who cared. But the life I lived was strictly my own choice, and how it turned out is totally my responsibility. Ezekiel 18:20 tells us, "The soul that sinneth, it shall die. The son shall not bear the iniquity of the father, neither shall the father bear the iniquity of the son: the righteousness of the righteous shall be upon him, and the wickedness of the wicked shall be upon him." Parents' sins do not fall on their children, so don't expect children to be like their parents. Help them to be productive, successful people.

A person's character is developed during the hard times and not when times are good. My father's lifestyle and poor reputation followed me throughout my life. He had a violent temper, a major problem with telling the truth, and lived an adulterous lifestyle. When I was doing my student teaching at the high school where I had graduated, my former English teacher could not believe that I turned out as I had. She did not expect me to be what she considered a quality person because of who my father was. She asked me, "How did you turned out as you have with such a home life as you had?" Many other people have felt the same way she did. My answer to my former teacher's question was each person makes their own choice in the direction they want their life to go. I chose my direction in life, which happened to be opposite of my former teacher's expectations of me.

During my teaching career, I saw the reflection of myself in the attitude and approach to learning in some of my students. They did not put much effort into their approach to learning in my classroom, and I would tell them that I was concerned. They needed to make some changes to their approach to learning, or I could not see them as becoming successful people.

Some of them were facing tough home lives, and I saw them making poor choices. The good thing about these young people is that many of them eventually made changes. I was always thrilled to hear that they had become very successful people.

I was and still am one of those people who is not good at accepting or asking for anyone's help. I became so accustomed to being my mother's helper around the farm and not letting other people know what I needed that I never learned how to accept or receive help from others. It can be said that there was a huge discrepancy between my giving of and accepting help. As I dealt with my life situations, I figured things out for myself. There were no other options for me. No one was there to teach me how to accept help from other people. Self-reliance is all that I ever knew. It was and still is difficult for me to ask for or accept help but easy to step in and do for others. My instincts have always been to give the help other people need when they need it. This self-reliance was at times very beneficial for me, because I never looked for others to do the work I was capable of doing myself. The negative aspect of my self-reliance is that I often did not allow people to experience the blessing that comes from doing things for me. I once was told by a dear friend, when I needed help and wouldn't freely accept it, something that has stayed with me, and

I have used his comment a number of times myself. He said, "Are you going to deprive me of my Christian duty?" How do you answer that? You can't say no to anyone, or you are depriving them of their Christian duty.

I read a story somewhere about twin boys growing up in the same home with an alcoholic father. One twin became an alcoholic just like his father, and the other twin never drank a drop of an alcoholic beverage. When asked why they turned out as they had, both twins replied, "I watched my father." The twins had exactly the same environment but had different ways of seeing their situation and how they chose to be.

One's perspective in life will determine one's actions, beliefs, morals, integrity, and character. Bible scripture informs us that we will be known by our "fruits," by our words and actions. "Ye shall know them by their fruits. Do men gather grapes of thorns, or figs of thistles? Even so every good tree bringeth forth good fruit; but a corrupt tree bringeth forth evil fruit. A good tree cannot bring forth evil fruit, neither can a corrupt tree bring forth good fruit. Every tree that bringeth not forth good fruit is hewn down, and cast into the fire. Wherefore by their fruits ye shall know them" (Matthew 7:16–20).

We are either like trees planted by a source of water or like trees planted where no water source is present. "And he shall be like a tree planted by the rivers of water, that bringeth forth his fruit in his season; his leaf also shall not wither; and whatsoever he doeth shall prosper" (Psalm 1:3). We either bear fruit in our lives or we are barren, unproductive, and useless, failing to achieve the desired results or outcomes.

My family has always been immensely important to me, and during some of our family time when my children got old enough, I would take them fishing at a pond in our sandhill pasture. I wanted my children to experience the joy of fishing, just as I had during my growing-up years. Fishing was the only time I can remember having what could possibly resemble a kind of quality time with my father. My son was like me and learned to love going fishing together. He caught his first fish at three years of age. He had a tiny little fishing pole with a small hook on his line. He placed this baited hook about six inches from the bank of the pond. At three years of age, his patience in watching for a fish to bite the baited hook was lacking. He would play in the water at the edge of the pond, trying to catch little frogs and tadpoles. The important thing was not catching fish; it was the time we spent together. While he would be playing at the bank of the pond, fish would often pluck the bait off of his hook.

One evening while my son was playing along the bank of the pond, all that was left of his bait was the head of a minnow. Even with only this tiny bit of bait left on his hook, a fish bit on that dead minnow's head. I was fishing about ten yards away from where my son was playing. I continually kept my eye on him, and one time when I looked at him, he had his tiny fishing pole in his hands, and a fish was pulling him into the water. I sprinted to him, grabbed him, and then grabbed the pole while he reeled his first catch into the bank of the pond. That very first fish he caught in his life was a five-pound channel catfish. From that moment on, he had permanent fishing fever, which he has passed on to his children. The desirable aspect of all this was that both he and my daughter were able to spend quality time with me.

My daughter also loved to go fishing. When the fish were not biting well, she would use her baited hook to catch musk turtles at the edge of the pond. One day, she caught what I remember as forty, but my son says she caught sixty-one of those turtles in a couple of hours of fishing. Musk turtles are an endangered species, except in our pasture pond, and we wanted to preserve them. We just didn't want any of those turtles eating the fish in the pond where we enjoyed fishing. So, we took all of them to a river one and a half miles away from the pond to dispose of them. We released all of those turtles into that river, which made for an interesting sight, seeing all forty or sixty-one turtles floating down the river in one place at one time.

A few years after my son caught his first fish, he caught a very small carp about the size of a goldfish. My sister and her husband had a small goldfish pond in their backyard. I asked my young son if he wanted to take the little carp and play a joke on his uncle. Of course, he thought that would be a great idea. So, we took the little dark carp and put it into his uncle and aunt's goldfish pond. When his uncle went to feed the fish the next morning, he saw the orange goldfish swimming around with something dark that wasn't supposed to be there. My son's uncle became excited and ran into the house to inform my sister that there was something dark in the goldfish pond that shouldn't be there. My sister went to check out this strange creature that her husband saw in their pond. When she saw the creature, she recognized it immediately as a small carp. The thing that puzzled them was how did this carp get into their pond? My brother-in-law first thought that a bird possibly dropped this little fish into their small pond. My sister and her husband eventually ruled out all possibilities except someone was pranking them by placing this little fish in their pond. They proceeded to try to find out which of their friends had done this to them. It took them quite a while to figure out who had pranked them. About six months after the incident happened, I asked my sister how her fish pond was doing. She told me the story about what had happened. After she saw me smiling, she realized who had pranked them. She then began to tell me about a story concerning their rain gauge.

At the same time we put the little carp into the fish pond, my son and I filled my sister and her husband's rain gauge with water. It was a rather large rain gauge, which held up to five inches of water. It happened that the next day it rained a small amount, and when my brother-in-law went out to see how much it had rained, to his surprise, his rain gauge showed five inches of rain had fallen. After telling a lot of people about the amount of rain he received at his house, he came to the realization that he was a recipient of a prank. No one else, even his neighbors, had received more than one quarter of an inch of rain. As I was laughing, my sister realized it was me and my son who had pranked them again.

Quality fishing time with my son, at times, was exciting. When my son was thirteen years old, he caught thirty-eight large-mouth bass in less than two hours. He used two fishing poles, and for those two hours, all I did was bait the hooks and take the fish off of the hooks to release them. Now, when I take my grandchildren fishing, all I do is bait their hooks and take the fish off of the hooks to release them. Sometimes we do keep enough fish for a meal. What is important is the time we spend together.

When my son was young, he had a very soft heart for animals. One evening, when we were driving home after spending time fishing, I accidentally drove over a cottontail rabbit that ran in front of our pickup truck. Being so softhearted, my son requested that I stop the pickup, back it up to where the dead rabbit lay, get out of the pickup, walk over to the dead rabbit, kneel down, and apologize to the rabbit for accidentally driving over him. Since that was what my son wanted done, that's what I chose to do. I wanted my son to know that his feelings were important to me.

God has given us the responsibility of working with the souls of our children, and we are to teach and cherish them. Ephesians 6:4 gives us the responsibility of raising our children correctly. There it says, "And, ye fathers, provoke not your children to wrath: but bring them up in the nurture and admonition of the Lord."

CHAPTER 17

PROFESSIONAL TIPS, HINTS, AND POINTERS

As I see it, since the mid-1960s, there has progressively become a lack of respect for human life and for those in authoritative positions. Terminating the innocent unborn child's life has become acceptable, OK to do, while the death of an animal or bird is considered an atrocity. We, as a people, are losing, if we have not already lost, the respect for human life, and I cannot imagine that the God of heaven is pleased with our society. Proverbs 6:16–19 tells us that God hates the shedding of innocent blood, and nothing can be more innocent than the unborn child. "These six things doth the Lord hate: yea, seven are an abomination unto him: A proud look, a lying tongue, and hands that shed innocent blood, An heart that deviseth wicked imaginations, feet that be swift in running to mischief, A false witness that speaketh lies, and he that soweth discord among brethren." Police officers are shot and killed in what seems to be daily. It is hard for me to understand, but there are actually people who consider that as acceptable.

As a teacher, I experienced student disrespect. An example of the lack of respect for authority occurred after I retired from teaching and while still coaching basketball and substitute teaching for the school district. One day as I was talking with a female teacher during the classroom passing period, a student walked by this teacher and me. The student had the hood of his hoodie pulled up over his head, which was against the school rules. This female teacher asked the student politely to remove his hoodie three times, but the student ignored her requests and walked into the main office at the school building. I looked at the teacher and said, "I'll be right back." The teacher knew exactly what was about to occur. I followed that student into the main office of the school building, and we had a ten-minute discussion about respect for those in authority and following school rules. During our discussion time, that student used an unacceptable word, at least ten times, in referring to me. The discussion ended with our faces a few inches apart and my explaining to this disrespectful student that it would be in his best interest for him to remove his hood from his head on his own, or I would remove it for him. He tried to explain to me that I could not touch him, but I clarified in no uncertain terms that I would be removing the hood from his head if he did not remove it himself. At that point in our discussion, the student realized that I meant every word I said, and when I would remove his hood, he wouldn't like the way it would be done. So, not to have me remove his hood in a way that he didn't like, he removed his hood himself. At that point, I informed him that he would not have had to put up with me being in his face if he had just honored his teacher's request.

Of course, the administration gave no punishment for that student's actions, his disrespect, or his use of unacceptable language. That in itself explains why the student acted the way he did. He knew there would be no consequences for his unacceptable behavior. But he also realized that I would have taken action, and there would have been consequences if he did not comply to his teacher's request. The administrators of our school systems have only made things worse because of their lack of proper student discipline. They fear litigation, and thus, they often do not hand out proper punishment for the students' improper behavior. The fear of litigation has paralyzed the public school system, and we the people, who have made up the juries, have caused this problem. Juries are not holding people accountable for their own inappropriate actions. We grant monetary rewards for frivolous lawsuits. We, the people who make up those juries, can help solve the problems we have caused.

To improve the public educational system in our country, we must change the attitude of the student toward the learning process and teach them to respect those in authoritative positions. Changing student attitude is done through effective discipline, and effective discipline makes the student not want to face the consequences of their actions again.

Along with this lack of proper student discipline, teachers have been blamed for poor student performances, and in so doing, we have simply taken accountability away from the student and placed the students' accountability on the teacher. It is far past time to stop blaming the teacher for poor student performance. It is time to make the students accountable for their own performance in the classroom. I sat next to a person from the Department of Education in Washington, DC, on a flight from Kansas City to Nashville. I started a conversation with this person. As we talked, I told this person I thought education in America could be greatly improved if approached properly. This individual then inquired about how I thought the educational process could be improved in our country. That was her mistake! I explained that teachers needed to stop being blamed for poor student performance and put the emphasis on making the student accountable for their learning.

Upon hearing what I said, this individual was skeptical about my taking the responsibility for learning away from the teacher and putting most of it back on the student. I promptly explained that student work ethic and accountability are what is needed if our educational system is to be improved. I told this individual that she could pick the best teacher she could find and allow me to pick the twenty-five students in that classroom, and the learning process would be very limited. She could pick what she considered a deficient teacher who would present the class material to be learned and let me pick the twenty-five students for that classroom, and learning would take place. The difference would be one classroom would have twenty-five problem students who did not care about their education, and the other classroom would have twenty-five self-motivated students who would take the material presented and learn from it. It all boils down to expectations, the student's attitude, their desire to learn, and their cooperation. Unfortunately, parents are often a major problem in their child's learning endeavors because they defend their child's unacceptable behaviors, resist their child's accountability, and try to be their child's best friend instead of parenting.

Along with changing the student's approach to learning, the flawed "everybody gets a trophy" philosophy has hurt our society's young people greatly. Young people no longer feel that they have to work to be successful to get a reward. They expect things to just be given to them, even if they haven't earned it. Since they do not have to work to earn their rewards, young people do not develop a work ethic. I read in a publication a few years ago that many high school students receive A averages, but their standardized testing scores, like SAT or ACT, are falling. This grade giving without earning it is even happening in colleges and universities. Graduation rates are up, which should make people happy; however, high school and college students show signs of being ill-equipped to function properly in the real world. Just have restaurant or department store employees try to figure out proper change without the aid of a cash register or calculator, and you will see how ill-equipped young people are today. I read somewhere that around 50 percent of the freshmen entering college either flunk out or drop out by the end of their first semester. If this is true, what our educational system has prepared them for is failure. We even are seeing people defacing their bodies to the point of making themselves unemployable and wondering why they can't get a job.

What we should be realizing is the "everybody gets a trophy" philosophy has taught our young people that they do not have to work for their grades or present themselves with a proper appearance for employment.

Grades are just given to students; thus, we are failing our young people by not teaching them to develop a high work ethic and what it is that enhances one's employment. It is far past time for our young people to learn to work for and earn their successes.

Of course, teachers can also improve their teaching skills and methods. I am confident that teachers will not like hearing what I have to say next, but if teachers want to improve their teaching skills and methods, they should find an effective sports coach and observe how that coach handles his/her athletes. Coaching is nothing more than teaching. A team's practice sessions are the classroom, and the games are the tests. By watching how effective coaches interact with and handle their players, teachers can learn much. If you watch a team's practice sessions (classroom) and then its performance (their tests), you will see how effective their practice sessions (classroom sessions) have actually been and how disciplined they are.

In my coaching and teaching career, I was very fortunate to have coached and taught many great people. During my forty-three years of coaching basketball, I have had the pleasure of coaching 471 girls and 318 boys. I have enjoyed being involved in 549 wins and tolerated 274 loses. I have found that the by-product of helping my players and students get what they wanted was that I got what I wanted also. So, a person will get all he or she wants in life if he or she helps enough other people to get what they want. If the players I coached wanted to win a league championship, play in a state championship game, or get a scholarship to play basketball beyond high school, and I did everything I possibly could to help them accomplish what they wanted, I received what I wanted as well. If I treated my players and students well, I had friends for life. If I did everything I possibly could do to prepare my players, I got to experience league championships and state championship games. If I worked to help my players to receive basketball scholarships, I got the satisfaction of watching them play the game at the next level and sometimes on TV.

On September 9, 2016, my girl basketball players, my boy basketball players, and assistant coaches were responsible for me being inducted into my school district's Athletic Hall of Fame. This induction was a great honor for me, and I realized they were truly the ones responsible for the Hall of Fame honor and all of the Coaches of the Year Awards I received. My classroom students were responsible for my receiving the five Who's Who Among America's Teachers Awards as well. To reiterate that good choices result in successful endeavors, four days after my induction into the Athletic Hall of Fame, my sister was honored as well. She was awarded the Health Care Hero Award by the business community of the large city near where she lives. Health Care Heroes honors companies, individuals and organizations for their contributions to improving health care. My sister successfully spent her career as an administrator of a number of health care clinics and did it all without a college education.

Unfortunately, people will say, "It doesn't matter if you win or lose but how you play the game." This statement is actually contradictory and counterproductive. If you do not play to win the game, your effort is deficient, and your deficient effort matters greatly. Playing to win or be successful is important. So, if you do not put every ounce of effort into winning, how you played that game was not good enough.

I hated losing, but I tolerated every loss until we had the next opportunity to win. Then I gave my best effort to win. That concept of winning and losing is what I tried to instill within my players. Hopefully, I instilled in my students and players a work ethic that is beneficial for them out in the real world of living productively.

Early in my coaching career, which was applicable to my teaching career, I realized that the important part of coaching basketball was not in the X's and O's of the game. It was about each individual person I coached. The same applied to the students I taught. I wanted to first get to know my players and students before I coached or taught them on how to play the game and learn in the classroom. I wanted my students and players to be able to trust me before we got down to the nitty-gritty of player and team development and student learning. There aren't any magic plays in the game of basketball, and there aren't any magic formulas of learning. Repetition is the best teacher, which can easily be seen in a sports classroom, and the classroom teacher can observe that in sports practice sessions. A coach must recognize the skill level and hidden or unused talent each player possesses and blend his/her players into a united team. A teacher must recognize the unused ability within each student as well. Divided or fragmented teams will never experience the success they could have if they were united. The same applies to the educational classroom setting, any organization, or society.

The character and integrity of each individual person has more to do with their individual or team's success than their physical skills. The same applies to the student in the classroom. Character is really about who we are because of what we do. Talent is a gift from God, but our character is our choice. And each individual person chooses what his/her character will be like. Our integrity is based on what we do when no one is there watching us. We cannot be one way when people are around us and different when no one is around to see how we are or what we do. Unfortunately, many people do not realize that someone is always there to see what we do or don't do. The God of heaven is omnipresent. He is there at all times, and He sees us for who we really are! The scriptures say in Colossians 3:17, "And whatsoever ye do in word or deed, do all in the name of the Lord Jesus, giving thanks to God and the Father by him." So, whatever we do, we do it in the name of Jesus Christ, and if we put forth an inadequate effort into whatever we are doing, we are inadequately representing Jesus Christ.

I am convinced that courage, resolve, trust, passion, integrity, and strength of character are the main predictors of success in all avenues of life and that failure and adversity should never determine who we are. Everyone will face tough times, adversity, and failure. How we handle tough times, adversity, and failure is important and should improve and perfect us into being better people, instead of dragging us down.

I always told my basketball players that they needed to have their priorities of life in the proper order. I would tell them to have God first in their lives; nothing is more important than that. Then they needed to have their families second, others third, their education fourth, basketball fifth. When I coached girls, boys should be no higher prioritized than sixth, and when I coached boys, girls should be no higher prioritized than sixth until they reached twenty-two years of age. At that point in their life, the sixth priority could move up the priority list. In my parent meetings, I would inform the parents exactly what I would be telling their children. If they had a problem with that, they needed a different coach. I told them that I would never cuss or swear at their child. There is absolutely no acceptable reason to cuss, swear, or use unacceptable language for any reason and especially not at young people. I also told parents that I would do whatever correction needed to be done in private.

I believe the greatest achievement of a coach or teacher has very little to do with victories or classroom performance and a lot to do with the influence and impact that they have on a players' or students' lives. My former players' and students' lives will expose my effectiveness as a teacher and coach. One has to examine the lives of the players and students I have coached and taught twenty, thirty, and forty years after they left my tutelage to be able to determine my true effectiveness. If my players and students are upstanding citizens, with good character and integrity, and are good moral people, I was an effective teacher and coach.

We need to be able to trust each other in all aspects of life, be totally committed to whatever endeavor we choose to pursue, and truly care about the things that we choose to be involved in. If a team of players, a classroom of students, an organization of members, or a society of people are composed of individuals who can be trusted, who are committed, and who care about what they are involved in, great things will happen.

CHAPTER 18

WHAT'S IMPORTANT

This is the last chapter of my story. You may wonder why I wrote this account of my life experiences. I wrote this account for eight reasons.

1. I wrote this book for myself. Writing this narrative was therapeutic for me. For a good portion of my life, I was deceived by a person who I should have been able to trust. I did not realize the extent of the deception until many years later. I lived with rejection for reasons I did not fully understand, and in fear of losing my life. Putting all that happened to my family into print helped me make sense of many things I faced in my life. Some of what I wrote made me sad, some made me angry, and some made me smile. I now have a greater understanding of how all that has happened to me over my lifetime has formed me into the person I have become.

2. I wrote this book to help people understand that no matter how tough the situations they face in life are, there is always hope in their pursuit of acceptance, encouragement, recognition, success, and love.

3. I wrote this account because people tend to make unjustified judgments of others based on inaccurate perceptions, causing children who are in situations that are beyond their control to feel rejected, inferior, and inadequate. How we treat others is important, especially the children.

4. I wrote this narrative to help young people realize that the person they are and will become is the result of the choices they have made and will make, and that they are accountable for those choices, no matter how undesirable the situations are that they face. Things can always change with better choices.

5. I wrote this book as a way of reminding each of us that every person has value and needs to be treated that way.

6. I wrote this account to help people understand that God and Jesus Christ are the answer to everything.

7. I wrote this narrative to inspire people to examine their past, make the necessary changes needed in their lives, and create a more fulfilling life for themselves and others.

8. I wrote this account to encourage people to engage in discussions about how things that have happened to them have formed them and how others were affected by what happened. As I have stated in previous chapters, life gives us many challenges and choices, some difficult to make and others more painless. It is my hope that all people, and especially children, meet their challenges in life with determination, integrity, humility, character, and love. If they do, this world can become a kind of refuge or sanctuary for them, and they will enjoy a life of praising and glorifying God. In 1 Corinthians 10:31, it says, "Whether therefore ye eat, or drink, or whatsoever ye do, do all to the glory of God."

At a very young age, I developed a mental frame of mind that no matter what I was facing, I could handle it. This determination to prove myself carried me through many tough times. I could have easily gone in the direction that people expected me to go because of my father. Despite the fact that I thought of myself as inferior, I made the decision to prove my skeptics wrong and went in the right direction in life.

Even though I did not have a father who cared about me, I had God, Jesus Christ, and the Bible scriptures to direct my life. I had a grade school teacher/coach who gave me the responsibility of coaching my teammates when I was not allowed to play in a game. I had a high school teacher who recognized my interest in biology, saw something inside of me that others did not see, and chose me to be his student classroom aide. I spent three years as a surgery technician dealing with life-and-death situations. I had a mother who loved me and taught me to put God first in my life. She always told me that the Bible was the infallible Word of God and that I should live my life according to what those scriptures say, no matter what happens. She gave me the best advice that can be given to anyone. So, I am giving this same advice to you who are reading this book. Live your life according to the infallible Word of God. You have only two choices, to follow the truth or to follow a lie.

My mother left her mark in this world, so to speak, and the evidence of her mark is that both my sister and I have wonderful families. Both of us have been married for over fifty years to our one and only spouses. I have a wonderful wife and two exceptional children who are presently raising, with their outstanding spouses, seven impressive grandchildren. I am truly blessed and could not have asked for more in life than that. My sister and her husband have also raised two exceptional children who are presently raising, with their outstanding spouses, seven impressive grandchildren. My mother's fingerprints can be seen in us, and what an amazing mark to leave behind when one departs this life! But when all is said and done, the primary factor in who I am today is God and my desire to please Him by living my life as He wants me to live it.

A goal of mine was to have an excellent reputation, and I worked hard to try to achieve it. I never wanted anyone to think poorly of me, even though my home community's expectations of me did not support that goal of mine. One's reputation is important, and if one has just a good reputation, that isn't good enough. An excellent reputation is what each of us needs to strive to have. Without it, we aren't the "salt " or the "light" we are to be. Matthew 5:13–16 tells us we are to be "the salt of the earth," "the light of the world," and spiritual examples for those around us.

Salt carries the meaning of a preservative and a seasoning.

Salt protects food from spoiling and preserves it unchanged. We are to be salt by our lifestyle, example, character, behavior, and influence. We must be the preservers of what God has commanded as righteous. We must not make the choices in our associations and actions that will dilute our preserving and seasoning influence and character. Poor choices will only entangle us in things we ought not to be doing. We should be looking out for one another, preserving one another unchanged from our walk in Christ. It is our responsibility to communicate those things required for an acceptable life to God.

Just how does salt lose its preserving qualities? Salt loses its preserving qualities when it is diluted, and the more diluted it becomes, the less effective it is. When we allow our life to become tainted, we lose our saltiness, our desire to protect and to preserve. Dad lost his saltiness through poor choices.

Light carries the meaning of a source of light, a radiance. We are to be illuminating and radiating people who help to preserve and season and do the right thing because it is the right thing to do.

People may claim that my feeling of rejection from my home community was not really as I perceived it to be. However, a few years ago, a man who grew up as a neighbor to my sister and me and attended grade school with us made a comment to her. He basically said that he was surprised that she and I had grown up to be the successful people we have become, with the integrity, character, and moral standards we possess, since we faced so much rejection, ridicule, and deception in our lives.

How did my sister and I rise above the adversity we faced? In Proverbs 23:7, we are told, "For as he thinker in his heart, so is he." There is a definite connection between our thinking and our acting. My sister and I are the results of our thinking and actions, and because of our thinking and actions, we are not causalities of the situations we had to endure. It is important that every child realizes that no matter how serious and difficult the situations are that they face in life, they do not have to be a causality of those situations if they do not want to be.

Listen to young people like I was, looked down upon because of situations beyond their control, and they'll tell you of the importance of seeing and celebrating their God-given talents and strengths, encouraging them to focus on what they are good at doing, and being cared about.

I see people gravitate into groups, and when that happens, often someone is excluded, left on the outside looking in. If you are fortunate to be in a group, groups are great. But if you are the one on the outside of the group looking in, feeling excluded, groups are devastating. I was one of those kids on the outside of the group, feeling left out, inwardly talking to myself about why it was happening to me. Each person deserves to feel included and have a smile on their face. No one should be called disrespectful names or made to feel like a second-class citizen, because there is no such person. Everyone should be on the lookout for and talk to the outcast, the isolated, the friendless, the unloved, the abandoned, the lonely, the unwanted, the unhappy, and give them a hug because they are the ones hurting inside. If you have ever felt the excruciating pain of being excluded, unwanted, or friendless, you know exactly what I am talking about.

When I think about why things are happening the way they are in our society, I realize that each successive generation has become more secular in their thinking and actions than the generation before them. Why has this happened? As I see it, the pursuit of pleasure and sensual self-indulgence has progressively been forced into the thinking of the young people.

I see less and less emphasis on living according to the will of God. What 2 Timothy 2:15 says has been and is gradually being ignored. There it says, "Study (plan, practice, give diligence) to shew thyself approved unto God, a workman that needeth not to be ashamed, rightly dividing the word of truth." People are losing their interest in being diligent in rightly dividing the word of truth. With this lack of interest in biblical things, Bible authority has gone by the wayside, and the lack of study or giving diligence to studying the scriptures has caused people to be unable to cut straight, handle correctly, properly divide, or understand "the word of truth." If only people would realize that the Bible message is as relevant today as it was when it was written, their lives would be more productive, and they would be more satisfied with life. Sadly, there are people claiming that the scriptures have become old-fashioned, outdated, or obsolete, but they have not. The scriptures are authoritative and need to be seen that way. If one rejects any part of God's authoritative Word, they have, in essence, actually rejected all of it. It is an all or none thing. There is no fence sitting when it comes to Bible authority. People are fast becoming what is said in Hosea 4:6, "My people are destroyed for lack of knowledge."

When I reflect on my life and all I have experienced, I see God's hand in every aspect of it. I survived a tough home life, a father who didn't care about me, an untreated poisonous snake bite, four broken vertebrae from a twenty-foot fall, and cancer. God isn't finished with me yet. He had a purpose for the pain I endured and a reason for my struggles. The hard times I faced progressively helped prepare me for the rest of my life. I know that I am a work in progress and need to keep improving no matter how tough life becomes. My prayer is that I am on life's road to becoming the person God intended me to be.

When we face problems, it isn't God who created our problems. He provides the solutions. When we face what seems to be a locked door, it is God who provides a key.

I am confident that God is not interested in how many basketball games my teams have won or lost, how many years I've coached the game of basketball, how many years I taught school, or how many games I played in myself. I am confident that God is interested in how I have lived my life, if I was obedient to His will, how many lives I influenced in a positive way, and how many people I helped change for the better.

I never wanted one of my students, one of my players, and especially not one my family members to ever feel that I didn't care about them. I pray that I have influenced, inspired, taught, and empowered as many people as I possibly could have during my lifetime and brought more glory to God, who I ultimately serve. I pray that I have taught my children the importance of obedience to the infallible will of God, the Bible, and taught them the importance of humility, character, integrity, and truthfulness. It is essential that my children continue to live godly lives and teach their children to do the same.

As I was growing up, like many people do, I thought that I was a Christian until I studied the scriptures for what they had to say. Through careful examination, I came to realize that I was merely a Christian in name only. I had not met God's requirements to be a child of His. I had not been obedient to His will. Sure, I was living what people considered to be a good life, but I hadn't followed God's prerequisites to become His child. So, as the scriptures instruct, I confessed Jesus as the Son of the living God, repented of my sins, and was baptized for the remission (forgiveness) of my sins as Peter commanded the first Christians to do in Acts 2:38. There it says, "Then Peter said unto them, Repent, and be baptized every one of you in the name of Jesus Christ for the remission of sins, and ye shall receive the gift of the Holy Ghost." I hadn't put Christ on as Galatians 3:27 tells us to do. "For as many of you as have been baptized into Christ have put on Christ." Until then, I didn't realize just how important baptism was for one's salvation, for reconciliation with God. I just thought it was something you do! I was like many people who do not understand that baptism is an essential part of being saved, as 1 Peter 3:21 says it is. "The like figure whereunto even baptism doth also now save us (not the putting away of the filth of the flesh, but the answer of a good conscience toward God,) by the resurrection of Jesus Christ." If this verse is to be believed, baptism is required for salvation. If that is not to be believed, none of the Bible can be believed. "All (every one of them) scripture is given by inspiration of God, and is profitable for doctrine, for reproof, for correction, for instruction in righteousness: That the man of God may be perfect, thoroughly furnished unto all good works" (2 Timothy 3:16–17). What has been written on the pages of the Bible is there for our learning. But if we never read them or study them, we will remain ignorant of God's will for us and reap the consequences of our ignorance one day.

I was like many people who hold to the idea that Ephesians 2:8–9 teaches that faith or belief is enough. "For by grace are ye saved through faith; and that not of yourselves: it is the gift of God: Not of works, lest any man should boast." I was mistaken. Grace is freely given, but it must be accessed. It is there for the taking through obedience. James 2:24 says, "Ye see then how that by works a man is justified, and not by faith only." James 2:19 says, "Thou believest that there is one God; thou doest well: the devils also believe, and tremble." If all that one needs to do is believe, demons will also be in heaven, and we know demons will not spend eternity with God. I studied the scriptures and became obedient to God's will. I hope and pray that you do the same.

Even though my father and I never had a close relationship, before my father passed away, I went to see him and expressed my concern about the spiritual condition of his soul. I knew that his spiritual condition was in great need of change. Unfortunately, he saw no need for changes to take place in his life and told me not to be concerned because he was just fine the way he was. My father's worldly life caused him to feel that he never really did anything wrong. But he never showed any concern for his family or love. As far as I know, he was unrepentant to the day he died. He never apologized to my mother, sister, or me for what he put us through. He expressed regrets but never asked for our forgiveness. Of course, I am saddened that my father never expressed to us a repentant heart for what he did to us. I am told that late in his life, my father went to his sister and shared some regrets with her in tears, concerning how poorly he had treated our mother. Unfortunately, regrets with tears do not translate into repentance. Repentance demands a change in the direction of one's life and asking for forgiveness. My sister and I are truly saddened that he was never able to share those regrets with us or ask for forgiveness.

Throughout his life, my father demonstrated that he loved the world and the things that are in the world (1 John 2:15–17). My sister and I so wish that he hadn't. Because of our life experiences, my sister and I have come to understand that what has happened to us or will happen to us cannot define or destroy us unless we allow it to.

With all of this in mind, as my sister and I reflect on our lives, we are saddened by the fact that we never experienced a normal home life or what it was like to have a loving father in our lives. We have truly been tested; we were strengthened; we overcame the trials we faced; and we were formed into the people we are today. We have truly faced the fires of adversity and came out stronger for it, with a determination to be more than what was expected of us. We have overcome much. And, yes, it is true: my sister and I were truly fashioned and forged in the fire of life.

Printed in the United States
by Baker & Taylor Publisher Services